ALABAMA FOUNDERS

THE UNIVERSITY OF ALABAMA PRESS
TUSCALOOSA

ALABAMA FOUNDERS

*Fourteen Political
and Military Leaders
Who Shaped the State*

HERBERT JAMES LEWIS

The University of Alabama Press
Tuscaloosa, Alabama 35487-0380
uapress.ua.edu

Typeface: Adobe Garamond Pro

Cover image: Digitally restored map of Alabama constructed from the surveys
in the General Land Office and other documents by Scottish mapmaker John
Melish in 1818; courtesy of the Alabama Department of Archives and History
Cover design: David Nees

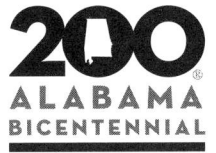

Library of Congress Cataloging-in-Publication Data

Names: Lewis, Herbert James, author.
Title: Alabama founders : fourteen political and military
leaders who shaped the state / Herbert James Lewis.
Description: Tuscaloosa : The University of Alabama Press,
[2018] | Includes bibliographical references and index.
Identifiers: LCCN 2017052788| ISBN 9780817319830 (cloth) |
ISBN 9780817359157 (pbk.) | ISBN 9780817391836 (ebook)
Subjects: LCSH: Alabama—Biography. | Alabama—
History. | Alabama. Constitutional Convention (1819)
Classification: LCC F325 .L49 2018 | DDC 976.1—dc23
LC record available at https://lccn.loc.gov/2017052788

CONTENTS

FIGURES

ACKNOWLEDGMENTS

In 2004, a couple of years before I retired from the US Department of Justice, I presented a paper at the annual meeting of the Alabama Historical Association in Birmingham. That paper was about my third great-grandfather Henry Wilbourne Stevens, a graduate of the Litchfield Law School, who immigrated to Alabama from Connecticut in 1814. Shortly after I retired in January 2006, this paper was published in the April 2006 issue of the *Alabama Review*. Between 2007 and 2009, I wrote numerous articles concerning early Alabama history for the comprehensive *Encyclopedia of Alabama*. During this time, I also had begun research on a book covering early Alabama all the way from colonial times to Alabama's secession from the Union. This book, titled *Clearing the Thickets: A History of Antebellum Alabama*, was published in March 2013 by Quid Pro Books in New Orleans, Louisiana. Shortly after *Thickets* was published, the History Press (now merged with Acadia Publishing) approached me to write a book about the lost capitals of Alabama. I did so, and *Lost Capitals of Alabama* was published in November 2014. The present book, *Alabama Founders: Fourteen Political and Military Leaders Who Shaped the State*, contains a series of detailed biographies of those who played prominent roles in the founding of Alabama almost two hundred years ago.

In writing this book, as well as my other publications, I was fortunate to have received critical inputs, support, assistance, and encouragement from a virtual "who's who" of Alabama's history community. Those who have in one way or another helped me in any of my endeavors include Dr. Leah Rawls Atkins, former director of the Auburn University Center for the Arts and Humanities; Dr. Wayne Flynt, in his capacity as editor-in-chief of the *Encyclopedia of Alabama* (EOA); Dr. Jeff Jakeman, former editor of the *Alabama Review*; Edwin C. Bridges, director emeritus of the Alabama Department of Archives and History; Steve Murray, director of the Alabama Department of Archives and History; Jay Lamar, executive director of the Alabama Bicentennial Commission; Dr. Paul Pruitt Jr., Collection Development & Special Collections Librarian, Bounds Law Library, University of Alabama School of Law; Christopher Lyle McIlwain Sr., attorney and author of *Civil War Alabama*; James L. Noles Jr., attorney, author and former chairman of the Board of Directors of the Alabama Humanities Foundation; Robert Stewart, former director of the Alabama Humanities Foundation; Mike Bunn, Director of

Operations at Historic Blakeley State Park; Martin Everse, former director of the Tannehill Historical State Park and Brierfield Ironworks State Park; Dr. James S. Day, associate professor of History at the University of Montevallo and chairman of the Alabama Historical Commission; Garland Cook Smith, Wilcox County Historical Society; Bobby Joe Seales, former president of the Shelby County Historical Society and currently honorary Ambassador for the Alabama Bicentennial; Elizabeth C. Wells, former coordinator of the Special Collections Department, Samford University Library, Birmingham, Alabama; James P. Kaetz (deceased), former managing editor of the *EOA*; Claire Wilson, senior content editor of *EOA*; Christopher Maloney, content editor of *EOA*; Laura Newland Hill, communications director of *EOA*; Meredith McDonough, as well as the research staff of the Alabama Department of Archives and History (ADAH), Montgomery, Alabama; and the staff of the Linn-Henley Library, Birmingham, Alabama.

ALABAMA FOUNDERS

INTRODUCTION

This book contains extensive biographies of the key political and military leaders who laid the foundation for the political and economic infrastructure of Alabama as it sought and achieved statehood. Regarding the founding of the United States, Robert B. Morris is among many historians who recognize founders such as George Washington, John Adams, Benjamin Franklin, Thomas Jefferson, James Madison, John Jay, and Alexander Hamilton. In addition to these, most historians also recognize all the signers of the Declaration of Independence and the framers of the US Constitution as founding fathers. Some historians expand the designation further to mean an even larger group, including not only the signers and framers but also others who participated in any significant way in securing American independence and creating the United States of America.[1]

The Alabama founders highlighted herein certainly fit within the expansive view of a founding father, but this is not intended to be an exhaustive list of all the state's founders. Therefore, the fact that someone is not included in this book is not necessarily indicative that the person is not worthy to be labeled as such. There is no official list of such people, in any event. The reason for choosing those included in this book is that the author believes that they were all key figures, either in clearing the territory for settlement, serving in the territorial government, working to achieve statehood, serving in a key role at the Constitutional Convention of 1819, or serving in important offices in the first years of statehood.

Those founders who readied the Alabama Territory for statehood include Judge Harry Toulmin, Henry Hitchcock, and Reuben Saffold. The political movers and shakers who used their influence to obtain statehood for Alabama include Charles Tait, William Wyatt Bibb, Thomas Bibb, LeRoy Pope, and John Williams Walker. These founders were from an area in northeast Georgia referred to as the Broad River region. Historian J. Mills Thornton III coined the phrase "Broad River Group" to signify these men, as well as others who migrated from Georgia to Huntsville and Montgomery prior to statehood.[2] Those who were instrumental participants in the Constitutional Convention of 1819 and served the state well in its early days include John W. Walker, Clement Comer Clay, Gabriel Moore, Israel Pickens, and William Rufus King. Military figures who played a role in the clearing of the territory for further settlement and development include General John Coffee and Samuel Dale.[3]

The first founder examined is Judge Harry Toulmin, an immigrant from England, who was appointed by President Thomas Jefferson as a territorial judge in the Tombigbee District of the Mississippi Territory.[4] He was soon to be Alabama's first significant leader and his actions readied the Tombigbee District for territorial status and eventual statehood. Known as the "Czar of the Tombigbee District,"[5] Judge Toulmin ruled the area for fourteen years, during which he boldly transformed his remote frontier outpost into a more civilized community ready for statehood. Judge Toulmin was versatile in many areas, including codifying the statute law of the state of Alabama, earning him the name of the "frontier Justinian."

The Tombigbee settlements grew as more settlers streamed into the area, causing frictions to increase between the newly arrived settlers and the Creek Nation. After the Fort Mims massacre, a call to arms brought volunteers under the command of Andrew Jackson into Alabama to quell the Creek uprising. Those involved in the defeat of the Creeks certainly helped pave the way for an increasing population that in turn made the area eligible for statehood. Two such people of prominence were Samuel Dale and General John Coffee. Dale was a scout, frontiersmen, soldier, and public servant in the development of Alabama. Coffee served with distinction in Alabama[6] and Louisiana under the command of General Andrew Jackson during the War of 1812, and was one of the principal founders of Florence in Lauderdale County.

After the Creek War of 1813–1814 and the resulting cession of millions of acres of Creek lands, the influx of settlers into the area was so great that it was called "Alabama Fever." Also, responding to the availability of land opening in the Tennessee Valley were LeRoy Pope, known as the "Father of Huntsville,"[7] and Thomas Bibb, brother of William Wyatt Bibb and second governor of Alabama, who were both in the Broad River Group. Within a few years other Georgians from that area were ready to follow Pope and Bibb. The group had become politically powerful in Georgia before setting their sights on Alabama, which to them was inviting because the area was rich in lands to be gobbled up, as well as in patronage to be taken advantage of.

Most influential of the Broad River Group were Georgia senators Charles Tait and William Wyatt Bibb. Both Tait and Bibb were popular senators in Georgia, but both ran afoul of the electorate when they voted in favor of an act that effectively doubled the pay of all congressmen. Thus Bibb was defeated in his bid for reelection and resigned his Senate seat in the fall of 1816. He then headed for Alabama where, because of his connections within the Georgia faction, President Monroe appointed him as governor of the Alabama Territory in 1817. Senator Tait wished to follow Bibb to escape the wrath of the protest created by their pay increase votes. However, John W. Walker, a former Georgian then serving as a representative in the Alabama territorial legislature, persuaded Tait to retain his Georgia senatorial seat until he could shepherd the Alabama admission bill through Congress.

Also focused upon are key founders who were not from the state of Georgia. Among them is Gabriel Moore from North Carolina. Moore migrated from North Carolina in 1810, and he became the first Speaker of the House of Representatives in the Alabama Territorial legislature. He did not seek reelection as Speaker for the second session because his wife petitioned for, and the legislature granted her, a divorce from him as well as for permission to revert to her maiden name. John W. Walker of Madison County succeeded Moore.[8] Despite this embarrassment, Moore was not harmed in the long run—he was one of the representatives from Madison County in the Constitutional Convention of 1819, Alabama's fifth governor, a member of the US House of Representatives, and then a member of the US Senate. Another key founder from a state other than Georgia was Henry Hitchcock, who had emigrated from Vermont, arriving in the Alabama Territory in January 1817. Hitchcock served as the territory's first secretary and went on to serve in the Constitutional Convention of 1819, was Alabama's first attorney general, and served as chief justice of the Alabama Supreme Court. Another key founder during the territorial period was Reuben Saffold, who was from Wilkes County, Georgia. As soon as he arrived in the territory he joined the local militia and served in the Creek War. He was later elected to the territorial legislature, was a delegate to the Constitutional Convention of 1819, and became chief justice of the Alabama Supreme Court.

As mentioned, several key founders were delegates to the Constitutional Convention of 1819. Alabama's Enabling Act had called for a convention to be held in Huntsville, commencing on July 5, 1819, for the distinctive purpose of creating the twenty-second state. John W. Walker's biography includes an examination of his service as president of the convention. Also thoroughly scrutinized is Clement Comer Clay, chairman of the Committee of Fifteen, which was given the responsibility to produce a draft of the constitution. Clay, although not from the Broad River region of Georgia, initially allied himself with, and became a leading member of, its powerful political machine when he arrived in Alabama from Tennessee in 1811. Eventually he held himself out to the electorate as a Jacksonian Democrat and was successful in securing office as a state legislator, a US congressman, a governor, and a US senator. A subcommittee of just three delegates—including founders William Rufus King[9] of Dallas County, Henry Hitchcock of Washington County, and Judge John M. Taylor of Madison County—were given the task of reducing the rough draft of the entire committee to a form suitable for presentation to the convention as a whole for debate and adoption. After submission of the constitution to the Congress, on December 14, 1819, President Monroe signed the resolution that enabled the Alabama Territory to officially become the twenty-second state in the Union. The first three governors of the state were William Wyatt Bibb, Thomas Bibb, and Israel Pickens. As previously mentioned, the Bibb brothers were from the Broad River region in Georgia. Israel Pickens was from North Carolina. At first, Pickens aligned himself with Governor William Wyatt Bibb and the powerful Georgia faction. But in 1820, he began to distance himself from the Georgians as he started to sense that the poorer yeoman farmers would win the day.

◆

Alabama's founders were obviously all white men, as they were the only members of the early Alabama populace empowered to participate in politics and government. African American slaves, ever since they had been imported into Mobile by the French in 1721, were without substantive legal rights. As their numbers increased, King Louis XV ordered Governor Bienville to institute the Code Noir, the first formalized laws applied to slaves in the area in what was to become Alabama. These laws placed very severe restrictions upon slaves, such as prohibiting slaves of one master from gathering to meet those of another master; forbidding them from carrying weapons, unless hunting with the permission of their master; and forbidding them from selling any commodities without the permission of their master. More humane provisions provided for prohibitions against torture, separation of husbands and wives by sale, or separation of young children from their mothers. It even allowed slaves to buy their own freedom. But the Mississippi Territory's first governor, Winthrop Sargent, did not adopt those humane provisions. There would be future codes governing slavery that were even more restrictive. Although the following description was made much later, it reflected how the status of slavery had always been perceived in the eyes of the law: "The status of a slave, under our law is one of entire abnegation of civil capacity."[10] Perceived as property, enslaved people were obviously disenfranchised with respect to all civil rights.[11]

As for women, they were the nucleus of the frontier family and were responsible for providing for the general welfare of their families. As cotton became king, women often helped immensely in the running of the plantation and, in some instances, overseeing the work of their plantation's slaves. They too, however, could not vote, hold office, or sit on juries. Also, married women generally were not allowed to make contracts, devise wills, take part in other legal transactions, or control any wages they might earn.

I

JUDGE HARRY TOULMIN

Czar of the Tombigbee District

Figure 1.1: Judge Harry Toulmin, "Czar of
the Tombigbee District." Courtesy of Transylvania University Photographic Archives.

The Mississippi Territory was created by the US Congress on April 7,
1798. With the territory's creation, scores of settlers came rushing
into the areas that are now the states of Mississippi and Alabama. Many of
these were veterans of the Revolutionary War who responded to the lure of
the newly created territory as economic opportunities began to wane in the
Upper South because of a diminishing supply of fertile lands and the decline
of their markets for tobacco and rice. One of the lures to the new territory
was the ever-expanding cotton culture.[1]

When the Mississippi Territory was established, the Tombigbee District consisted of a few Tory refugees of the American Revolution, a few planters of French descent, numerous fugitives from American justice, debtors escaping enraged creditors, and several backwoodsmen ill suited for interaction with civilized society. Most of the settlers who came after 1798 and before the establishment of the Federal Road in 1811 came by the way of the Ohio, the Tennessee, and the Mississippi Rivers to Natchez and then overland to the Tombigbee District. Others came through the Tennessee and Alabama River basins. When they arrived in this wayward outpost on the southern frontier, they found themselves isolated from the United States. In this regard, Spain controlled the waterways into the Tombigbee District, the district was surrounded by hostile Native Americans, and the nearest neighbors were in Georgia to the east and in Natchez to the west. Each location was more than 150 miles away and the only communication was via horseback through hostile Indian territory.[2]

The isolation of the district only made the Bigbee settlers feel more exposed to the Spanish and local Native Americans, along with the feeling of being ignored by their own government in faraway Natchez. Historian Robert V. Haynes declared that the Bigbee settlers had a "morbid suspicion and hatred of Indians and Spaniards, a jealousy and resentment of their more fortunate Mississippi neighbors, a sense of insecurity, and a bitter feeling of neglect by the United States Government." With new settlers continuing to migrate into the Tombigbee District due to settlers' complaints of being isolated from the government in Natchez, territorial governor Winthrop Sargent created Washington County—located in present-day southwest Alabama—by proclamation on June 4, 1800, when the new county had a total population of 1,250,733 whites and 517 African American slaves. McIntosh Bluff, located about forty miles north of Mobile, was named the county's first seat. The county seat took its name from Captain John McIntosh, a British officer who had served in West Florida and had been awarded a land grant in 1775.[3]

With the creation of Washington County, American government was implemented at the local level for the first time in what was to become the state of Alabama. In June 1800, Governor Sargent appointed six men to serve as justices of the county's first courts. The first county court did not meet until 1803. The superior court of Washington County met in September 1802 when it held its first session at McIntosh Bluff with Seth Lewis, chief justice of the Mississippi Territory presiding. In June 1800, Governor Sargent, realizing that a permanent territorial judge was needed in the eastern section of the territory, consented to allow one of the Natchez judges, Daniel Tilton, to depart for the Tombigbee District in order "to give due tone to judicial proceedings" there. Unfortunately, Judge Tilton never made it past New Orleans, as he was stopped there on a matter of personal business. It would not be until July 1804 that Ephraim Kirby would be appointed as the first federal judge for the eastern portion of the Mississippi Territory by President Thomas Jefferson.[4]

Ephraim Kirby, a land-speculating Connecticut lawyer, had been appointed by President Jefferson in 1803 as one of three land commissioners in the eastern part of the territory. Kirby and two other land commissioners met at Fort Stoddert to adjust land titles east of the Pearl River to provide claimants with clear titles where possible. On July 6, 1804, President Jefferson persuaded Kirby to accept an appointment as the first federal judge in the Alabama portion of the territory. The president also imposed tasks beyond Kirby's official duties, including the providing of intelligence to the government concerning the area's topography, the traits of American settlers, and the strength of nearby Spanish settlements. In one of his reports back to President Jefferson, Kirby gave a very unflattering account of American settlers, stating that "the present inhabitants (with few exceptions) are illiterate, wild and savage, of depraved morals, unworthy of public confidence or private esteem; litigious, disunited, and knowing each other, universally distrustful of each other." He was not much gentler in describing local officials of whom he said were "without dignity, respect, probity, influence or authority."[5]

Kirby also reported to President Jefferson his concerns about anti-Spanish sentiments in the district that could lead some to take matters into their own hands in freeing Mobile from Spanish control, ridding themselves of exorbitant Spanish duties, and gaining access to the Mobile River that ran through Spanish West Florida. To put a stop to American filibustering against Spanish territory or property, Kirby began an investigation to identify local filibusters, particularly James Caller, who was a colonel in the local militia. A filibusterer is an adventurer who engages in an unauthorized military expedition into a foreign nation to start or support a revolution.Unfortunately, Kirby died in his quarters at Fort Stoddert on October 20, 1804, before he could conclude his investigation. He was buried the next day with full military honors in the fort's cemetery.[6]

To succeed Kirby, President Jefferson chose Harry Toulmin, who at the time was Kentucky's secretary of state and had political ties to Jefferson.[7] Toulmin, born in 1766 in Taunton, England, was the son of Joshua Toulmin and Jane Smith Toulmin. Joshua Toulmin was a noted theologian, a Dissenting[8] minister, and was a friend of Joseph Priestly, a fellow Dissenting clergyman and also a renowned scientist. Harry was educated by reading in his mother's bookstore and by listening to the intellectual and vigorous conversations his father had with such notable theologians as Priestly and Theophilus Lindsey. He also attended Hoxton Academy for a time and prepared for the ministry under Rev. William Hawes of Bolton and Dr. Thomas Barnes in

Manchester. In 1786, at the age of twenty, Harry Toulmin began preaching; he served two congregations of Protestant Dissenters in Lancashire, one near Manchester between 1786 and 1788 and one near Chowbent between 1787 and 1793. The young Toulmin drew many followers with his radical Unitarian preaching and writing. Indeed, Theophilus Lindsey described Toulmin's Chowbent congregation as "one of the largest and most enlightened." About the time that Toulmin began preaching at Chowbent in 1787, he married Ann Tremblett, with whom he would have nine children—four of whom died at a young age.[9]

Many of Toulmin's mentors and supporters championed the French Revolution. However, their praise for the revolution and its concepts of liberty and independence were at times suppressed by the British government and the subject of attacks by intolerant mobs. For example, on the second anniversary of Bastille Day, Priestley's laboratory, home, and meetinghouse in Birmingham, England, were attacked and destroyed. Also, an effigy of Thomas Paine was burned at Joshua Toulmin's door. Harry Toulmin also drew the attention of anti-dissenting forces when a mob surrounded his house while he was away. However, when he heard of his family's danger he hurried home, and with the use of his diplomatic skills was able to disperse the crowd. Nevertheless, in 1793 Toulmin's Chowbent church was subjected to a recruiting party, which the night before had "huzzaed" (shouted in triumph) and knocked at the houses of Dissenters and then passed by the chapel with drums and fifes. After the service, members of the mob wanted to put a cockade in Toulmin's hat just as they had forced one on many members of the congregation. Getting wind of their intentions, "Toulmin took off out of another door."[10]

Tiring of anti-dissenter attacks, a high tax burden, an inability to elect lawmakers representing the interests of the Dissenters, a legal system rigged for the privileged, being a subject rather than a citizen, and the corruption of the ruling elite, in 1792 Harry Toulmin began to contemplate a new country in which to live. He chose America because he found it to be a land where "you are not compelled to pay towards the propagation of a faith which you do not believe . . . you are not threatened with fines or imprisonment for any articles of your creed . . . You may calmly inquire after the truth." He visualized America as "a fine field for the diffusion of religious knowledge. The minds of the people are not shackled by articles and creeds. Their senses are not captivated by the pomp of superstition, nor their judgments fettered by the trammels of authority. In America, to contend for the faith, is not to contend for power; to publish the truth, is not to preach sedition."[11]

Toulmin's praise of America prompted his congregation to collect enough money to send Toulmin and his family to America in 1793 in hopes that they might find land where members of the congregation might settle. Sailing with his wife and children, and armed with letters of introduction from Priestley to Thomas Jefferson and James Madison, Toulmin sailed to Norfolk, Virginia. In route to America his ship was stopped by a French privateer who allowed him to proceed when shown Toulmin's letters of introduction. He presented one of the letters to James Madison at Montpelier and visited Jefferson and Monroe at their homes in early August 1793. Jefferson and Madison were delighted with Toulmin's political interests. In this regard, Jefferson described him as a "person of understanding, of science, and of great worth," as well as "a pure and zealous republican." With the encouragement and recommendation of these influential Virginians who were both future presidents of the United States, Toulmin and his family set out for Kentucky.[12]

Upon settling in Kentucky, Toulmin decided to relinquish his position as a clergyman and to become a scholar and teacher instead. What prompted that decision is not known for certain, but in February 1794 Toulmin was elected to the prestigious position of president of Transylvania Seminary in Lexington, Kentucky. Established in 1780 by an act of the Virginia Assembly and supported by Governor Thomas Jefferson, Transylvania Seminary was the first institution of higher learning west of the Alleghenies. There is little doubt that Jefferson pushed for the selection of Toulmin as president of Transylvania based upon his letters of recommendation and his personal observation.[13]

During his tenure at Transylvania, Toulmin launched a demanding curriculum of languages, science, mathematics, philosophy, and political science, all of which were taught to an ever-increasing student body. In these years, Lexington presented a scene of intellectual and political turmoil, with ongoing discussions of a republican form of government and deism. About this time, Thomas Paine's *Age of Reason* was making the rounds in America and was the subject of much debate, both for and against. Toulmin's short tenure was fraught with conflict between the Presbyterians who had begun the seminary and the more liberal board members who had elected Toulmin. A legislative amendment required a unanimous vote of the board to reelect the president. From his first days at Transylvania, he was closely watched by a Presbyterian faction on the school's board of trustees who viewed him as a Dissenter and had opposed his election. Continuing interventions in university undertakings propelled Toulmin to resign in April 1796.[14]

Toulmin's two-year tenure at Transylvania was contentious because his liberal Unitarian views conflicted with those of the Presbyterians who had founded the seminary. Toulmin's resignation in April 1796 was sealed when James Garrard, a liberal former member of the Transylvania board, was elected governor in 1796 and appointed Toulmin secretary of state of Kentucky. He would hold this position for eight years during the administration of Governor Garrard, a Jeffersonian Republican. As secretary of state he was required to certify acts of the legislature, which he did in signing Kentucky's Resolutions of November 1798, by which Kentucky nullified the Federalist-sponsored Alien and Sedition Acts. Thomas Jefferson had drafted the Kentucky Resolutions nullifying these acts. Toulmin also believed that these acts represented unwarranted government intrusion into freedom of thought, association, and free speech, thus outing himself as an advocate of "states' rights" and positioning himself for a future presidential appointment during the Jefferson administration.[15]

In between his official duties as secretary of state, Toulmin read law and sold sets of Blackstone's *Commentaries*, which put him in good stead when he was appointed by the legislature as one of two revisors of Kentucky's criminal law. Toulmin and the other revisor, James Blair, were appointed to make the revision and to "collect from the English reporters and from all such other writers on the criminal law as they think proper." Their finished product, *A Review of the Criminal Law of the Commonwealth of Kentucky*, was published in 1804. In another effort at bringing the law closer to the people, in 1802 Toulmin had published a work titled *Magistrate's Assistant: Collection of the Acts of Kentucky*. Toulmin's published legal digests put him on the road to becoming what Toulmin biographer Paul M. Pruitt Jr. referred to as a "scholarly lawgiver" or as "frontier Justinian" as he would later be known.[16]

Toulmin's recent experience with legal publications led him to write Secretary of State James Madison on May 1, 1804, to request that he be appointed to the newly created Tombigbee judgeship in Washington County of the Mississippi Territory. In his letter, Toulmin enclosed recommendations from Senator John Breckinridge of Kentucky and another Kentucky Republican, Caleb Wallace. Wallace, a longtime friend of Madison, had graduated from the College of New Jersey in Princeton in 1770. After being admitted to the bar, he moved to Kentucky in 1783, where he served as judge of the Kentucky Court of Appeals from 1792 to 1813. Wallace's letter of recommendation, dated April 20, 1804, indicates that Toulmin had advised him "that a Judge is to be appointed for a District on the Tombigby [*sic*] river in the Mississippi Territory, and that he is anxious to obtain the appointment." Wallace then urged Madison to recommend Toulmin to the president "as a person who I think qualified for that office." Wallace did, however, stress that since "he never has acted as a Judge or Lawyer and is a native of England, it may be proper to suggest that about eleven years ago he came to this State with letters of recommendation from Mr. Jefferson, yourself, and several other respectable characters; of which he was for some time employed as the principal teacher in the Transylvania Seminary." Other emphasis was recommended for his service as Kentucky's secretary of state and his appointment to make a compilation of the criminal common law. Summing up, Wallace stated, "And with pleasure I subjoin that he is a Gentleman of liberal Education, good Genius, agreeable manners, and remarkeable [*sic*] attention to any business he engages in. He is also a very inteligent [*sic*] Republican, and I believe his political principles induced him to adventure to America, where, in every sense of the word, he has become naturalized." Of course, President Jefferson followed these recommendations and in November 1804 appointed Toulmin as superior court judge for the Tombigbee District of the Mississippi Territory.[17]

While Toulmin waited for President Jefferson's official appointment to the Mississippi territorial bench,[18] he delivered a memorable Fourth of July address in Frankfort, Kentucky, in which he defended Jefferson's purchase of Louisiana and described in no uncertain terms the destruction that would have undoubtedly ensued had the French or English assertively inhabited the new territory. He further emphasized that it was fortunate that a Republican administration had diplomatically negotiated the acquisition rather than devotees of federalism utilizing force or duplicity. While Toulmin was optimistic about the viability of republican institutions, he was aware of the turmoil of borderline politics. He was surely not a proponent of an absolute democracy as evidenced in his Fourth of July address, wherein he noted, "Some opposition to the will of the majority may be necessary for the purpose of keeping them within the bounds of reason, of justice, and constituency."[19]

On November 5, 1804, Toulmin wrote to Secretary of State Madison, "I am preparing to remove to the Mississippi Territory, and hope to be ready by the time that the water will be sufficiently high to admit of my descending the Ohio with my family." He went on to ask for guidance as to where he was to reside in the territory, requesting that such information reach him prior to his embarking on his journey to the territory, indicating that he would probably take a route by the way of the town of Mobile. To make matters easier, he requested that he be given a letter of introduction "to some person of respectability in that place." Finally, Toulmin offered to "serve the government, by obtaining a knowledge of such facts as may be important to it" as had been done by his predecessor. He further stated, "I esteem it the duty of a public officer, not only to discharge the immediate duties of his station, but to be ready at all times, and at all times anxious, to devote his time and his talents to his country's good."[20]

Toulmin brought his family down the Mississippi River by flatboat, and then by sailing ship from New Orleans to the port of Mobile, which was under control of the Spanish government. From Mobile the family traveled up the Mobile River to Fort Stoddert, which was an American military out-post near the confluence of the Tombigbee and Alabama Rivers in Wash-ington County and just above the thirty-first parallel, which served as the boundary between the United States and Spanish West Florida. Upon his arrival, Toulmin moved the Washington County seat from McIntosh Bluff to a site approximately eight miles north that he named Wakefield after Oliver Goldsmith's novel *The Vicar of Wakefield*. It is said that Judge Toulmin held the first permanent federal court in Washington County in the fall of 1804, but this does not square with the fact that his appointment was not made until November 22, 1804, and a report that Toulmin and his family had arrived in the Tombigbee District in the summer of 1805.[21]

As the only federal official within the Tombigbee District, in addi-tion to presiding over the territorial district court, Judge Toulmin assumed many other responsibilities. Like Kirby before him, he was an emissary and reported to federal officials in Natchez and Washington. He also represented American citizens in disputes with Spanish officials, primarily regarding the excessive duties imposed for use of the area's river system or a shutdown of trade altogether. Additionally, he served as the district's postmaster, and he contracted to run a mail route from Fort Stoddert to Natchez between 1806 and 1810. He also officiated at marriages and funerals, practiced medicine, and entertained dignitaries. Judge Toulmin's standing in the community was enhanced by the fact that one of his daughters married Edmund Pendleton, the commandant at Fort Stoddert, and another daughter married the son of General James Wilkinson, the controversial senior officer of the US Army. Probably to Toulmin's dismay, his son married the daughter of James Caller, who became his rival as a filibusterer against the Spanish.[22]

In his capacity as territorial judge, Toulmin's immediate aim was to bring order and stability to this remote frontier post. He later reflected that he had been against what he called "that baneful ascendancy which the most abandoned men, have obtained among us."[23] He also recognized Ephraim Kirby's earlier curtailed efforts against such a group of rough-edged frontiers-men and the efforts of others who had departed the area "shutter[ing] at the idea of sacrificing [themselves] to such men." Despite the difficulties that lay ahead, Toulmin began what would be a fourteen-year career of dispensing justice from a primitive log courthouse in Wakefield, which was across the road from the jail on the road from St. Stephens to Mobile.[24]

To tackle the job of bringing order to the Tombigbee District, Toul-min could not just hold court in Wakefield. Indeed, his territorial authority extended over an area 340 miles long and 330 miles wide covering seven counties, mostly in present-day Alabama. Having to hold court twice a year in each county led Judge Toulmin to complain in a letter to William

Lattimore, a territorial representative to Congress, that a minimum of two new judges was needed to adequately cover such a large circuit. Toulmin rode the circuit on horseback, usually accompanied by his young African American slave, Tony. It was a long and hazardous excursion through the dense backwoods, encompassing an area that was sparsely settled by Europeans but teeming with Native Americans, many of whom were antagonistic to the ever-increasing white settlers.[25]

Amidst all his other duties and responsibilities, Judge Toulmin was tasked by the government in Natchez with compiling the laws of the fledgling territory. Thus, he compiled the laws of the new territory in a volume titled *1807 Statutes of the Mississippi Territory*. Legal historian Paul M. Pruitt Jr. has observed that the completed work revealed Toulmin's "understanding of his work and the verities of legal business on the borderlands." As Pruitt further observed, "Clearly, he was determined to blaze a clear path for future judges, for he devoted more than 200 pages to laws and statutes pertaining to judicial proceedings, including such detail-oriented subject headings as 'Demurrers, when frivolous' as well as an interesting section on the licensing and conduct of attorneys." Toulmin next gave considerable attention to the territory's land laws and even more to its criminal laws. Reflecting the international intrigue prevailing in the borderlands, there were quite a few quasi-military offenses within federal jurisdiction, including treason, manslaughter in a fort, assaulting a foreign minister, accepting a commission from a foreign power, launching a military expedition or a ship against a foreign government, and participating in the international slave trade.[26]

In enforcing these laws, Judge Toulmin had to strike a delicate balance between representing the interests of his citizens, who were resentful of US or Spanish authority, and imposing the will of his federal superiors. This balancing act would be necessary in dealing with his fellow settlers who objected to Spanish control of Mobile Bay. On behalf of the settlers, in 1805, Toulmin called upon Congress and the Spanish government for relief from exorbitant tariffs, embargoes, and confiscations. Unsuccessful in gaining any relief, Judge Toulmin hoped to fend off an attack on Mobile or any other filibustering activities. In the meanwhile, Toulmin played a role in the arrest of Aaron Burr, who was believed to be leading a conspiracy of some sort to establish an independent state in the Southwest. Many of the inhabitants of the Tombigbee District would probably have allied with Burr in an expedition against Spain in Mobile, since Burr had been in contact with filibuster James Caller before he was arrested. The precise object of the conspiracy was difficult to ascertain, however, because, as historian Thomas Perkins Abernethy put it, "The whole trouble with the Burr Conspiracy is that there were too many liars mixed up in it."[27]

Figure 1.2. Aaron Burr. Toulmin played a significant role in the arrest of Burr. Courtesy of the Alabama Department of Archives and History.

Whatever the exact object of the conspiracy, Burr surrendered to civil authorities in January 1807 in response to a proclamation that had been issued by President Jefferson on November 27, 1806, calling for his arrest. The territorial judges and grand jurors in Natchez then reviewed the charges against Burr, while Toulmin observed the proceedings as a spectator. Although the judges and grand jurors struggled to understand the alleged conspiracies, they were apparently reluctant to bring charges against Burr in any event because they believed, whatever crimes he had committed elsewhere, no crime had been committed in their jurisdiction. To some extent, they could have been influenced by the fact that many citizens were sympathetic to Burr's expedition if it involved taking Mobile away from Spain. Finally, Judge Peter Bruin was one of Burr's friends, a fact that surely clouded his judgment.[28]

When the territorial judges released Burr, Judge Toulmin was infuriated and, not wanting Burr to get away, issued arrest warrants for Burr and his principal coconspirators. Chief Judge Thomas Rodney then stepped in and took the case way from Toulmin, stating that he had no authority beyond his eastern Tombigbee District. Rodney was hampered, however, when the territory's attorney general, George Poindexter, declined to bring charges because Burr had committed no crime within their jurisdiction. Judge Rodney therefore commenced to take depositions on his own to submit to the grand jury. The grand jury, purportedly consisting of Federalists and friends of Burr's, then proceeded to exonerate Burr of all charges, including treason. Although the grand jury was discharged, Judge Rodney refused to release Burr from his bond and instead added a requirement to the bond that Burr remain in the vicinity indefinitely at the discretion of the judge. Just two days after the grand jury was discharged, Burr failed to obey a summons to appear before the territorial court, which resulted in his bond being forfeited; an award of $2,000 was announced by the territorial governor for Burr's apprehension. Ironically, Burr was eventually captured on February 19, 1807, near Judge Toulmin's town of Wakefield. He was held at Fort Stoddert until March 5, 1807, before being sent to Richmond to face trial for treason. Although Burr was acquitted due to Chief Justice John Marshall's strict construction of what evidence was admissible regarding the act of treason, Judge Toulmin was successful in his efforts to disrupt Burr and his cohorts from enlisting Bigbee settlers to filibuster against Spain in Mobile or West Florida.[29]

Even though the Burr arrest may have diluted filibustering activities for a while, the "Mobile Society," which comprised James and John Caller, Joseph P. Kennedy, Reuben Kemper, and Sterling Dupree, began to set their sights on Mobile. This group was allied with an obscure revolutionary organization, the Convention of Baton Rouge, whose leaders had recently annexed several "Florida Parishes" from the Spanish. The Mobile Society and other "Bigbee" settlers continued to be considerably exercised over Spain's imposition of a 12 percent duty on ships bound to and from Fort Stoddert through the Spanish-held port of Mobile. The Caller brothers preyed upon their fellow settlers' bitterness over these heavy duties imposed on necessary imports by threatening to capture and burn any Spanish ship drifting into American waters above the thirty-first parallel. Judge Toulmin understood the vital importance of Mobile to the Tombigbee District and expressed his indignation in a letter to Secretary of State James Madison for the heavy duty imposed by Spain: "Such an extraction as this, you may well conceive, must be ruinous to this country, and is moreover the source of perpetual hearburnings [sic] and contention between our citizens and the subjects of his Catholic majesty."[30]

Judge Toulmin, however, knew that any annexation of territory or corrective action should be relegated to official military or diplomatic action of the United States rather than to the likes of the Mobile Society. Although he was determined to keep the peace and evade international incidents, Toulmin was sympathetic with the Bigbee settlers' exasperation over Spanish control of the waterways. Even as he rode herd over the Mobile Society's activities and sought to deter potential lawbreakers, he took on a quasi-diplomatic role in putting out feelers to see if the Spanish government was interested in ceding Mobile of their own accord. This proposal fell on deaf ears and in November 1810, Reuben Kemper finally led an attack on Mobile, albeit with a force of drunken combatants. On December 9, 1810, Judge Toulmin had Kemper and his leading abettors arrested. On the next day, the Spanish commander at Mobile attacked the remaining filibusterers' camp, thus putting an end to the expedition. The leaders of this filibustering attack were put on trial but were acquitted on March 11, 1811, of all charges due to a widespread feeling in the community that Judge Toulmin was too soft on the Spanish and too zealous in arresting Kemper and his men.[31]

More criticism was heaped upon Judge Toulmin when he was believed to be instrumental in preventing an attack by American forces against the Spanish at Mobile. He and officials in Washington believed that such an attack might result in the Spanish burning down Mobile. Thus, in February 1811, federal officials were ordered to leave the port in Spanish control, at least temporarily. Although Toulmin could always count on support from a core group of official and legal friends, he was nevertheless the subject of abuse and threats throughout the Tombigbee District, including a threat of assassination against him by Joseph Kennedy and his narrow escape from an angry mob. His enemies even convinced a grand jury in newly created Baldwin County to indict him on multiple charges of abusing his judicial powers and an implication that he carried on treasonable negotiations with Spain. The indictment was provided to the territorial legislature, which in turn forwarded it to the US House of Representatives in November 1811. An investigating committee found no evidence to sustain the indictment and the investigation was closed in May 1812, with a report commending Toulmin's "vigilant attention to the duties of his station."[32]

With filibustering effectively under control for the time being, Judge Toulmin's next challenge was presented by the increasing number of white settlers within the district who interrupted the delicate peace prevailing within the borderlands. After the renowned visit of Tecumseh, a Shawnee chief from the Ohio Valley, to encourage southern Creeks to defend their tribal lands, the white and Métis (mixed white and Creek blood) communities of the Tombigbee District began to gradually experience difficulties with their Native American neighbors. Noting the concern of white settlers as he rode the circuit, on March 10, 1812, Judge Toulmin made a report of his observations to a State Department official in which he indicated that "a considerable consternation pervades the upper settlements—particularly in the forks of the Tombigbee and Alabama—of an immediate attack upon them by Creek Indians." Toulmin was not convinced himself, believing that the perceived dangers of the settlers were blown out of proportion. Although an immediate all-out attack did not occur, the settlers' anxiety was increased when they learned of the murder of two local citizens by a roaming band of Creek warriors on March 26 and April 29. Anxiety increased yet again after a series of Indian raids well to the north in the Tennessee Valley and America's declaration of war against Great Britain. With war declared against Great Britain and the seizure of Mobile from Spain, settlers in the Mississippi Territory were anticipating that the British would stir up ill will against Americans among the surrounding Native Americans, with the Spanish in nearby Pensacola likely becoming their allies. Judge Toulmin, however, supported Indian agent Benjamin Hawkins and urged calm and a restraint of governmental action.[33]

By August 1813, the situation had deteriorated to the point that Judge Toulmin concluded "that war exists between a part of the Creek nation and the people of the United States." This statement was made after an engagement at Burnt Corn Creek, near present-day Monroeville, occurring on July 27, 1813,[34] between a group of militia led by Toulmin's nemesis, James Caller, and Creek warriors, who were returning home from Spanish Pensacola where they had sought ammunition and supplies. Caller was embarrassed when he let his troops lose their early advantage gained from a surprise attack by letting their guard down as they ransacked the Indians' packhorses. This allowed the Creek warriors time to regroup and launch a surprise attack of their own, causing confusion and sending the Americans into a humiliating retreat. As the news of this debacle spread, the Bigbee settlers hurried to hastily construct forts for protection, an action that was referred to as "forting up." Toulmin reported to Governor David Holms that he was seeking refuge for himself and his family at Mount Vernon, a new fortification close to Fort Stoddert. On August 30, 1813, the Creeks (led by William Weatherford) attacked nearby Fort Mims in retaliation for Burnt Corn Creek, massacring some 250 settlers, including women and children. This massacre would become the rallying cry for American forces to come into the territory and annihilate the Creek Nation.[35]

Judge Toulmin survived the Creek War and continued to rule the Tombigbee District. With the defeat of the Creeks at Horseshoe Bend and the Treaty of Fort Jackson, millions of acres of Creek lands were ceded to the United States. With this came "Alabama Fever" and the pressure for statehood. After the Creek War, the settlers of the eastern Alabama section of the Mississippi Territory favored admission of the whole territory as one state, while the western section of the territory favored division of the territory into two states. This was a complete reversal of positions of the sections that had existed before the war. The settlers in the eastern section changed their position in large part due to the fact of the increasing population in the east caused by the acquisition of Mobile in 1813 and the cession of millions of acres of Creek lands in 1815. The easterners thought that they could gain control of the territorial legislature and perhaps even have the territorial capital moved to St. Stephens.[36]

In October 1816, a convention of eastern citizens in favor of the admission of the entire territory as a single state was held in the house of John Ford on the Pearl River. The convention selected Judge Toulmin to take their resolutions opposing division of the territory to Washington. Judge Toulmin's appearance before congressional committees and lobbying efforts was to no avail, however, as congressional sentiment favored division of the territory so as not to upset the balance of power between slave and non-slave states. Accordingly, on March 1, 1817, Congress passed an enabling act for the admission of the western portion of the territory into the Union as the state of Mississippi.[37]

Just a few days later, the Alabama Territorial Act of March 3, 1817, granted territorial status for the eastern section of the territory. This legislation set the boundaries for the new territory, made applicable the laws of the old Mississippi Territory until overridden by the new Alabama territorial legislature, established St. Stephens as the territorial capital, provided a new judge so as to allow the establishment of a three-judge territorial court, and created a House of Representatives and a Council (Senate) to comprise all the previous members of the Mississippi Territorial Legislature who had represented districts in the Alabama portion of the old territory. The act further provided that the governor and secretary would be appointed by the president, possessing the same powers, performing the same duties, and receiving the same pay as the previous governor and secretary of the Mississippi Territory.[38] Judge Toulmin remained as one of the three judges who were all to be presidential appointees. The judges were expected to ride circuit and to preside over "superior courts" in the counties. They were also required to meet twice a year at St. Stephens to hear appeals and to exercise federal jurisdiction within the territory. For the remainder of the territorial existence, Toulmin shared the three-judge bench with John W. Walker of Madison County, who would become one of Alabama's first US senators, and Henry Y. Webb of Perry and Greene Counties, who later served as a state circuit court judge—which made him a member of the first Alabama Supreme Court.[39]

Not surprisingly, Judge Toulmin was elected as a delegate to the Constitutional Convention of 1819. Although he was not put on the select Committee of Fifteen to draft a proposed constitution, nevertheless this committee drafted a constitution containing a liberal suffrage provision like those of Toulmin's Kentucky and that was more democratic than those of the older southern states. Paul Pruitt proffers that Toulmin's status as a "good Jeffersonian" made it likely that Toulmin also supported the liberal provisions that afforded slaves basic legal protections and judicial rights, banned the slave trade, and required humane treatment, among others. His role in the convention was otherwise rather limited and ineffective. In this regard, he was unable to make more definite the provisions regarding religious freedom nor to apply the federal three-fifths ratio as a basis for reapportioning state senate districts. His one modest success was supporting a provision requiring for the popular election of sheriffs, but he was unable to successfully oppose a provision allowing the popular election of clerks of court.[40]

As soon as the first elections were held for circuit court judges who would also sit collectively as a supreme court, Toulmin sought to be elected to the First Circuit, but he was surprisingly trounced by Abner S. Lipscomb, a former territorial legislator, by a vote of sixty-three to five. Toulmin was still Czar of the Tombigbee District, but he obviously did not fare well outside of his district as shown by the failure of the 1819 legislature to elect him to a circuit court judgeship.[41] He was, however, elected to the 1821 legislature. By now, however, the strains of the frontier, its wild inhabitants, filibusterers, and traveling throughout and tending to seven circuit courts twice a year were getting to him. Thus, generally fatigued at this point, Toulmin was glad to accept the offer of the 1821 legislature to study, revise, and digest the state's statute law. He produced an outstanding work consisting of almost a thousand pages of text titled *1823 Digest of the Laws of the State of Alabama.* He still had other important responsibilities. He was an emissary for and reported to federal officials in Natchez and Washington. He also represented American citizens in disputes with Spanish officials, primarily regarding the excessive duties imposed for use of the area's river system. Toulmin did not live to see his work in final print, but before he died he succeeded in securing a promise of $1,500 from the 1822 legislature to finish the project.[42]

Toulmin died on November 11, 1823, on his cotton plantation near Fort Stoddert, ending a remarkable career on the frontier of the Old Southwest. In his will, Toulmin provided for the emancipation of his loyal slave, Tony, dictating that he be allowed to go to any state where he could be granted his freedom and declaring that he felt "towards him almost as one of my family rather than a slave."

Toulmin's career was summarized by this author in a previous work. "For a period of fourteen years, he brought order and balance to a remote area of the nation that was filled with raucous characters and international intrigue. Fearing no one, whether a former vice president, prominent filibustering local citizens, or rowdy backwoodsmen, Toulmin courageously transformed his remote frontier outpost into a civilized community ready for statehood."[43]

As Paul Pruitt Jr. said of the "frontier Justinian": "What he left behind, apart from printed pages, was a legacy pointing toward the supremacy of the law. It could justly be said of him that neither distance, hardship, danger, intrigue, politics nor political persecution could shake his faith in the rule of law. . . . A judge and legal scholar, Toulmin could not suppress the anarchic features of frontier life. But he could help to determine the structures that would stand when chaos had run its course."

2

SAMUEL DALE

Frontiersman and Hero of the Canoe Fight

In this chapter we examine the life of Samuel Dale, a scout, frontiersmen, soldier, and public servant who played an important role in carving the state of Alabama out of the Mississippi Territory. His exploits in the Creek War of 1813–1814 earned him hero status among early Alabamians and the nickname of the "Daniel Boone of Alabama." He is particularly known for his participation in the legendary "Canoe Fight" in which he and two other militiamen took on a canoe full of Creek warriors who outnumbered them three to one and killed each of them in hand-to-hand combat.

Samuel Dale was born in 1772 in Rockbridge County, Virginia, to Scotch-Irish parents Samuel and Mary O'Brian Dale, who had just moved from the vicinity of Carlisle, Pennsylvania. When Samuel was three years old, the family moved again to the forks of the Clinch River in Washington County, Virginia. There they purchased a piece of property where they united with several neighbors to build a stockade called Glade Hollow Fort for protection against Indians in the area. After several ambushes and massacres, however, the families, including the Dales, moved westward river by river. Before leaving for Georgia, young Samuel had seen the extremely gruesome results of several Indian attacks.[1]

In 1783 Samuel's family moved to the vicinity of Greensborough, Georgia, where the family anticipated more tranquility than they had experienced on the Clinch River. But within a few months of their arrival, the surrounding Creeks and Cherokees began to stir up trouble to the extent that the Dales, along with thirty other families, had to seek shelter at a place called Carmichael's Station, which consisted of several log cabins built around a small square with usually a blockhouse in the center. During his stay at Carmichael's Station, Samuel witnessed several Indian attacks and killed at least one Indian himself.[2] As for his youthful experiences, Dale summarized them as follows: "Inured to every hardship, living on the coarsest food, earning our bread with our rifles cocked and primed, often witnessing the ruin of homesteads, and the murder of families, my own life constantly in jeopardy,

Figure 2.1. Engraving of Sam Dale in his legendary canoe fight. Courtesy of the Alabama Department of Archives and History.

yet ever hopeful, ever relying on Providence, ever conscious of my duty to my fellow-men, never counting a personal risk for others as a merit, but only as a duty, and, in spite of privation and danger, loving the wilderness to the last."[3]

Both of his parents died in 1791, leaving nineteen-year-old Samuel responsible for his eight orphaned brothers and sisters. He was for a while overwhelmed as he owned no land, was burdened with debt, and had eight mouths to feed, and the deep wilderness around their cabin was teeming with hostile warriors. Despite these obstacles, Samuel was able to provide for his siblings. In 1793, conditions were such that he even felt comfortable leaving an older man in charge of his farm, along with his brothers and sisters, so that he could volunteer to join a cavalry troop organized under the authority of the governor of Georgia to fight Creeks who were disgruntled at the continuing encroachment of whites. Young Dale indicated that their accoutrements consisted of a "coonskin hat, bear-skin vest, short hunting-shirt and trowsers of homespun stuff, buckskin leggings, a blanket tied behind our saddles, a wallet for parched corn, coal flour, or other chance provisions, a long rifle and hunting-knife." After his troop had scouted for a few months, they were mustered into the service of the United States. The money Dale earned for this, along with what the children made from tobacco, allowed him to pay for one-half of their land and to stockpile provisions. The next year Dale could extinguish the entire debt on their land. In 1794, Dale's troop was called out again when Creeks resumed burning houses and running off horses and cattle. During this period of service, Dale was involved in several skirmishes with raiding warriors. In one of these, Dale's troop followed warriors to the

Okfuskee village on the Chattahoochee River, where they killed thirteen warriors and captured ten before burning the village to the ground.[4]

When the troop disbanded in 1796, Dale traveled to Savannah, Georgia, where he founded a wagon business engaged in the transportation of goods. He ran this business in the winter and returned to his farm in the spring to help his brothers with planting. The business prospered such that Dale could invest what little capital goods he had on a trip to trade among the Creeks in 1799. Soon thereafter, in response to the increasing migration of settlers from Georgia and the Carolinas into the Mississippi Territory, Dale contracted to transport families into the territory by wagon and then return to Savannah with Indian trade goods. Because of the name he made for himself in trade with the Indians of the region, in 1803 Dale was appointed as a guide for federal forces mapping a road through the Cherokee nation in northwest Georgia. While in the Cherokee lands, Dale witnessed the death of Doublehead, the great chief of the Cherokees. His death resulted from a feeling among his warriors that he had committed treason by selling a piece of their country near the shoals of the Tennessee River to a company of American speculators.[5]

For a few years, a farm in Jones County, Georgia, was Dale's and his siblings' home. In 1811, however, Dale accompanied US Indian agent Benjamin Hawkins to the annual grand council of the Creeks at the ancient town of Tuckabatchee on the Tallapoosa River in present-day Elmore County, Alabama. With rumors swirling that northwestern Indians were heading south, some five thousand people including many Cherokees and Choctaws were in attendance. The day after the council commenced, the celebrated Shawnee chief, Tecumseh, made a grand entrance with a few of his warriors. Big Warrior of the Creeks gave Tecumseh and his band a cabin in which to congregate. The visitors danced at night in a style familiar to the northern tribes, and every morning Tecumseh sent word that he was ready to address the council, only to later indicate that the "sun had traveled too far" and so he would have to wait the next day to make his address.[6]

Agent Hawkins became impatient and, despite Dale's encouragement to stay, he left the council. Dale went with him for about twelve miles, at which point he convinced Hawkins to stop for a day or two. Dale then returned to a point where he could hear Tecumseh when he finally addressed the council. According to Dale, the speech's "prevalent expression was a sneer of hatred and defiance; sometimes a murderous smile; for a brief interval, a sentiment of profound sorrow pervaded it; and, at the close, a look of concentrated vengeance, such, I suppose, as distinguishes the arch-enemy of mankind." Tecumseh's incendiary speech encouraged the Creeks to remove white settlers from their lands. He reportedly said, "Let the white race perish. They seize your land; they corrupt their women; they trample on the ashes of your dead! Back whence they came, upon a trail of blood, they must be driven. . . . Burn their dwellings! Destroy their stock! Slay their wives and children! The Red Man owns the country, and the Pale-faces must never enjoy it."[7]

During this period, Dale was still engaged in the business of transporting settlers into the Mississippi Territory through the Creek Nation. During his travels, Dale learned while in Pensacola that the lower Creeks were becoming increasingly hostile and disgruntled, and that the Spanish were covertly supplying them with arms and ammunition.[8] In June 1813, with rumors abound of an imminent attack by the Red Stick Creeks, Dale was engaged to move Judge Reuben Saffold and his family to the Tombigbee District. To maximize safety, Dale wanted to join a detachment of troops that had been ordered from Fort Mitchell to Mobile, but the convoy had left two days prior to Dale's arrival at the fort. Dale nevertheless pushed on and safely delivered Reuben and his family to their new home in Clarke County. During the journey with the Saffold family, Dale became convinced that the Creeks had determined on war against the encroaching white settlers. A deposition taken from Sam Maniac bolstered Dale's belief of an impending war. Maniac stated in the deposition that a Creek party was headed to Pensacola armed with a letter from a British general to the Spanish governor allowing them to get all the arms they needed. High Head Jim, a Creek leader, told Maniac that once they got the arms and ammunition that they wanted from Pensacola, Creeks "on the Coosa, Tallapoosa, and Black Warrior would attack the settlements in the forks of the Tombigbee and Alabama." Due to the urgency of the information in Maniac's statement, Dale forwarded it to Colonel James Caller, Commanding Officer of the Clarke County, Fifteenth Regiment Militia of the Mississippi Territory. Caller, in turn, sent a communication to Brigadier General Claiborne, based in part on information provided by Dale, informing him that they deemed it advisable to call up the militia to attack McQueen's party on their return trip from Pensacola.[9]

To recruit for such an attack, in July 1813 Dale headed to Point Jackson on the Tombigbee River, where settlers were constructing a stockade called Fort Madison to shelter their families. Of these settlers, Dale could recruit about fifty men and took them to join Colonel Caller and his command of 180 men. On July 27, 1813, Dale led a scouting party that quickly discovered an advance party of Creeks with packmules near Burnt Corn Creek as they peacefully lunched. As the main body of men joined the scouts, Dale was wounded on his left side with a ball eventually lodging against his backbone. One of his men reloaded Dale's rifle for him so he could continue despite the wound. It turns out Dale suffered probably the first injury of the first engagement of the Creek War of 1813–1814. This engagement, however, turned into a rout of the Americans because they lost their advantage of surprise when many of them spent valuable time ransacking the pack mules while the Creek warriors were rallying from their initial retreat. Dale asserted after the battle, however, that the rout would not have occurred had not someone yelled "retreat!" which caused confusion among the raw and undisciplined troops who fled from the field of battle. Indeed, but for use of the word "retreat," Dale believed that they would have achieved a total victory. However, to make matters worse, Colonel Caller and a Major Wood became lost after the battle and were not found until about August 10, 1813, both near death. Dale indicated that although no one who knew Caller or Wood would question their courage, "the disaster drew down on them much scurrility."[10]

After the Battle of Burnt Corn Creek, Dale went back to Fort Madison in Clarke County to recuperate from his wounds and to help defend the women and children there seeking protection from Creek war parties.[11] At this time, Dale painted a bleak picture of the Tombigbee District: "The condition of the settlements had become deplorable. Immigration was suspended; the mails cut off; several murders had occurred; the fields were abandoned; houses burned; cattle and crops destroyed; and the citizens crowded into ill-constructed stockades with insufficient supplies, afraid to venture out for provisions, and scourged within with typhus, scarlatina and dysentery." Despite these observations, Dale took charge of Fort Glass, a small stockade only about a quarter of a mile away from Fort Madison. Here Dale was responsible for fifteen families. Soon thereafter Colonel Carson, the commanding officer of Fort Madison, was ordered to abandon it. He reluctantly obeyed the order, and his troops headed to Mobile, St. Stephens, or Mount Vernon as needed. As Carson's troops marched out of Fort Madison, Dale, who had decided to stay, and a group of about fifty men, marched in.[12]

In November 1813, about two months after the massacre at Fort Mims, Dale was contacted by General Claiborne to send two of his best scouts from Fort Madison with two of Claiborne's men to reconnoiter the so-called Wolf-path trail near Burnt Corn that led to Pensacola, so as to remove roaming bands of Creek warriors from the area. Dale thus struck out with some seventy troops, consisting of thirty Mississippi Territorial volunteers and forty Clarke County militiamen. On November 12, 1813, Dale and sixty of his men eventually came upon the mouth of Randon's Creek on the Alabama River where they encountered a party of eleven Creek warriors paddling in their direction. Despite being outnumbered three to one,[13] Dale was determined to take them on. With a majority of his troops across the river, Dale ordered a free African American named Caesar to paddle a small dugout canoe that could only hold himself, Jeremiah Austill, and James Smith. As Caesar paddled toward the Creek canoe, Dale, Austill, and Smith all attempted to fire their rifles, but two of the weapons did not fire because the river water dampened their priming. When the canoes soon came into contact, Dale leaped up and placed one foot in each boat. Dale soon clubbed two warriors to death, saving Austill from a likely death. No longer able to keep a foot in each canoe, Dale leapt into the Creek canoe, causing his own canoe to float off. Dale nevertheless proceeded to kill two of the remaining warriors in the Creek canoe, while Austill shot one more. That left the chief who recognized Dale and, purportedly, shouted in English, "Big Sam, I am a man—I am coming—come on." The chief then struck Dale with his rifle, which dislocated Dale's shoulder. Dale in turn bayonetted the chief to death.[14]

This fierce hand-to-hand skirmish, forever hence known as the "Canoe Fight," lasted only about ten minutes, but it earned its American participants instant fame as their fellow soldiers watched from both sides of the river, cheering as the bodies of dead warriors were thrown into the river. Dale's leading role in this skirmish attained him hero status, and he became as legendary to Alabamians as Daniel Boone and Davy Crockett were to Kentuckians and Tennesseans, respectively. Historian Joel Campbell DuBose looked upon the skirmish as follows: "This is one of the most desperate engagements that ever tested individual heroism and manly prowess."[15]

Just a few weeks after the Canoe Fight, Dale accompanied General Ferdinand Claiborne's federal troops to attack many Creeks who had gathered at Econochaca, or the "Holy Ground," located on the Alabama River in present-day Lowndes County. Prophet Josiah Francis had established this settlement as a safe haven "at a spot made sacred by the great spirit . . . never to be sullied by the footsteps of the real white man." Because of this, they were convinced that an impenetrable barrier protected their village, across which a white man could not traverse. Due to this feeling, as well as in anticipation of a retaliatory strike by the Americans in response to the massacre at Fort Mims, many Red Stick Creek families left their old towns for the presumed safety afforded by this sacred village. However, before General Claiborne and his troops could set out, a group of officers signed a petition requesting that their commander abandon the proposed mission, citing such reasons as insufficient food and munitions; a lack of warm clothing and shoes; no roads or paths to transport supplies; and the fact that many soldiers' enlistments were due to expire within a few days. General Claiborne, on the other hand, was bound to proceed so that he could make amends for the embarrassment of his regiment's performance at Fort Mims.[16]

Notwithstanding their petition, Claiborne's officers pronounced that they would "cheerfully obey" the decision of their commander to press forward. According to Dale, the men told their commander that "they would follow him or die in the wilderness." On that note, on December 13, 1813,

Claiborne's army set out from Fort Claiborne to the strains of "Over the Hill and Far Away." The army consisted of the US Third Regiment, the Mississippi Territory volunteers under Joseph Carson; Choctaw chief Pushmataha and his warriors; Major Cassel's Cavalry Battalion; and Captains Bailey Heard and Samuel Dale. Claiborne's soldiers arrived near the Holy Ground on December 22, 1813. When they attacked the next day, the American forces were successful, except for the fact that they had left a gap where Prophet Joseph and his followers could escape to the Alabama River, as they did when they figured out that their mystical powers had failed them, allowing the white soldiers to break through their supposed impenetrable barrier. The most daring escape was the one undertaken by William Weatherford, who had been left high and dry by the Prophet and his followers. Dale witnessed Weatherford's escape, indicating that Weatherford "with difficulty escaped on a powerful charger, making his famous leap of twenty feet over a deep ravine, and down the bluff into the Alabama, which his gallant courser swam, the chief holding the rifle over his head, and shouting his war-whoop as soon as he descended the bank."[17]

Just considering the number of casualties, the Battle of the Holy Ground was not that momentous—only one of Claiborne's soldiers and an estimated thirty-three Red Sticks were killed. Although there was not much of military significance resulting from the battle, Dale emphasized its psychological impact: "The moral effect of this bold movement into the heart of the nation, upon ground held sacred and impregnable was great. It taught the savages that they were neither inaccessible nor invulnerable; it destroyed their confidence in their prophets, and it proved what volunteers, even without shoes, clothing, blankets, or provisions would do for their country."[18]

During the Battle of Burnt Corn Creek, a ball had lodged next to Dale's backbone; after the Battle of the Holy Ground, it was extracted by Dr. Neal Smith, a surgeon at Fort Claiborne. In March 1814, Dale joined several other men to farm for a while near Fort Claiborne in Monroe County. They had agreed to do this for Peter Randon, who had escaped from Fort Mims and who feared in his absence that someone might take over who would be hard to oust. Dale furnished a thousand bushels of corn from this farm to General McIntosh for the starving forces of Major Woolfolk at Fort Jackson. In late December 1814, Dale, who was at Fort Hawkins on business, was induced by Agent Benjamin Hawkins and General McIntosh to deliver a message to General Jackson in New Orleans. He arrived just as the Battle of New Orleans was commencing on January 8, 1815. General Jackson was so impressed with the speed in which the message had been delivered that he held up the dispatches and Dale's credentials from Colonel Hawkins and said to his officers, "This express has been brought from Georgia in eight days." He then complained that their expresses from Mobile were often en route for fourteen days. Jackson next ordered Dale to return to the Indian Agency in Milledgeville, Georgia, as fast as he had come.[19]

After his legendary dispatch mission to General Jackson, Dale returned to an area now known as Dale's Ferry on the Alabama River in Monroe County to engage in merchandising and farming. Dale's Ferry was not too far from the mouth of Randon's Creek, the site of the Canoe Fight. Dale's reputation was such that Mississippi territorial governor David Holmes appointed Dale as the colonel of the local militia, the tax assessor and collector for the county, and the commissioner to take the census and organize beats or precincts with blank commissions for justice of the peace, constables, and other civil offices. Governor Holmes indicated to Dale that he would rely totally on his discretion to fill these offices. In 1816, Dale was elected a delegate to a convention seeking a division of the Mississippi Territory, with the western portion to form a state and the eastern to become the Alabama Territory. In 1817, he was elected as a representative to the first General Assembly of the Alabama Territory. While serving in that legislative body, Governor William Wyatt Bibb commissioned Dale as a colonel in the Alabama militia. Dale soon had to leave his legislative post to call up thirty volunteers to go to the scene of murders committed by Savannah Jack in Butler County. In a September 23, 1813, letter to Governor Bibb, Dale reported on several scouting expeditions he had made in response to these murders and concluded, "I am under a full belief there is [sic] no Indians of the disaffected in this quarter." He then asked about the future of the fort he established in Butler County: "You will be so obliging as to saying what manner, I shall dispose of the publick [sic] arms and other stores which is now at this post, and whether the post will still be kept up." He later served in the state's legislature from 1819 to 1820 and again from 1824 to 1828. In 1821, he was appointed a commissioner to establish a public road from Tuscaloosa to Pensacola and then on to Blakeley in Baldwin County and Fort Claiborne.[20]

The 1821 session of the Alabama legislature granted the first pension in the state's history to Samuel Dale. In this regard, it adopted resolutions praising Dale's military service and bestowed upon him the rank of brigadier general by brevet, with lifetime benefits of a colonel in the Army of the United States—to be paid during his life half the pay now allowed by the United States to such colonels. Recognizing that he had protected many vulnerable frontier settlers from the "barbarities of savage warfare," and recognizing that services during the Creek War had subjected him to "privations, hardships and difficulties that have impaired his constitution and reduced him to indigence," the legislature resolved that it had a duty "not only to remunerate him from losses actually sustained, but also to compensate him for his distinguished services." Deliberating in this vein, the legislature also discharged an indebtedness of just shy of $230.00 owed by Dale for the collection of taxes in Monroe County for the year of 1817. In the 1822 session, however, a group attempted to take Dale's pension away because of a concern for the inequity of singling out just one person for a pension, and because of the belief that the public treasury was not intended for charitable purposes. Although the attempt to take away the pension failed, the anti-pension faction was able to take away Dale's designation as brigadier general. During the 1823 session, however, his pension was withdrawn altogether. In an effort to retain his pension, Dale went to court, but the Alabama Supreme Court ruled that the legislature was within its province to withdraw the pension.[21]

The Marquis de Lafayette of France, the last surviving general of the Revolutionary War and a former allied aide to General George Washington, visited Alabama as part of a nationwide visit to the United States honoring the nation's fiftieth anniversary. In 1825, while serving in the state legislature, Dale also served on the committee to meet Lafayette at the Fort Mitchell crossing of the Chattahoochee River and escort him to Montgomery. Dale recalls that also on this committee were John Murphy, a future governor of Alabama, Colonel Freeman, Bolling Hall, and John D. Bibb, a brother of the first two governors of the state. Lafayette arrived at the Fort Mitchell crossing on March 31, 1825, where his Georgia escorts turned him and his entourage over to the Alabama welcoming party, including Samuel Dale. To Dale, the most noteworthy aspect of the reception was the enthusiasm displayed by the Creeks under the leadership of Chilly McIntosh, son of General William McIntosh, in greeting Lafayette by marching past the general in single file, each one giving him their hand.[22]

In 1831, Dale was appointed along with Colonel George Struthers Gaines to help remove the Choctaw Indians to their treaty-mandated territory on the Arkansas and Red Rivers. The Treaty of Dancing Rabbit had mandated their removal and the cession of all their prime lands in Alabama and Mississippi. Dale found the Choctaw party to be very sad as they had made no arrangements to leave until the last moment. They thus hung around their humble cabins and returned repeatedly to the resting places of their dead. In the meanwhile, on November 21, 1831, a Choctaw named Ia-cha-hopa sold his reserve of two sections of land to Dale for $700. The land consisted of approximately 1,280 acres near Dale's new residence in Lauderdale County, Mississippi. Dale was now ready to collect and transport the Indians remaining on the ceded lands, but he was unable to complete the journey because of severe injuries he sustained when his horse fell and rolled over him early in the trip.[23]

Samuel Dale spent most of his remaining years in Lauderdale County,

Mississippi, where he became that county's first representative in the Mississippi legislature in 1836. He traveled to the nation's capital, where he visited with President Andrew Jackson and other leading political figures of the time, including John C. Calhoun, Henry Clay, Daniel Webster, and Thomas Benton. Alabama senator William R. King sent word to Dale on his visit to the nation's capital that President Jackson would like to see him. Dale met the president as he was walking on the lawn in front of the White House. As President Jackson approached he grabbed Dale by the hand warmly and told him that no introduction was necessary: "I shall never forget Sam Dale." Their conversation ran the gamut from a discussion of nullification to Dale's claims against the government due him for corn and other supplies furnished to the troops in service of the United States. Despite his efforts, and the influence of his powerful friends, Dale failed in getting his claim satisfactorily settled.[24]

During peacetime, Samuel Dale was greatly admired by the Creeks—so much so that he served as a groomsman at the wedding of his old foe, William Weatherford. Legend has it that Choctaw chieftain Greenwood LeFlore was heard to say at Dale's grave, "You sleep here, Big Sam, but your spirit was a chieftain and a brave in the hunting-ground of the sky."[25] In turn, Dale "entertained a strong attachment for the Indians, extolled their courage, their love of country, their patience, their tenderness to their children, and their reverence for the dead." Dale showed his kindness to those Indians that were homeless and oppressed by letting them camp on his plantation and subsist on Dale's crops. According to Dale's early biographer, J. F. H. Claiborne, Dale's physical characteristics were much like that of the Creeks and Choctaws, who surrounded him in life. Claiborne reports that Dale was "six feet two inches, erect, square-shouldered, raw-boned, and muscular, noted particularly for great strength and length of arm. In many respects, physical and moral, he resembled his antagonists of the woods. He had the square forehead, the high cheek-bones, the compressed lips—in fact the physiognomy of the Indian, relieved, however, by a fine, benevolent Saxon eye. Like the Red Man. . . . He was habitually taciturn; his face and manner grave; he spoke slowly, and in low tones, and seldom laughed."[26]

Samuel Dale died on May 24, 1841, and was buried near Daleville, Lauderdale County, Mississippi, which was named for him. Although, no official record has been found that Dale ever married or had any children in his book, *Thunder in Meridian*, author Hewitt Clarke indicates that Dale indeed had a Creek Indian wife and children in Alabama. In Alabama, Dale County is also named in his honor. Dale was certainly in the early vanguard of those founders who carved the state of Alabama out of the wilderness. His life was full of adventure and importance.[27]

3

GENERAL JOHN COFFEE

Military Hero, Land Surveyor, and Founder of Florence, Alabama

John Coffee served with distinction under the command of General Andrew Jackson during the War of 1812 in Alabama and Louisiana and was one of the principal founders of Florence, situated in Lauderdale County. After the Battle of New Orleans in January 1815, Coffee settled in north Alabama, where he became a surveyor, land developer, and planter. In March 1818, he joined other influential investors to form the Cypress Land Company and subsequently established the town of Florence at the foot of the Muscle Shoals on the Tennessee River.

John Coffee was born on July 2, 1772, in Prince Edward County, Virginia, the same year as Samuel Dale, less than one hundred miles from Dale's birthplace in Rockbridge County, Virginia. Coffee's parents were Lieutenant Joshua Coffee (1745–1797) and Elizabeth Graves (1742–1804), whose great-grandfather had been one of the first settlers in Jamestown in 1607. In 1775, Joshua, a tobacco planter, moved his family from Virginia to Granville County, North Carolina, and later served in the Revolutionary War, during which he commanded "a company of mounted gunmen in the service of the colonies."[1]

After the close of the Revolutionary War, Joshua Coffee moved to Rockingham County, North Carolina, where he died in 1797. In addition to his widow, he left three children, Thomas Graves Coffee, John Coffee, and Mary Coffee. In his will, he left his eldest son, John, five slaves, specifying that they were to be sold to acquire land for him and his mother. Waiting to execute what his father had stipulated in his will, John Coffee briefly became a resident of Alabama while the younger children moved to Tennessee. In April 1798, finally fulfilling the direction to sell the family's slaves for land, Coffee joined his mother at the village of Haysborough, on the Cumberland River near the present village of Madison, a few miles above Nashville. There, Coffee became a merchant and a surveyor.[2]

At some point during his early years, John Coffee met and became the loyal friend of future US president Andrew Jackson and remained so until his death. In 1804, Coffee formed a business partnership with Jackson, as

Figure 3.1. General John Coffee, military leader and land surveyor. Courtesy of the Alabama
Department of Archives and History.

well as John Hutchins, a nephew of Jackson's wife, Rachel. These partners opened a tavern and dry-goods store four miles from Jackson's plantation at the Hermitage. In all, Coffee was engaged as a merchant for five years—from 1802 until 1807. He and his partners also invested in land in north Alabama. In 1807, Coffee was appointed as a surveyor of public lands on the Elk and Duck Rivers in Tennessee. The surveying business proved to be very profit-able for Coffee, enabling him to pay off the debts from the mercantile busi-ness and allowing him to reserve several valuable tracts of land to himself.[3]

Coffee endeared himself further to Andrew Jackson by participating in a duel with Nathaniel A. McNairy on March 1, 1806. Thomas Swann, a Vir-ginia lawyer, had made disparaging remarks about Jackson, and then encour-aged McNairy to challenge Jackson to a duel. Jackson responded through Coffee that he would cane Swann, and in fact did so, as he did not consider Swann a gentleman worthy of satisfaction through a duel. Therefore, it was left to Coffee, representing Jackson, to duel McNairy, standing in behalf of Swann. The duel occurred just over the Tennessee line in Kentucky. McNairy unintentionally fired before the word had been given authorizing the duel to commence, slightly wounding Coffee in the thigh.[4]

On October 3, 1809, Coffee married Mary Donelson, a niece of Rachel Jackson. This would, of course, further strengthen Coffee's ties to Jackson. It was a true May–December marriage, as Coffee was thirty-seven years old and Mary Donelson was a bride of sixteen. Mary was the youngest of thir-teen children, and she and John would have ten children of their own. For a

Figure 3.2. Andrew Jackson. Coffee was a lifelong
friend and business partner of Jackson. Courtesy of
Alabama Department of Archives and History.

dowry, her father gave Mary a farm on Stone's River, about ten miles from
the Hermitage in Rutherford County, Tennessee. Andrew Jackson gave the
bride of his former partner a wedding gift in the form of canceled notes representing a debt that Coffee had incurred with the senior partner in the mercantile firm.[5]

Soon after John and Mary Coffee settled into their Stone's River
farm, John was selected to serve as clerk of the County Court of Rutherford County. He occupied this office and ran the Stone's River farm until
the onslaught of the Creek War of 1813–1814 led him into military service.
Andrew Jackson soon recommended Coffee as colonel of one of the regiments
to be raised in Tennessee. Not surprisingly, with such a recommendation,
Coffee was made a colonel of the Second Regiment of Volunteer Mounted
Riflemen, which was composed mostly of Tennessee militiamen, except for
one company of volunteers from Madison County, Alabama. The so-called
Natchez Expedition resulted from a call by President James Madison for fifteen hundred volunteers for the defense of New Orleans. It turned out, however, that New Orleans was not at that time threatened by the British. While
Jackson—then a major general of the Tennessee militia—was itching to get
into military service, Colonel Coffee had raised a troop of cavalry numbering
670 for the Second Regiment of Volunteer Mounted riflemen to join Jackson
in Natchez. Jackson went by river in flat-bottomed boats to Natchez with two
regiments of infantry, commanded by Colonels Thomas Hart Benton and
William Hall. They left Nashville on January 7, 1813, while Colonel Coffee's

regiment was assembling at Franklin, Tennessee, for their march overland to Natchez. Their march down the Natchez Trace finally commenced on January 19, 1813. On February 16, all three regiments of Coffee and Jackson met in Natchez in anticipation of moving on to New Orleans. After months of inactivity, however, an order came from the War Department in Washington for the regiments to disband. Instead of disbanding, a disappointed General Jackson led the entire force back to Nashville at his own expense.[6]

Not long after their return to Nashville, the news reached them of the Fort Mims massacre occurring on August 30, 1813. As the news of this tragedy quickly spread nationwide, there were outraged cries for revenge and a call for arms. On September 24, 1813, the Tennessee Legislature, responding to the urging of Governor Willie Blount, gave the governor authority to call up five thousand men for a three-month tour of duty. Andrew Jackson in turn was authorized to call out two thousand militiamen in a retaliatory invasion of the Creek Nation. In his plea for recruits, Jackson stated, "Your frontier is threatened with invasion of the savage foe . . . with scalping knives unsheathed to butcher your wives, your children, and your babes." In response to the legislative action authorizing a call to arms, Coffee was promoted to brigadier general after raising two additional mounted regiments, and was given the command of a brigade consisting of approximately 1,300 cavalrymen, which included his former Second Regiment of Volunteer Mounted Riflemen.[7]

Colonel Coffee and his troops assembled at Fayetteville, Tennessee, with General Jackson and his militia. Coffee and his regiment of cavalry and mounted gunmen set out first and reached Huntsville on October 4, 1813. Ten days later they were joined by Jackson and his forces. In a letter to his wife, Mary, just prior to the arrival of Jackson, Coffee painted an optimistic picture of this expedition: "I am sufficiently strong to go anywhere without any kind of danger, and when General Jackson comes on with his 2,500 men, now at Fayetteville, we shall be able to overrun the Creek nation, and I fear we shall never see an Indian for, as they hear of our strength, they will fly before us and never risk an action."[8]

Colonel Coffee soon headed south to the hastily constructed Fort Strother on the Coosa River, located about thirty miles south of present-day Gadsden, whence General Jackson dispatched troops to attack nearby Red Stick towns. The goal of these troops was to ultimately construct a military road to Mobile, connecting Tennessee with the Gulf of Mexico. General Jackson shortly ordered Coffee to take about six hundred cavalrymen on a mission to forage for food for his troops, who were underfed and inadequately supplied. Coffee wrote to his wife, "As I have this moment arrived here [headquarters twenty-four miles south from Ditto's Landing] from a rout into the

Indian Country of ten days, have been to the Black Warrior Towns, where Mrs. Crawley[9] was carried and find them all deserted by the Indians, leaving their corn and some other plunder behind." Coffee had marched two hundred miles in ten days, burned two towns, and obtained three hundred bushels of corn. The legendary David Crockett[10] was attached as a scout in Coffee's command, and was present at the burning of Black Warrior's Town. While gathering the fruits of their efforts, Crockett observed, "In the field where we gathered the corn, we saw plenty of fresh Indian tracks, and we had no doubt they had been scared off by our arrival."[11]

After this forage raid, General Coffee, who had doubted the willingness of the Red Sticks to fight, would soon find out that they would fight until the last man was left standing, allowing no quarter. Upon learning of the presence of a sizeable Red Stick stronghold nearby, on November 2, 1813, Jackson dispatched his right-hand man, General Coffee, and 900 mounted troops to destroy the Creek town of Tallushatchee, thirteen miles east of Fort Strother. Arriving the next day, Coffee divided his troops into two columns, which then encircled the village. Early the next morning, Coffee's troops had progressed to within a mile of Tallushatchee, at which point they split and surrounded the Red Stick village. Two detachments of scouts were then sent into the heart of the village to draw the warriors into a trap. Red Sticks rushed to the outer perimeter of federal soldiers, where a hail of lethal gunfire drove them back. Fighting lasted until the last warrior fell. In all, 186 Red Sticks were killed, including several women and children. The remaining women and children were taken prisoner. Coffee's troops, by contrast, suffered only five killed and forty-one wounded. Coffee thus was victorious in the first battle of Jackson's foray into Alabama. Crockett, who was still assigned to General Coffee, said of the battle that they "shot them like dogs" and others were burned to death when the house they sought refuge in was set ablaze. Sensitive to the criticism aimed at the death of Creek women and children, Coffee said that their killing was unintentional and blamed the warriors for seeking refuge in their houses with their families. Nevertheless, General Coffee was pleased with his triumph, telling his wife, "Our men are in excellent spirits—we shall very soon finish the working of destruction of those wretches and return home." General Jackson was jubilant over Coffee's victory, writing to Governor Blount in Tennessee, "We have retaliated for the destruction of Fort Mims."[12]

One of the effects of the destruction of the village of Tallushatchee was to convince many Creek villages of the need to ally themselves with the American forces under General Jackson, even though William Weatherford warned of an assault on any town or village doing so. The village of Talladega chose to defy that warning, thus prompting Weatherford, as promised, to attack the village with a thousand Red Stick warriors just as Coffee's men were returning from the victory at Tallushatchee. To get word to Jackson of their need for help, on November 7, 1813, a Talladega chief escaped to Fort Strother disguised in the skin of a hog to request help. Responding to this plea for help, General Jackson quickly headed south toward Talladega with 1,200 infantry and 800 cavalry and mounted riflemen. These combined forces arrived on November 9, 1813, and surrounded the besieging Red Sticks encircling Talladega in an effort to replicate Coffee's successful tactics at Tallushatchee. While inflicting approximately 300 casualties and breaking the siege, a gap in the encircling forces permitted William Weatherford and 700 of his warriors to escape and live to fight again. Jackson described this result as the "faux pas of the militia," yet he nevertheless praised the troops for their high spirits and bravery. Only fifteen Americans were killed during the battle.[13]

In January 1814, Coffee engaged many of the warriors who had escaped at Talladega in the Battle of Emuckfau Creek. General Jackson with new inexperienced troops headed out from Fort Strother in pursuit of a large contingent of Red Sticks camped in a bend of the Tallapoosa River near the mouth of Emuckfau Creek. On January 21, 1813, Jackson's forces camped for the night about three miles from the Red Sticks who were gathered at Emuckfau Creek. Jackson's forces were attacked early the next morning by the Red Sticks, who were on the offensive. After thirty minutes of fighting, Jackson's left wing under General Coffee charged and ran the Red Sticks from the field. Lacking confidence in his raw troops, General Jackson decided not to attempt to take the town at Emuckfau but instead to head back to Fort Strother to await another chance to attack the Creeks settling into the Horseshoe Bend. Only twenty of Jackson's men were killed while seventy-five were wounded. Some of these casualties had occurred at Enotochopco when the Americans were headed back to Fort Strother. Coffee was seriously wounded at Emuckfau, and was led off the battlefield on a litter. The next day, however, General Coffee mounted his horse in anticipation of a fight at Enotochopco and conducted himself with "his usual calm and deliberate firmness." After this engagement, though, Coffee convalesced for several weeks before rejoining Jackson in March 1814, just in time for the decisive Battle of Horseshoe Bend.[14]

On March 24, 1814, General Jackson set out to engage the Red Sticks in what he hoped would be the last major campaign against the Creek Nation. Waiting for Jackson and his troops at Horseshoe Bend (Tohopeka) were approximately 1,000 Red Stick warriors and another 350 women and children. At 6:30 A.M. on the day of the battle, General Jackson dispatched Coffee along with seven hundred cavalry and mounted gunmen, as well as six hundred friendly Cherokees and Creeks, to take up a position across the river

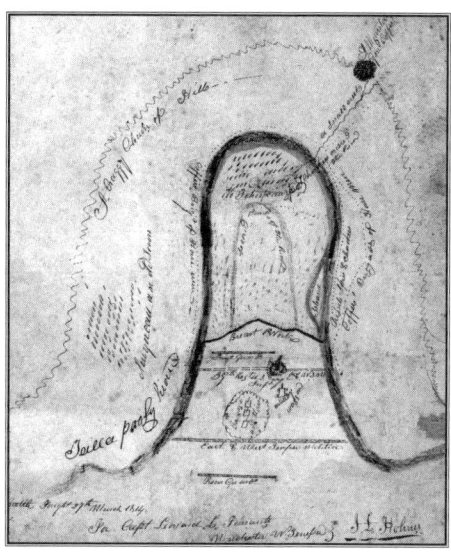

Figure 3.3. Map of Horseshoe Bend. Coffee played a significant role in the defeat of the Creeks at the Battle of Horseshoe Bend. Courtesy of the Alabama Department of Archives and History.

from Tohopeka where they could prevent the Red Sticks from escaping by crossing the river. The remainder of Jackson's men positioned themselves and their artillery in front of the breastworks that the Creeks had built blocking the top of the horseshoe. As the bombardment of the fortifications had begun at the top of the horseshoe, some of the allied Indians assigned to General Coffee swam across the Tallapoosa River to capture enemy canoes, which could be used for escape. They then used the canoes to ferry troops across the river to attack the village at the bottom of the horseshoe. After capturing the village, the troops could move up the shoe to commence firing at the breastworks from the rear, while General Jackson continued his frontal assault. Although greatly outnumbered, the Creek warriors kept up the fight for several more hours until darkness prevailed. In the meanwhile, many Red Sticks attempted to escape across the river as had been anticipated, but Coffee's troops shot them as they swam.[15]

The Battle of Horseshoe Bend in effect ended the Creek War of 1813–1814. Over 800 Creek warriors lost their lives in this battle, while only 49 Americans were killed and 153 wounded. Of the Creek casualties, it is estimated that approximately 250 to 300 warriors were killed trying to cross the river. Also, some 350 women and children were taken as prisoners. After the battle, Jackson and his men marched down the Tallapoosa River to its confluence with the Coosa River and built Fort Jackson, which was adjacent to the old French outpost at Fort Toulouse. Red Stick leader William Weatherford boldly walked into the fort and surrendered himself to General Jackson. Jackson was so impressed that he spared his life despite those who wanted to see him executed. Jackson, however, demanded a harsh peace, and on August 9, 1814, a treaty was signed resulting in the cession to the United States of approximately twenty-two million acres of Creek lands. This opened the floodgates as new settlers rushed into Alabama.[16]

Citizens fervently cheered Jackson's forces as they made their way back to Tennessee in May 1814. Waiting for them in Huntsville was a planned daylong celebration, which was hosted by LeRoy Pope and other town leaders. After they were saluted in the town square, the artillery company headed by General Jackson and his staff, and accompanied by General Coffee,[17] formed ranks at LeRoy Pope's newly completed brick mansion named "Poplar Grove," where there was a presentation of the colors. Later in the afternoon a dinner was served on the green immediately behind Pope's house in honor of Jackson and his staff, with upward of one hundred people in attendance. Among those believed to be in attendance were John W. Walker, William Wyatt Bibb, Thomas Bibb, Gabriel Moore, Clement Clay, Hugh McVay, and Dr. Henry Chambers—five of whom became governor of Alabama, and all of whom were prominent in the founding of the state. There were some nineteen toasts at the dinner, including ones to General Jackson, General Coffee, and the Tennessee Militia. Later that evening, a ball was held in honor of the Tennesseans at the Bell Tavern. The next morning, the festivities having been completed, the troops continued their march back home to Tennessee.[18]

Not long after the troops returned home, Jackson ordered Coffee, who was recruiting soldiers in Nashville, to join him in Mobile to prepare a defense against an expected British invasion. In response to this order, Coffee and his 2,000 men completed a 470-mile forced march in just eighteen days. After participating in a brief raid on the British garrison at Spanish-held Pensacola, Coffee's troops moved westward to Baton Rouge, Louisiana, in anticipation of the next British move against New Orleans. When the British general John Lambert took over Villere's Plantation near New Orleans, Coffee led his men on another forced march of 135 miles in only three days, and engaged in a night battle against Lambert's forces on December 23, 1814. This attack temporarily halted the British advance, giving Jackson more time to set up his breastworks defending New Orleans. When British reinforcements arrived at Villere's Plantation, Coffee's mounted riflemen dropped back to cover Jackson's left flank, playing only a marginal role in the Americans' decisive victory at the Battle of New Orleans, which occurred on January 8, 1815.[19]

After the battle, an eyewitness described Coffee's and his men's march through the city of New Orleans: "Their appearance was not very military. In their woolen hunting shirts and copper-dyed pantaloons, with slouched hats or caps made of the skins of raccoons and foxes with belts or untanned deerskin, in which were stuck their hunting knives, but were admiral soldiers remarkable for endurance and possession of that admiral quality in soldiers of taking care of themselves. At their head rode their gallant leader [Coffee], a man of noble respect, tall and herculean in frame, yet not destitute of natural dignity and ease of manner. His appearance upon a fine Tennessee thoroughbred was stately and impressive."[20]

After the Battle of New Orleans, General Coffee and his men left New Orleans and headed back home to Tennessee. On their way, they stopped at the Choctaw Agency, where Coffee received a letter from his brother-in-law, Lemuel Donelson, informing him that his first son, John Donelson Coffee, had been born. Colonel Denis de Laronde, one of Coffee's officers, sent a barrel of oranges to Mrs. Coffee in recognition of the birth of Coffee's son and heir. The oranges were shipped from New Orleans to Rutherford County, Tennessee, but commercial transportation was so slow that Coffee, who was on horseback, arrived at home before the oranges. Oranges were such a rarity in their part of the country that General and Mrs. Coffee threw a party so that they could share this rare fruit with their relatives and friends.[21]

With the end of the War of 1812, John Coffee gave up his military career, spending most of time as a land surveyor and a land speculator. On October 4, 1815, Coffee was appointed by President James Madison to survey the boundaries created by the Treaty of Fort Jackson after the Creek War of 1813–1814.[22] In March 1817, Coffee was appointed by President James Monroe as surveyor general of the public lands. He first supervised the survey of public lands in the northern Mississippi Territory, which included what is now Alabama, and then all the lands in the territory. These appointments were secured primarily due to the efforts of Huntsville's John W. Walker, with whom Coffee had formed a friendship when he and Andrew Jackson visited Walker on their journey south to take on the Creeks.[23]

In 1818, Coffee decided to move from his Haysborough home in Rutherford County, Tennessee, to what was to become Florence, Alabama, where he initially built a log cabin. The Coffees would stay in this primitive house until 1825 when they built a much bigger house, which they called Hickory Hill. Coffee made this move to become involved in the Cypress Land Company. A steady increase in land sales had caught the attention of influential investors and, as a result, Coffee and James Jackson, both protégés of Andrew Jackson, were the principal organizers of this powerful company. Prominent investors included Andrew Jackson, President James Monroe, future Alabama governor Thomas Bibb, LeRoy Pope (the "father of Huntsville"), and John McKinley, future associate justice of the US Supreme Court. Under Coffee's leadership, the Cypress Land Company bought at government auction a desirable tract of land consisting of 5,515 acres at the foot of Muscle Shoals, which became the site of the town of Florence. Under the supervision of Coffee, the new town was laid out by Ferdinand Sannoner, a young Italian engineer who had served as a surveyor for Napoleon. Sannoner was allowed to name the town Florence in honor of the city of that name he had surveyed in his native Italy. The lots from this tract went on sale on July 22, 1818, and sold within just a few days, bringing in $223,580, which would have a relative value today ranging between $3.4 and $4.4 million. This rapid development led Coffee to relocate the land office from Huntsville to Florence in 1823. With no concern for ethical considerations, the Cypress Land Company's office was in the new land office.[24]

The influence of Coffee's business partners no doubt resulted in Coffee's appointment to assist in the survey of the boundary lines separating Alabama, Mississippi, and Tennessee. Coffee continued to invest in real estate, including a large tract purchased on March 4, 1825, from the trustees of Cotton Port,[25] located on the Tennessee River in Limestone County. During this time, the federal government appointed him to assist in negotiating several treaties with the Chickasaw and Cherokee nations in Alabama. Because of these treaties, Coffee could acquire large tracts of land for the United States, obtaining most of the Chickasaws' lands east of the Mississippi River by 1832.[26]

In addition to being a business partner with Andrew Jackson, Coffee remained a confidant of Jackson until Coffee's death in 1833. Soon after Jackson's election as president of the United States, his beloved wife, Rachel, died on December 22, 1828, more than two months before he was inaugurated. President-elect Jackson wrote to his trusted friend John Coffee, "My mind is so disturbed . . . that I can scarcely write—in short my dear friend my heart is nearly broke." Before he left the Hermitage, the president-elect wrote to Coffee again sharing his innermost thoughts: "Whether I am ever to return or not is for time to reveal, as none but that providence, who rules the destiny of all, now knows."[27]

Because of Jackson's absolute trust in Coffee, it is not surprising that the federal government appointed him to negotiate with the Choctaws. Coffee and Secretary of War John Eaton negotiated the Treaty of Dancing Rabbit Creek with the Choctaw nation. Signed on September 27, 1830, it was the first removal treaty negotiated under the terms of the Indian Removal Act of 1830. The treaty ceded about 11 million acres of the Choctaw nation in Mississippi in exchange for about 15 million acres in the Indian territory in what is now the state of Oklahoma. The treaty was ratified by the US Senate on February 25, 1831. Coffee had commenced negotiations with the Chickasaws, but the United States did not conclude a treaty with the Chickasaws until after Coffee's death. A few months before his death in 1832, Coffee was summoned to Washington by President Jackson to testify before Congress concerning his negotiations pertaining to the Indian Removal Act. While in Washington, he visited Jackson at the White House for the first and only time. On his way home in mid-winter, Coffee took ill and died in Florence on July 7, 1833, at the age of 61. He was buried in the Coffee family cemetery located on the grounds of Hickory Hill near Florence.[28]

Following his death, John Coffee was remembered as the "perfect citizen-soldier." Andrew Jackson was perhaps closer to Coffee than anybody outside of his family. Sometime in the spring of 1824, Jackson was visiting a plantation he had purchased at Melton's Bluff in Lawrence County, Alabama, where he grew cotton with sixty slaves. As this plantation was near Coffee's Hickory Hill, Jackson visited Coffee while he was there, musing over whether he should have been drawn into the presidential election of 1824. With this on his mind, he gave this description of Coffee's life: "How much your situation is to be envied and how prudent you have been to keep yourself free of political life, surrounded as you are by your lovely children, and amiable wife, you ought not to abandon it for anything on earth." When Coffee died, one of Coffee's children asked President Jackson to compose an epitaph for his tombstone. Jackson readily agreed, and composed an epitaph that preserves "the memory of General John Coffee. . . . As a husband, parent, and friend he was affectionate, tender, and sincere. He was a brave, prompt and skillful general, a disinterested and sagacious patriot, and unpretending, just, and honest man."[29]

4

LEROY POPE

Broad River Pioneer and "Father of Huntsville"

Figure 4.1. LeRoy Pope, known as the "Father of
Huntsville." Courtesy of the Alabama Department
of Archives and History.

As observed in the last chapter, when Andrew Jackson and John Coffee were honored at Poplar Grove, the newly built mansion of LeRoy Pope in Huntsville, many of Alabama's future leaders were in attendance. Most of these, including Pope, were originally from the Broad River region in northwest Georgia. Historian J. Mills Thornton III defined these Georgia leaders as "an alliance of relatives and friends who dominated Alabama politics in the territorial and early statehood periods." They were also instrumental in the establishment of Huntsville and Montgomery, both of which became financial and business centers in the state.[1]

Most of the Georgians had migrated from an area near Charlottesville, Virginia, to Georgia, where they established tobacco farms on the banks of the Broad River just above the town of Petersburg where the Broad and Savannah Rivers meet. They had left Virginia primarily because most of their tobacco lands were exhausted. The area in Georgia near the Broad River had been visited by General George Mathews of Albemarle County, Virginia, during the Revolutionary War when he traveled to the newly created Wilkes County, Georgia, and was impressed with the suitability of its fertile soil for growing tobacco, so much so that he purchased a disputed title to a large tract of land in the area. When Mathews got back to Virginia, he spread the word of his discovery in Albemarle and Augusta Counties. These lands were readily obtainable under Georgia's grant system, which allowed heads of families settling in Georgia to receive a two-hundred-acre grant of land. Hearing about Mathews's discovery, in 1784, a group under the leadership of Francis Meriwether and Benjamin Taliaferro made their own investigative trip to Wilkes County, Georgia. They were just as impressed as Mathews, and likewise bought land on their initial trip. They then went home merely to retrieve their families and then return to settle in the Broad River region. For the next decade, many more would follow them.[2]

Of those who migrated from Virginia to the Broad River region, most were affluent and brought with them valuable possessions, including furniture, books, cattle, and slaves. Their common tastes and their sense of camaraderie as Virginians were such that they "formed a society of the greatest intimacy." Once they arrived in Georgia, they established tobacco farms, married into the local planters if not already married, and acquired great social standing within their close-knit community. Among the emigrants from Virginia were the Gilmers, Taits, Bibbs, Crawfords, Taliaferros, McGehees, Popes, and Walkers. Because of the influx of these families and others, as well as the expansion of the tobacco production, the town of Petersburg was established. At its height, Petersburg had a population of between seven and eight hundred, and for twenty years it was known for the wealth of its residents. In addition to planting tobacco, the close-knit emigrants became politically powerful in Georgia, producing two governors, three US senators, a US secretary of the treasury, and several congressmen and state legislators. Of these, several would be involved in Alabama's road to statehood, including Senators William Wyatt Bibb and Charles Tait, as well as US Secretary of the Treasury William H. Crawford.[3]

Alabama's opening for settlement after the Creek War of 1813–1814 came at a time when residents of the Broad River region had begun to be concerned with continuing to produce tobacco in view of "King Cotton" beginning to emerge in Alabama. By 1810, Petersburg only had 332 residents, and was quickly fading as the prominent town it once was. LeRoy Pope was a part of an initial group of Georgians who set out to purchase lands situated in Madison County, Alabama, offered for sale by the US land office in Nashville.[4]

LeRoy Pope was born in Westmoreland County, Virginia, in 1764, the son of John Pope and Elizabeth Mitchel Pope. Little is known of his early life other than that he was educated in Virginia and he purportedly served in the colonial army at the age of fifteen during the Revolutionary War. According to one unconfirmed account, he was a courier for General Washington during the Battle of Yorktown in 1780. At some point after the war, Pope married Judith Sale of Amherst County, Virginia, before joining a group heading to Georgia's Broad River region in 1790. Pope became one of the wealthiest men in the Petersburg area and was appointed one of the commissioners to govern Petersburg. The eminence of his family in the Broad River region was such that it became referred to as "the Royal family." As mentioned, after almost two decades in the Broad River region, Pope struck out for Madison County, Alabama, to acquire fertile lands near Huntsville. Others migrating at this time in search of new lands were Pope's cousins Thomas and William Bibb, both future governors of Alabama, and Pope's son-in-law, John Williams Walker, one of Alabama's first senators. The sale of Madison County land began in August 1809 in Nashville, and, in just a few weeks, almost 24,000 acres had been auctioned off at a sale price of over $67,000. A private government sale of land at a minimum price of $2.00 per acre followed, which allowed Pope to buy up the best land surrounding Huntsville in the Tennessee Valley.[5]

Before the 1809 land sale, Madison County had been primarily settled by yeoman farmer squatters, many of whom were unable to purchase the land they had toiled to clear due to the exorbitant sales prices. Even John Hunt, who had first settled the area near Huntsville in 1805, could not purchase the land on which he had built a cabin overlooking a spring he called "Big Spring" (later referred to as Hunt's Spring). Hunt's inability to purchase the lands where he had squatted paved the way for LeRoy Pope to become the principal owner of acreage that would become the town of Huntsville, including Big Spring. Pope and two of his associates paid the astronomical price of $23 per acre to obtain the quarter-section of land at Hunt's Spring. To secure his holdings, Pope purchased an additional 1,120 acres west and south of the spring. Others acquiring property in the Madison County sale of 1809, in addition to Pope, were John W. Walker, James Manning, Robert Thompson, Peyton Cox, and Thomas and William Wyatt Bibb. It is believed that these influential Georgians purchased almost one-half of the lands offered for sale at that time.[6]

On July 5, 1810, upon the recommendation of a legislative commission, the area surrounding Hunt's Spring was designated as the county seat of Madison, and at the urging of Pope was given the name Twickenham, which was in honor of the estate of English poet Alexander Pope, who some believe was a distant relative of LeRoy Pope.[7] The older settlers of more moderate means, many of whom were squatters who had lost their lands, were so outraged with the arrogance of Pope and his associates with respect to the land sales and the change in the town's name that they made the name change an issue in the next legislative election. As a result, they were successful in defeating two of the three candidates put up by Pope's Georgia faction, including John W. Walker. Meanwhile, in its first action, the county's new legislative delegation succeeded in having the name changed to Huntsville in honor of John Hunt, who was the original squatter on the land at the Big Spring. The new town of Huntsville was incorporated on December 9, 1811.[8]

Despite the setback regarding the town's name, and the defeat of two of Pope's Georgians seeking election to the territorial legislature, Pope remained the most prominent and powerful citizen of Madison County, generally thought of as the "Father of Huntsville." Pope's influence earned him the distinction of serving as the first justice of the quorum of the inferior court, or county court, of Madison County. He served with four associate justices—Edward Ward, William Dickson, John Withers, and future governor Thomas Bibb. The inferior court is believed to be the first court to convene in Madison County, with its first session being held on the first Monday of January 1810. Pope's son-in-law, John W. Walker, was the first lawyer admitted to practice in the Madison County courts.[9]

John W. Walker had married LeRoy Pope's daughter Matilda on January 30, 1810. After deciding to move to Madison County, Walker purchased two quarter-sections in the sale of 1809. In 1810, he purchased another quarter-section as he would in 1811, 1812, and 1814. In June 1810, Walker and his new wife, and the remainder of the Pope family, set out for Madison County. John Walker's decision to leave Petersburg sprang out of ambition and love, both of which was bound up in the "Royal family" led by LeRoy Pope. John and Matilda Walker built a cabin they named Oakland about eight miles north of Hunt's Spring. Within a few months, on December 2, 1810, Matilda gave birth to their first child, whom they named Mary Jane. While John and Matilda were settling in and starting their family, LeRoy Pope was amassing even more wealth. The 1815 tax list reveals that Pope was probably the wealthiest citizen in Huntsville, owning 1,480 acres of land, eighteen town lots each worth $2,000, and 104 slaves. Pope, along with Thomas Bibb and James Manning, were the only substantial planters because they each had at least fifty slaves.[10]

Pope was not shy about showing off his wealth, as both he and Thomas Bibb rode through town in four-wheeled carriages. To further display his wealth, Pope constructed a huge brick mansion on the highest hill overlooking the entire town of Huntsville to replace his modest cabin. The bricks, made in Tennessee, were carried down the river on flatboats and then were carried to town by wagon. Anne Royall, visiting in 1818, said of the house that Pope named Poplar Grove, "If I admired the exterior, I was amazed at the taste and elegance displayed in every part of the interior; massy plate [heavy sterling silver], cut glass, chinaware, vases, sofas, and mahogany furniture of the newest fashion decorated the inside." The house was completed in 1814, just in time to host General Andrew Jackson and his officers to a dinner on the grounds as they headed home after the Battle of Horseshoe Bend.[11]

On December 11, 1816, the Mississippi Territorial Legislature authorized commissioners to open books at Huntsville for a subscription to the capital stock of the first banking corporation organized in Alabama, styled as "The President, Directors and Company of the Planters' and Merchants' Bank, of Huntsville." The commissioners, led by LeRoy Pope, also included John P. Hickman, David Moore, Benjamin Cox, John M. Taylor, Thomas Fearn, Jesse Searcy, Clement C. Clay, and John W. Walker. Soon after settling into the showplace of the county, Pope became the president of the Huntsville bank. His reign as bank president once again brought him into a confrontation with the yeoman populace who knew very well of his history of arrogance—the Twickenham controversy, his treatment of squatters, and his showing off his wealth. With the onset of the Panic of 1819, the common man was hit hard by the suspension of specie payment and the bank's failure to renew loans. They naturally made their opinions known, and Pope undiplomatically responded to these concerns to William B. Long of the *Huntsville Democrat*, who in turn reported to his readers that Pope had repeatedly stated that "the country people were a parcel of ignorant animals and not able to determine whether this Bank acted correctly or incorrectly." To Pope's chagrin, however, the Huntsville bank never fully resumed specie payments and lost its charter early in 1825. Pope was its first, and only, president.[12]

Before the bank lost its charter, it had come under the scrutiny of US Secretary of the Treasury William H. Crawford, who was a leading member of the Broad River Group. The increased scrutiny came because the bank had been made a federal depository. Crawford's natural goodwill toward the Huntsville bank was damaged in part over Pope's reluctance in the summer of 1819 to honor the government's drafts for the land-sale funds. Pope expressed his increasing antagonism in a letter to Judge Charles Tait in November 1819, yet another colleague from the Broad River Group. Although both men knew Pope from Petersburg, and all three were leading members of the Georgia faction, Secretary Crawford referred to the Huntsville bank officers as "a set of public swindlers," who "think themselves reputable after having practiced fraud not

Figure 4.2. Pope's mansion, Poplar Grove, which still stands today. Courtesy of the Alabama Department of Archives and History.

only upon the government, but upon the unfortunate and necessitous." When Pope was soundly defeated by Gabriel Moore in an election for a state senate seat, Crawford's stinging assessment was that Pope could not "acquire popularity anymore there [Madison County] than in Elbert county [Georgia]."[13]

Despite LeRoy Pope's shortcomings, he was passionate in the development of Huntsville. Alabama historian Thomas McAdory Owen quoted a local Huntsville historian regarding Pope's service: "Col. Pope was called upon to serve his people in varied capacities, and was the moving spirit and dominating influence of nearly all positive action in the life of the settlement." As an example, Pope was one of the promoters of the Indian Creek Navigation Company, which was a lock and dam project designed to make the Big Spring Branch and Indian creek a commercial pathway to the Tennessee River, and then to outside markets. The project got under way when the Alabama legislature chartered the Indian Creek Navigation Company on December 21, 1820, with Pope, Thomas Fearn, Stephen S. Ewing, Henry Cook, and Samuel Hazard as commissioners to open books for subscriptions to stock in the corporation. The canal was to run from the spring at Huntsville to the town of Triana, which was the locale of the mouth of Indian creek. The company was given the power to remove obstructions along the way and was given the power of eminent domain to aid it in this regard. While some progress was made on this project thanks to its president, Dr. Thomas Fearn, the canal finally gave way to the emergence of rail traffic.[14]

Pope was also one of the founders of the first Episcopal Church in Huntsville, which was not organized until June 15, 1830. His piety, however, was challenged by journalist Anne Royall, who, like others, expected more of him in view of his status as a wealthy public figure. In this regard, Royall reported about her first attendance of missionary preaching in Huntsville, during which the evangelist was able to collect several hundred dollars "to convert the heathens." The day after the preaching, it was reported that some of the women in attendance were complaining that Colonel Pope put only 25 cents in the hat. Royall reacted, "Such a man of his wealth—to give a quarter—Did you ever see the like! They would have given all they had! It was beyond doubt, the worst laid out quarter he ever spent."[15]

When LeRoy Pope died in 1845,[16] he left a widow, Judith Sale, originally from Amherst County, Virginia. Among his surviving children was Matilda Pope, who married Alabama's first senator, John Williams Walker. John and Matilda had a son named John Pope Walker, who was born on February 17, 1817. He was a devoted supporter of states' rights and secession, serving in several positions of the Confederacy, including as secretary of war. Interestingly, he successfully defended notorious outlaw Frank James, brother of Jesse James, who was charged with robbery in Muscle Shoals in 1883.

Although LeRoy Pope may not have given but a quarter to the evangelist preacher, he gave a lot to the town of Huntsville, including his risk-taking investments, his participation in land sales, and his service to the community. He has been accurately called the "Father of Huntsville" and as such was instrumental in the development of Madison County and was a contributor to the founding of Alabama. He is buried in the Maple Hill Cemetery in Huntsville, located east of the Twickenham Historic District. Others buried there include five governors of Alabama, five US senators, and numerous other figures of local, state, and national note. Included among these are John Williams Walker, Clement Comer Clay, Clement Claiborne Clay, Jeremiah Clemens, Reuben Saffold, and Thomas Bibb.

5

WILLIAM WYATT BIBB AND THOMAS BIBB

Alabama's First Two Governors

Figure 5.1. William Wyatt Bibb, Alabama's territorial governor and first governor of the state. Courtesy of the Alabama Department of Archives and History.

William Wyatt Bibb and Thomas Bibb were born to Captain William Bibb, an officer in the Revolutionary army and a member of the Virginia legislature, and Sally Wyatt Bibb in Amelia County, Virginia—William on October 2, 1781, and Thomas on May 8, 1783. Their mother considered William Wyatt Bibb to be a promising genius, and she predicted that he would someday become the president of the United States. While William did not become president, he seved as Alabama's first governor, and his brother, Thomas Bibb, served as the state's second governor. The genesis of their political careers stemmed from their becoming part of the Broad River Group after their family migrated to Georgia around 1784 with many

Virginians, led by General George Mathews. The Bibbs were one of the first families in Elbert County, Georgia, located between the Savannah and Broad Rivers, where, as we have seen, numerous others would settle and become a close-knit group. Many moved on to Alabama where they would continue their cohesiveness and retain their political prowess.[1]

Captain William Bibb died in 1796, leaving Sally to care for William, Thomas, Peyton, John Dandridge, Joseph, Benajah Smith, Dolly, and Martha. Captain Bibb, however, left his family in relatively good financial shape as both William, the oldest, and Thomas were able to receive educations. William attended William and Mary College in Williamsburg, Virginia, for two years, then earned a medical degree from the University of Pennsylvania in 1801. He then returned to Petersburg, Georgia, the busy commercial center of Elbert County, to practice medicine. His neighbor and good friend there was John Williams Walker who, along with Bibb, would be among the founders of Alabama. In 1803, William married Mary Freeman of Wilkes County, Georgia, with whom he would have four children, only two of whom lived to adulthood.[2]

Soon William Bibb enjoyed politics more than he did the practice of medicine. Indeed, in 1803, at the age of twenty-two, he was elected to the Georgia House of Representatives, where he served until 1805. His popularity was such that in 1807, he convincingly won a seat in the US House of Representatives, where he served for six years and gained the confidence of President James Madison by regularly supporting his policies. His political career continued to rise when he was selected in the fall of 1813 to fill the US Senate seat held by William H. Crawford—a neighbor in the Broad River region—because of Crawford's appointment by President Madison as the US minister to France. Bibb served in the Senate until November 9, 1816.[3]

Dr. Bibb was at the height of his popularity in Georgia in 1816 and could have reasonably expected to keep his Senate seat for as long as he wanted. His fate, however, took a drastic turn when he joined the majority in voting to pass an act that effectively doubled the pay of all congressmen. Many so voting were forced to resign or were not reelected by their infuriated constituents. One of the more notable congressmen who failed to get reelected—purportedly because of his vote on the salary bill—was Representative Daniel Webster of New Hampshire. Bibb himself resigned his Senate seat in November 1816 after losing his bid for reelection to George M. Troup, and headed for Alabama where his brother Thomas had been entrenched in the Tennessee Valley since 1810. Bibb and his family, however, settled initially in the territorial capital of St. Stephens on the Tombigbee River. Georgia's other senator, Charles Tait, a Broad River man who also voted for the Salary Act, was ready to join the Bibbs in Alabama, but he was encouraged by John W. Walker, who addressed him as the "Patron of Alabama," to stay long enough to shepherd the Alabama admission bill through Congress.[4]

Bibb's fall from grace in Georgia did not end his political career; rather, it opened other opportunities for him in Alabama. As we have seen, his brother Thomas was already there along with other Broad River men such as LeRoy Pope and John W. Williams. Bibb's influential connections in both Georgia and Alabama, particularly with Secretary of the Treasury William H. Crawford, as well as his steady support of President Madison's policies, earned him appointment as Alabama Territory's governor in 1817. According to historian J. Mills Thornton III, the Broad River faction's support for Alabama's imminent statehood was based upon a political quid pro quo whereby it would support Alabama statehood in return for being able to control important patronage in the future state.[5]

Upon becoming the governor of the Alabama Territory in April 1817, William Wyatt Bibb began immediately to press for statehood with his Georgia allies. He also called for the first territorial legislature to meet in St. Stephens on January 19, 1818. Seven counties that had existed when Alabama was part of the Mississippi Territory sent twelve representatives to the lower house of the territorial legislature. From this group, Gabriel Moore was elected as the first Speaker of the House. Only one senator appeared initially, as another died and a third resigned. A selection process involving the president was utilized to select three more senators.[6]

On January 20, 1818, Governor Bibb delivered a written message to the members of the new territorial legislature. Since there were no government buildings in St. Stephens, the members assembled in the Douglas Hotel. In his message, Bibb extolled the virtues of the new territory as "ample in extent, abounding in navigable waters, and rich in the advantages of soil and climate." Predicting a rapid development of the territory, he indicated that it would not be long before "the haunts of the savage will become the dwelling place of civilized man, and the forests of the wilderness be converted into fertile fields." He then requested the legislature to focus on education and internal improvements. He called for investments in transportation improvements, which would not only facilitate the flow of goods and people but also bind together the northern and southern regions of the territory. He further indicated to the assembled that he would wait to fill civil and military posts until after the legislature had a chance to set current county boundaries. Governor Bibb also took this opportunity to inform the legislature that he had deployed two companies of the territorial militia to Fort Crawford in Escambia County for a period of two months to aid in the defense of the southern frontier at the request of the commander of the US Army's southern military district. In closing, Governor Bibb urged the legislature to pass

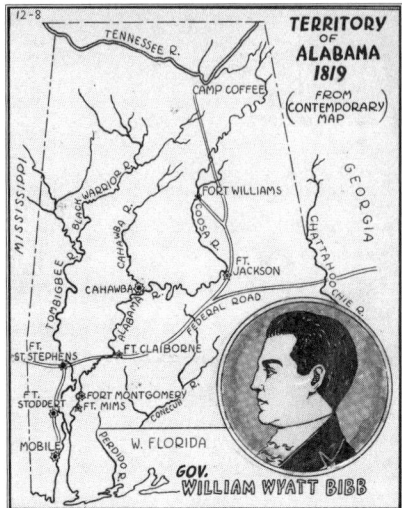

Figure 5.2. Map of the Territory of Alabama in 1819. Courtesy of the Alabama Department of Archives and History.

during that session an act authorizing a census to be taken prior to the next session to assist in justifying a petition for statehood.[7]

The legislature quickly responded to Governor Bibb's message by passing over fifty laws and resolutions in just twenty-four days, most of which were aimed at transitioning the new territory into a functioning government pre-pared for statehood. As Bibb expected, many of the first statutes pertained to the modification of existing county boundaries or the creation of entirely new counties. In addition to creating counties, the legislature provided a framework for the territory's judicial system requiring that a Superior Court of Law and Equity, a County Court, and an Intermediate Court meet for a specified number of sessions in each county. Additionally, a bill was passed that divided the counties into three judicial districts, each to be served by an attorney general (i.e., district attorney). Regarding education, the legis-lature chartered the first academy at St. Stephens, authorizing its trustees to raise up to $4,000 by way of a lottery. As for transportation, the St. Stephens Steamboat Company was chartered, the building of bridges were authorized in Washington County, and road commissioners were appointed to find the most suitable routes between the Falls of Tuscaloosa and the Tennessee River in north Alabama, and from the town of Blakeley on Mobile Bay to Clai-borne on the Alabama River in south Alabama. Among further significant action taken was the authorization of the governor to organize a militia, authorization for the taking of a census, chartering of the Tombeckbe Bank in St. Stephens, the repeal of the usury law, and the authorization for the emancipation of two slaves.[8]

Two bills passed by the first territorial legislature were of great benefit to the financial interests of the Georgia faction—one authorizing the Alabama Territory to purchase two-thirds of the stock of the Planters' and Merchants' Bank of Huntsville, and one that repealed the laws against usury. Regarding the bank bill, Governor Bibb surprised his fellow Georgians by vetoing the bill. In his veto message, he expressed fear that the territorial government would not have sufficient control over the bank and would be forced to accept the bank's notes at face value for all obligations due it. Also, he was reluctant to give power to a private bank to decide where to open branches within the territory. However, a very similar bill was passed over the governor's veto. The bank would eventually close, however, as it was perceived as an advocate for the wealthy and the enemy of the common man by overextending loans, speculating in government specie, and suspending specie payments. As for the repeal of the usury law, legislation was introduced allowing individuals to charge an unlimited rate of interest with the proviso that such interest rate agreement is reduced to writing. However, where there was no interest rate specified in the note, ceilings of six percent on bank loans and discounts and eight percent on personal loans were imposed. Despite these ceilings, the popular party in opposition to the Georgia faction regarded the act as hostile to debtors and provided too much protection for the moneyed interests. The unpopularity of the amendment to the usury law increased as the Panic of 1819 set in, so much so that the first legislature of the state of Alabama repealed it.[9]

During the next, and last, session of the territorial General Assembly in November 1818, John W. Walker, a member of the Georgia faction from Huntsville, was elected as Speaker of the House after Gabriel Moore resigned due to the notoriety surrounding his highly public divorce. Relieved of committee assignments, Speaker Walker was free to focus on statehood. On November 10, 1818, both houses of the legislature passed a joint memorial formerly petitioning Congress for statehood. Speaker Walker immediately sent the petition to Senator Charles Tait, who had remained in the Senate from Georgia to shepherd the Alabama Enabling Act through Congress.[10]

Bibb's Georgia roots not only linked him to powerful friends in the federal government, but also provided an extensive political base in Alabama itself. Former neighbors in the Broad River region, including his brother Thomas, were prospering in the Tennessee Valley through land speculation, planting, commerce, and their creation of the Planters' and Merchants' Bank of Huntsville. The yeoman farmers and the poorer settlers in north Alabama designated the group the "Royal Party." The interests of the landed gentry and the yeoman farmers necessitated that Governor Bibb exhibit great skills as governor of the territory. One historian described Bibb as having a "dignified but easy bearing," and suggested that "his uniform courtesy and kindness . . . won the respect of all classes." Another historian stated, "Dr. Bibb was a tall spare man, with head and features admirably expressive of his mild, benevolent temper, his sincere upright character, and good understanding." Having won the respect of the territorial legislature, Governor Bibb could nudge it into ambitiously enacting most of his proposals.[11]

But Bibb's own high-handed actions in the selection of a site for the capital of the new state of Alabama intensified the very sectional tensions he sought to ease and eroded his political popularity. Bibb was intent on locating the state's new capital in the Alabama/Cahaba River basin in the center of the state. This was contrary to the recommendation of a legislative commission chosen to find the most suitable site for the state's new capital. According to historian William H. Brantley Jr., who wrote extensively on this issue, two factions lobbied the legislative commission chosen to recommend the permanent seat of government—the Alabama/Cahaba River basin group and the Warrior/Tombigbee system group. Since Huntsville was so far from the geographical center of the state, it chose not to make a bid for itself, but rather supported Tuscaloosa, which was pushed by the Warrior/Tombigbee group. With the support of Huntsville and the Tennessee Valley, Tuscaloosa was the commission's choice for the permanent seat of government.[12]

While the factions lobbied, Governor Bibb became a strong proponent of the Alabama/Cahaba basin group probably because his fellow Georgians had purchased land within its confines. Bibb himself had purchased a plantation on the Alabama River near Coosada, in what was then Autauga County. On September 19, 1818, he wrote from his Coosada home to Georgia senator Charles Tait, "I have selected the mouth of the Cahawba for the seat of government which has given much displeasure to the Madison [County] folks and the people on the Warrior. Should the President yield the place, which I consider doubtful, I apprehend some collision in the legislature at their ensuing session. What I believed right I have done, and with the help of the Lord I shall pursue the same course thereafter; whatever may be the consequence. It was not possible to make a selection which satisfy all portions of the country." Despite asserting that he could not please everyone, he failed to state the obvious—that he had satisfied himself and his fellow Georgians.[13]

Anticipating that the legislative commission was stacked in favor of Tuscaloosa, Governor Bibb began an end-run around the commission, using his connections with Senator Tait and US Secretary of the Treasury William H. Crawford to obtain passage of a bill whereby the federal government would grant a free section of land for use as the territory's seat of government, and would give the governor the right to select the site for such purpose. Bibb's selection of a site at the confluence of the Alabama and Cahaba Rivers in contravention of the commission's report was not made known until he addressed the second session of the General Assembly in November 1818, during which he said that "the town of Cahawba promises to vie with the largest inland towns in the Country" in population and prosperity. With this unexpected announcement, Governor Bibb was able to push through the assembly a rider to an apportionment bill favorable to north Alabama to establish Cahaba as the "permanent" capital. Historian William Brantley Jr. concluded that Bibb's most effective arguments to win approval for the Cahaba site were the meager amount of funds in the state treasury that made free land very alluring and the veto hammer held by Bibb over the apportionment bill desired by north Alabamians. Also, while most north Alabamians favored Tuscaloosa, Speaker of the House John W. Walker, from Huntsville, and his followers reluctantly supported Cahaba due to his friendship with Bibb and others who were part of the Broad River Group. Walker, however, voiced his displeasure over the high-handed way in which Bibb had handled the matter. Finally, however, the northern representatives were successful in having Huntsville selected as a temporary capital while the town of Cahaba was being laid out.[14]

The legislature appointed Governor Bibb as a commissioner with the authority to lay out the town of Cahaba in a manner suitable to him. He then was to have the lots surveyed and sold to the highest bidders after giving a minimum notice to potential buyers through advertisements in all the newspapers published within the territory, as well as others outside the territory deemed appropriate by Bibb. The governor was also authorized to contract for the construction of "a building suitable for the temporary accommodation of the General Assembly of the territory or [anticipated] state." On May 23, 1818, President James Monroe proclaimed that lots in the town of Cahaba would be sold at the Federal Land Office in Milledgeville, Georgia, on the first Monday in October 1818. A month later, the president announced that after the October sale, the land office would move from Milledgeville to Cahaba so that it would be closer to the unsold quarter-sections of fertile land attracting the new settlers into the region.[15]

Bibb's decision to go against the legislative commission generated intense resentment, especially in the Tennessee Valley. This resentment led former North Carolinian Marmaduke Williams of Tuscaloosa to challenge Bibb for the governor's office of the new state of Alabama, campaigning through the summer of 1819 almost solely on the Cahaba issue. Thomas Bibb's popularity in northern Alabama helped to deflect the challenger's complaints against his brother. Friends elsewhere reminded voters of Bibb's useful political connections in the federal government, and the role played by him within the Georgia faction in Alabama's quest for statehood. In the September elections, Bibb narrowly defeated Williams by a vote of 8,342 to 7,140.[16]

When Bibb assumed office as the first governor of Alabama on

December 14, 1819, he entered an office adorned with less power than that of the office of the territorial governor whence he came. Alabama's constitution limited the state's governors to two consecutive two-year terms, and allowed the legislative branch to override gubernatorial vetoes with a simple majority vote. The assembly also elected state judges and the heads of executive departments. The most serious reduction of power by the constitution, as far as Governor Bibb was concerned, was the power granted to the General Assembly to select a permanent seat of government in 1825 without the involvement of the governor. If the assembly did not act, the capital would remain in Cahaba. However, the Warrior/Tombigbee group, with one vote to spare, was successful in moving the capital to Tuscaloosa in 1826.[17]

In a written address to the first General Assembly, Governor Bibb stated that "your present meeting will form a memorable epoch in our history; chosen to perform the first acts of legislation, for the state of Alabama, you cannot estimate too highly the great interests committed to your charge, or the important consequences which may flow from your deliberations." As he had in his address to the territorial assembly, he again stressed the importance of education and internal improvements. He also happily reported to the assembly that in May 1819, 182 lots had been sold in Cahaba for a total of $123,856. Of this amount, $10,000 was deposited in the Planters' and Merchants' Bank of Huntsville in accordance with the amount appropriated by the previous territorial legislature to erect a temporary state house at Cahaba. The governor also urged the assembly to select senators to send to Washington as soon as possible. The assembly eventually chose John W. Walker of Huntsville and William Rufus King of Dallas County. Governor Bibb wanted Charles Tait, formerly of Georgia, to be chosen over King, but he realized the unlikelihood of having two members of the Georgia faction selected by the assembly. In a letter, Bibb assured Tait that he wanted him to serve in the Senate with John Walker, but that the public must be sounded out "with caution and delicacy," because of Tait's brief residency in Alabama and the jealousy of the Georgia influence.[18]

Fueled by sales of lots in the town of Cahaba, construction of the first capitol building began sometime in May 1819. As construction on the capitol progressed, and not long after the Alabama Supreme Court completed its first session, Alabamians were shocked with the news of the governor's death on July 10, 1820. Governor Bibb, who was already in poor health, had been thrown from his horse while riding on his plantation near Coosada, bruising his head and kidney. He spent much of early 1820 bedridden and probably would have resigned as governor except for the fact that his brother, Thomas Bibb, was president of the state senate and was running the state from Coosada. In a letter to Charles Tait dated April 15, 1820, William Bibb said,

"My brother Thomas is with me and has been many weeks, and perhaps has exhibited as much solicitude and anxiety for my fate as ever was witnessed."[19]

As for his injuries, William Bibb, a trained physician, expressed concern to his friend Charles Tait that his "apprehensions that my health had not improved were well founded. . . . I have been confined 10 weeks to my room, and the greater part of the time to my bed; and I have suffered as much pain as ever fell to the lot of unfortunate men. So much for a little injury which at the time did not excite much alarm, and the consequences of which a little prudence might have avoided. . . . But whether I shall ever again leave my house, except for the last time, is now very uncertain." Governor Bibb died some two and a half months later. He was only thirty-nine years old, leaving behind his wife, Mary Freeman, and two children. His brother, Thomas, succeeded him as governor because of a constitutional provision calling for the president of the state senate to become acting governor in case of the governor's death or incapacity.[20]

The town of Cahaba lost its strongest supporter with the death of Governor Bibb. His death also left the state bereft of the political astuteness of perhaps its most significant founding father. Secretary of State Henry Hitchcock described Bibb's political philosophy as follows: "The sovereignty of the people, the accountability and the responsibility of officers, and the supremacy of the laws, expressions common and much discussed, have been with him themes of deep and solemn reflection." In an obituary notice, Hitchcock said that "in the discharge of his domestic duties he was zealous, constant, and parental." Regarding Bibb's standing in the community, Hitchcock remarked that "his enemies never contradicted the character given him by his friends," despite the presence of fierce political factions. When the General Assembly first met after Governor Bibb's death, a joint legislative committee eulogized him and "his revered memory," describing him as a "friend of liberty and of man," as well as a "pure republican . . . devoted to the service of his country." This joint committee also resolved that members would wear black crepe on their left arm during the legislative session then convened. In honor of the deceased governor, the assembly also passed an act changing the name of Cahawba County to Bibb County. Bibb County, Georgia, was also named in honor of Governor Bibb. William Wyatt Bibb is buried in a family graveyard on his property near Coosada in present-day Elmore County, Alabama.[21]

◆

Like his brother, Thomas Bibb was born in Amelia County, Virginia, to Captain William Bibb, an officer in the Revolutionary army and a member of the Virginia legislature, and Sally Wyatt Bibb. The family migrated to Elbert County, Georgia, probably sometime in 1784, with many Virginians who followed Revolutionary War general George Mathews. Although his elder

Figure 5.3. Thomas Bibb, Alabama's second governor and brother of William Wyatt Bibb. Courtesy of the Alabama Department of Archives and
History.

brother was educated at the College of William and Mary and the University
of Pennsylvania medical school, Thomas remained in Georgia and received
his education in Elbert County. In 1805, Thomas married Parmelia Thompson, daughter of Robert and Sarah (Watkins) Thompson, the former a native
of Amelia County, Virginia, who also moved to Elbert County, Georgia.
Thomas and Parmelia would have twelve children together, four of whom
died in infancy.[22]

While William was pursuing careers in medicine and then politics,
Thomas set out for the Tennessee Valley portion of the Mississippi Territory
in 1810, not long after his cousin, LeRoy Pope, and some six years before
William. By the time William arrived in Alabama, Thomas had become
established as a prudent businessman in Madison and Limestone Counties
and had developed valuable political and economic connections with the
leaders of Huntsville. Thomas Bibb's wealth was evidenced by the fact that
in 1815 he owned fifty-three slaves, more than eleven hundred acres of land,
and one town lot. To the irritation of the yeoman class, both LeRoy Pope
and Thomas Bibb rode through the streets of Huntsville in extravagant four-
wheeled carriages, which only worked to widen the gulf between the yeomen
and planter classes.[23]

LeRoy Pope and Thomas Bibb also became investors in the powerful
Cypress Land Company, which had been established mainly through the
efforts of John Coffee and James Jackson, both protégés of General Andrew

Figure 5.4. Artistic rendition of the State House at Cahaba. Courtesy of the Alabama Department of Archives and
History.

Jackson. In addition to Pope and Bibb, investors included President James
Madison, General Jackson, and future Associate Justice of the US Supreme
Court John McKinley. As we have seen, under John Coffee's leadership the
Cypress Land Company obtained a tract of land consisting of 5,515 acres at
the foot of Muscle Shoals for $85,235.24. This lucrative tract of land became
the site of the town of Florence.[24]

Although spending much of his time as a planter and a merchant,
Thomas Bibb dabbled in politics to a certain extent. In this regard, he
served as a justice of the quorum on Madison County's first inferior court.
LeRoy Pope served as the chief justice of the quorum; other justices included
Edward Ward, William Dickson, and John Withers. Later Thomas Bibb was
selected to represent Limestone County in the Constitutional Convention of
1819, and was also selected to serve on the Committee of Fifteen, which was
appointed by the convention to write an original draft of the constitution.
After the convention, Bibb was elected to the first senate of the state of Alabama, and thereafter was selected as president of the senate. A constitutional
provision called for the president of the senate to become acting governor in
the case of the incumbent's death, and so, as noted, Thomas succeeded his
brother William on July 10, 1819.[25]

Thomas Bibb was deeply saddened by his brother's death as reflected
in his address to the General Assembly, which met in Cahaba for the first
time on November 6, 1820. He lamented at that time that he had assumed
the office of governor "with the most peculiar sensations of pain . . . rising
not only from the reflection of the loss of a more experienced officer than
myself, but also from a recollection which is continually renewed, that of a
loss of a friend and brother." Appropriately, one of the first issues addressed
by Thomas Bibb as governor was the completion of the statehouse, which his
brother worked so hard to secure for Cahaba. In a message to the General

Assembly, Governor Bibb reported that the statehouse was almost complete, although not within the time specified in the contract with the builders. Governor Bibb nevertheless recommended that they go ahead and receive it with the stipulation of its completion shortly thereafter.[26]

Thomas Bibb served as governor from July 1820 to November 1821, during a relatively quiet period, consumed largely with the formation of effective state government. However, controversies did erupt over issues of reapportionment and state banking. In addition to overseeing the state government's formal move from Huntsville to Cahaba, the General Assembly, which met from November 6, 1820, to December 21, 1820, passed numerous acts concerned with local municipal government, authorized a state bank, chartered the University of Alabama, and implemented a patrol system to help prevent the escape of slaves.[27]

A major issue addressed during the legislative session was the question of reapportionment. The 1819 constitution required that a census be taken and an apportionment law be passed. Some members of the legislature did not want reapportionment until after the 1821 elections and succeeded in adjourning without enacting one. They did pass a law which required a census, the terms of which would be due by August 1, 1821. Historian William H. Brantley Jr. surmised that the Alabama/Cahaba River system faction was opposed to apportioning the legislature while Thomas Bibb was governor because they regarded him as an "accidental Governor," and ironically believed that he was anti-Cahaba, despite his brother's herculean efforts to get the capital located in Cahaba. Their delaying tactics regarding the census were to stall in hopes that Bibb would no longer be governor and the census returns would be available. They were hoping for the best apportionment possible to keep the capital in Cahaba.[28]

The fact that Thomas Bibb had already announced that he would not seek reelection, however, changed the timing of everything. The gubernatorial election to be held in August 1821 was already taking shape as a race between Dr. Henry Chambers of Madison County, a favorite in north Alabama, against Israel Pickens of St. Stephens, who was the favorite in south Alabama. Dr. Chambers supported moving the capital from Cahaba, while Pickens favored keeping it there. When it became apparent that Pickens was going to defeat Chambers, Bibb's colleagues and supporters in Madison, Limestone, and Tuscaloosa Counties, who were in favor of moving the capital from Cahaba, advised Bibb to call a special session of the General Assembly. They purportedly believed that the constitution required a new apportionment law prior to the 1821 annual session. Their real goal was to get a new apportionment before Pickens became governor. Governor Bibb agreed and called the legislature into a special session on June 4, 1821.[29]

Addressing the special session of the assembly in writing, Governor Bibb admonished its members for not passing an apportionment bill in the previous session as he asserted was required by the state's constitution. Drawing heavily upon hyperbole, Bibb also avowed that their failure to do so "threaten[ed] the very existence of the legislative branch of Government." The senate predictably objected to the governor's call for a reapportionment of its house, asserting that it could not be reapportioned until the expiration of the first terms of the state senators in August 1822. The house and senate jockeyed for position as to apportionment and finally agreed upon a bill that only provided for a new apportionment of the house. Governor Bibb then executed the first veto in state history. The senate passed the bill over the governor's veto, but the house did not have enough votes to overcome the veto.[30]

Another major issue during Thomas Bibb's term as governor involved the establishment of a state bank. The regular session of legislature had provided for the development of a state bank, though the bank was not established due to insufficient funds. On November 7, 1821, as the time left in Bibb's term as governor was waning, he addressed the 1821 Annual Session of the General Assembly. In the address, Bibb urged the assembly to begin setting up the Bank of the State and further recommended that the assembly incorporate a state university as had been authorized by the constitution of 1819, giving the university's trustees power to sell their lands and invest the proceeds in a state bank. He also commented on the suspension of specie payment by the Planters' and Merchants' Bank of Huntsville: "The depreciated value of a very considerable portion of our circulating medium, owing to the suspension of specie payments by one of the banks in this state, and the additional embarrassment to the Treasury from the fact that the bills of this Bank are receivable therein in payment of all dues to the state, is a subject of the most serious regret, and calls for some act of legislative correction." He also noted the unfairness of the state taking the paper of the Huntsville Bank at a depreciation of fifteen to twenty percent and proposed a plan that called for the private banks in the state to become part of "a general State Bank, with branches."[31]

As he closed his farewell address, Governor Bibb stated, "I have always endeavored to form my opinion from the best reasons my abilities could afford, and with a solemn deference and regard to the best interest and harmony of the community at large . . . and in retiring from public life, in addition to the satisfaction which I shall always feel of having discharged my duty with fidelity it will be a further source of pleasure to see that our government shall proceed with unanimity, harmony, and with satisfaction to the people." Several days after Bibb's farewell address, Israel Pickens was confirmed as the winner of the general election and was installed as Alabama's third governor.[32]

As predicted in his farewell address, Thomas Bibb retired from public life, except for a brief period representing Limestone County in the Alabama General Assembly in 1828 and 1829. He also served as director of the Huntsville branch of the State Bank for a while. Otherwise, most of his time was spent directing his business interests as a planter and merchant from his Georgian-styled plantation house located in Limestone County, which was completed in 1826 and named Belle Mina (known as Belmina during the nineteenth century). The town gets its name from Bibb's plantation home, which still exists along Mooresville Road, some seventeen miles west of Huntsville. The Bibbs named the sprawling 1826 home Belle Manor but, thanks to southern accents, the plantation soon became known as Belle Mina. Bibb also built a mansion on Huntsville's Williams Street for his daughter Adeline, who married James Bradley. The house was completed in 1836 and was purchased for only $2,000 by Bradley. This price probably represented a very favorable family discount. Unfortunately, Bradley lost the house during the Panic of 1837 when he became heavily in debt, and the grapevine had it that Adeline Bradley did not find out that the family had lost it until gardeners arrived to plant flowers for the new owner.[33]

Thomas Bibb died on September 20, 1839, at the age of fifty-seven. He apparently took ill very suddenly on a business trip to New Orleans. Legend has it that his corpse was preserved in a barrel of whiskey for his trip home to Belle Mina. He was first interred in the family plot there, but for some reason his grave was later moved to the well-known Maple Hill Cemetery in Huntsville. Thomas Bibb was survived by his wife, Parmelia, and eight children.[34]

6

JOHN WILLIAMS WALKER

President of the Constitutional Convention of
1819 and First US Senator from Alabama

Figure 6.1. John W. Walker, president of
the Alabama Constitutional Convention of
1819 and Alabama's first senator. Courtesy of
Huntsville-Madison County Public Library.

Associated with the Broad River Group, John Williams Walker was a neighbor and close friend of William Wyatt Bibb in Petersburg, Georgia. He was also a close friend of Senator Charles Tait, who was also part of the Broad River Group. The closeness of their friendship is reflected in a letter from Walker to Tait that was written about seven years after Walker left Georgia for Alabama, in which Walker said, "I shall never cease to indulge the warmest wishes for your health and happiness and fame. Time has not, as yet, in the least degree diminished my respect and attachment." He continued, "That you continue to cherish towards me similar statements, is a source of high and unmixed gratification." Walker would accompany yet another member of the Broad River Group, his father-in-law LeRoy Pope, to Madison County, Alabama, which then was located within the Mississippi Territory. A few years after settling in Madison County, Walker became active in politics. Interacting with the Broad River faction both in Alabama and in Georgia, he played a significant role in the founding of Alabama, serving as president of the Constitutional Convention of 1819, and as the new state's first US Senator.[1]

John Williams Walker was born on April 12, 1783, in Amelia County, Virginia, to Reverend Jeremiah Walker and Mary Jane Graves. In 1769, Reverend Walker was a prominent Baptist minister and began a fifteen-year pastorate in Amelia County. He also founded some twenty churches south of the James River. In 1783, soon after the birth of John, the Walkers were part of the group emigrating from Virginia to the Petersburg area in Georgia. In addition to his ministering, Walker earned the respect of his community, serving as a justice of the peace in Wilkes County, Georgia, in 1788, and, that same year, representing Wilkes County in the Georgia Constitutional Convention. Reverend Walker died a wealthy man in 1792, leaving his children 1,350 acres of land, several town lots, and an unknown number of slaves. A separate trust was set up for John, who was set to inherit 250 acres of river lands and several slaves when he reached his majority.[2]

Walker became an orphan at the age of nine when his mother died in 1793, a year after his father's death. Memorable Walker, one of John's four brothers, was appointed as his guardian. John learned about agricultural and commercial practices from his brothers, two of whom were Petersburg merchants. As he progressed through his teen years, John made many friends, and by the time he was seventeen he was accepted into membership of the popular "Junior Set" of Petersburg. For a while he worked in his brother's stores and collected debts for a friend. In 1803, he enrolled in Moses Waddell's Willington Academy, across the Savannah River in Vienna, Georgia. Waddell was an eminent antebellum teacher who taught future prominent politicians such as John C. Calhoun and William H. Crawford. Also in 1803, two of John's brothers died, Memorable and Jeremiah; his good friend and neighbor, Dr. William Wyatt Bibb, was elected to Congress to represent the Petersburg district; and he met his future wife, Matilda Pope, the daughter of LeRoy Pope, who was one of the wealthiest men in Petersburg and had done business with the Walker brothers. Since Matilda was only twelve years old at this time, John Walker turned his attention to managing his brothers' estates while also pursuing his education at Waddell's academy.[3]

While Matilda Pope headed off to a finishing school in Bethlehem, Pennsylvania, John Walker enrolled in Princeton in the spring of 1805. He was able to do so with his share of the proceeds from the settlement of his brothers' estates. During his stay at Princeton, he was very lonely at times and tentative as to what he was to accomplish in life. He also contracted a disease, believed to be tuberculosis, from which he recovered, but which left him unhealthy for much of the rest of his life. Despite these obstacles, he graduated with distinction from Princeton in the fall of 1806. In a letter to his brother, James S. Walker, he indicated that he was joyful for receiving a degree from a prestigious university, but unhappy at leaving the gratifying life he had had there.[4]

Due to having to repay a note he had cosigned for a friend, Walker had only enough money to make it from Princeton to Washington, DC. Even when he received a draft from his brother allowing him to come home, Walker decided to stay for a while to get a sense of what life in the capital was all about and to observe congressional debates with his old neighbor and friend, Representative William Wyatt Bibb. He soaked up the atmosphere of the nation's capital by reading its newspaper and attending balls, whist parties, and "tea conventions." His visit to Congress left him appalled at the propensity of the nation's treasury being "lightened by those eternal blabbers, none of whom can talk grammar or common sense."[5]

In the spring of 1807, when Walker was finally ready to ride back to Georgia with Bibb, his health required him to return by sea. Hence, he set out from Baltimore to return home. His stay in Georgia, however, was very brief because Walker had the bug to continue traveling. He traveled first to Charleston and then on to New Orleans. Not very impressed with the Crescent City and with his health worsening, Walker moved on to the town of Washington near Natchez in the Mississippi Territory to visit Thomas Percy, a friend from his days at Princeton. By the time of his arrival in Washington, Walker was seriously ill but was fortunate to be under the care of Dr. Sam Brown. As Walker's health improved, he could get out and survey the territory. His observations led him to be impressed with the Mississippi Territory, particularly its soil, which he described as "exceedingly fertile & productive, beyond all comparison superior to that of Georgia." He thought the planters to be "rich and hospitable," many of whom set a "sumptuous table." Walker also preferred the territory's slightly milder climate to that of Georgia's up-country. These factors led Walker to want to settle where "hospitality & health" abounded, and where he hoped to find "independence and wealth." Accordingly, in late 1809 and early 1810, Walker completed plans to move to Madison County, in what was to become Alabama, and finally courted and then married Matilda Pope on January 30, 1810.[6]

Earlier, in 1809, fertile lands of Madison County in the great bend of the Tennessee River had been offered for sale to the public. A large portion of these lands was purchased by Walker, LeRoy Pope, Thomas and William Bibb, and three other residents of Petersburg. It is estimated that these seven prominent Georgians purchased approximately half of the lands offered for sale at that time. During this sale, Walker purchased two quarter-sections, and by June 1810 the Walkers had joined the Pope family at their newly acquired lands. Upon his arrival, Walker added another quarter-section and, as we have seen, would do so in 1811, 1812, and 1814. As indicated earlier, John and Matilda Walker built a cabin they named Oakland about eight miles north of the Hunt's Spring, which had been discovered by John Hunt in 1805. About the spring Walker said, "Huntsville is situated around the finest spring in the world; and at a trivial expense the spring can be made navigable for batteaux to the Tennessee River, which is only ten miles distant." As for the land in Madison County, Walker said it was "the handsomest" he had ever seen.[7]

Although the cabin that the Walkers built was a modest structure, it was decorated with elegant furniture and fine china, which was shipped to them from their home in Petersburg. It was soon adorned with a baby when John's wife, Matilda, gave birth to a daughter, named Mary Jane, on December 2, 1810. The Walker household increased even more when John took in his sister, Polly Coleman, and her six children after the death of Polly's husband. John remained the children's guardians for the rest of his life and assumed the responsibility for the care of a number of slaves inherited by Polly from her husband. As they settled in their new home, John continued reading law, which he had commenced back in Petersburg. He was finally licensed to practice by Madison County's first Superior Court of Law and Equity in the fall of 1810.[8]

Early Huntsville historian Edwin C. Betts asserted that "of the brilliant and promising young lawyers of Huntsville who rose to eminence, he [Walker] was the most talented and popular." In May 1811, encouraged by his popularity, Walker sought election to the Mississippi Territorial Legislature. There were six candidates contending for three seats, but Walker was not one of the three elected. The Georgia Broad River political faction had not yet taken hold in the Tennessee Valley enough to get Walker elected. Walker blamed his loss on the fact that he was a "stranger" to many settlers, and that he had been the object of a smear campaign. The ill treatment that he perceived led him to say that it would "be the last time" that he would "be a candidate for public favor."[9]

Walker's brother, James Sanders Walker, was his political and economic advisor. As political advisor, he continually urged his brother to seek political office again, even suggesting that he go back to Georgia and seek election to the Georgia House of Representatives. John, however, stuck to his guns by continuing to elude political office, at least for a while. In the meantime, James managed the family's cotton output. In 1811 the prices had fallen to an unprecedented low of eight cents per pound, resulting in James being unable to find a profitable market for their cotton during the war years 1812–1813. By February 1815, however, the market recovered, bringing between fourteen and sixteen cents a pound, and by November 1815 it was up to twenty-five cents a pound. With increasing family fortunes in the production of cotton, James Walker decided to move to Tuscaloosa in 1816.[10]

During the Creek War of 1813–1814, General Andrew Jackson and his aide, General John Coffee, stopped at John Walker's cabin, Oakland, on their way to Indian country further south. Walker subsequently wrote to General Coffee, who by then was encamped at the Hickory Ground, offering his congratulations to him and General Jackson "on the brilliant season, and glorious success of the army." By now, Jackson had become Walker's new hero, second only to George Washington. Not surprisingly, soon thereafter Walker used his influence with the Georgia faction in obtaining a federal appointment for General Coffee to survey the boundary lines with the Creek Nation. In 1817, Coffee was bestowed with another appointment to survey lands in the northern part of the Mississippi Territory. In turn, in June 1817 General Jackson recommended Walker for the governorship of the eastern portion of the territory in case it be separated from the western portion. In a letter to President Monroe, Jackson stated "a firm belief that Major John W. Walker, a resident near Huntsville, is a man qualified to fill that important office with honor to himself and profit to the country."[11]

By 1814, Walker had become more engaged in political causes like those of which the newly arrived settlers seemed to favor, particularly a more liberal land policy, which allowed those who bought more than one quarter-section to direct all their payments to one quarter-section. This proposal was to help those who had to purchase more land than they needed to get at least one fertile quarter-section. Emerging from his earlier avoidance of politics, Walker played a key role in the establishment of the Alabama Territory and subsequent statehood. At the outset, he disagreed with those in the Natchez section who supported the admission of the entire Mississippi Territory as one state. Walker advised the territory's delegate to Congress, George Poindexter, that he was against it because the area was too large and if admitted it would have been the largest state in the Union. Although Walker supported a division of the territory, he supported an east-west line instead of a more favored north-south line. Under Walker's proposed east-west division, the Tombigbee and Natchez districts would be admitted at once as the state of Mississippi and the new Alabama Territory, each being in the northern half of their respective state and territory. After the Creek War, the Natchez group suddenly favored division while the Tombigbee group also flip-flopped by opposing division. Walker and his Madison County colleagues, however, continued to favor division for a while.[12]

Walker undoubtedly remained comfortable with his position on division because his close friend, Senator Charles Tait of Georgia, was chairman of the select committee dealing with the admission of Mississippi as a state. Senator Tait, from the Broad River region, in turn was a close friend of Secretary of the Treasury William H. Crawford, a former US senator from Georgia and minister to France. As secretary of the treasury, Crawford controlled patronage in Georgia to protect his friends, including those who had left Georgia for the Mississippi Territory, such as William Wyatt Bibb, Bolling Hall, and Walker. This group of men would become the core of the "Georgia Machine" that took hold of Alabama's politics. In January 1817, Senator Tait asked Walker how the territory was to be divided. Walker, who had abandoned his support of an east-west division, advised that he agreed with the senator that the territory should be divided on a north-south boundary, which, unlike an east-west boundary, would include a large part of the Tombigbee River and the port of Mobile.[13]

Walker's efforts in helping to create the Alabama Territory made him very popular and enabled him to get elected as one of Madison County's representatives to the Alabama Territory's first General Assembly to be convened at St. Stephens in February 1818. Meanwhile, Secretary Crawford commenced doling out patronage in the newly created territory. First, Crawford recommended to President Monroe that William Wyatt Bibb be appointed as territorial governor. Of course, Bibb was available because he had been defeated in his bid for reelection to his Senate seat because he had voted for an unpopular bill to increase congressional salaries. After the appointment of Bibb, Crawford, and Tait, without consulting with Walker, recommended Walker to the president to serve as Secretary of the Territory. In a letter to Tait, in February 1818, Walker said, "I see in the newspapers that the President has conferred on me the appointment of Secretary for this Territory." Walker, however, turned down the appointment primarily due to health reasons and what he considered an inadequate salary to support his growing family. Henry Hitchcock, grandson of the legendary Ethan Allen of Vermont, was appointed in Walker's stead.[14]

Having turned down the Secretary of the Territory position, Walker concentrated on his legislative duties in the first session of the Alabama Territorial Legislature. Historian Hugh C. Bailey asserts that "Walker played an unsurpassed prominent role" in this first session. Despite the prominent role he played, as indicated in a letter to Senator Tait, at first Walker felt uncomfortable, saying, "I have been a fortnight engaged in the business of legislation for the Territory, and have felt as awkward and ashamed as a new boarding-school miss on her introduction to the *beau monde*." Walker undoubtedly abandoned these sentiments quickly since he was appointed to the powerful Ways and

Means Committee. He was also named to the Committee on Enrolled Bills and a committee to oversee legislative printing. The first bill Walker introduced was a proposed amendment to the Mississippi Territory's Act of 1816 establishing the Planters' and Mechanics' Bank of Huntsville. The amendment first changed the name of the bank to the Planters' and Merchants' Bank of Huntsville, but, more importantly, it allowed the Territory to purchase two-thirds of the bank's stock. Because of his sponsorship of this amendment, Walker was seen as conservative and as an emerging leader of the "Georgia Machine." It should also be noted that Walker was one of the nine directors of the bank.[15]

Surprisingly, Governor Bibb went against his fellow Georgians and vetoed the proposed amendment. In his veto message, Bibb expressed fear that the territory would not have sufficient control over the bank and would be forced to accept the bank's notes at face value for all obligations due it. He also did not want to give to a private bank the power to decide where to open branches throughout the territory. Despite these arguments, Walker secured the passage of a very similar bill over the governor's veto. Walker also played an important role in the securement of an amendment to the Mississippi Territorial Act against usury, which would allow an unlimited rate of interest if reduced to writing. If not reduced to writing, the interest rate would be limited to eight percent. Walker lent his support to the amendment by securing a favorable report from the Ways and Means Committee. Opposed to this amendment was the popular party, known as the "Champions of the People," who, despite some protections to debtors, believed that overall it was hostile to debtors and provided too much protection to the moneyed interests, so much so that the first legislature of the new state of Alabama repealed the amendment.[16]

Walker supported more popular proposals during this first session of the territorial legislature, including a bill allowing the territorial militia to expand beyond only one brigade. This bill also authorized the governor to call up the militia at his own discretion and appropriated $2,000 for use of the quartermaster in arming and supplying members of the militia. By the close of the first session in mid-February 1818, Walker had the distinction of having introduced more bills that were ultimately enacted than anyone else. Included among these was a bill that allowed Madison County to levy a special tax to finance the completion of its public buildings, another which authorized the governor to petition the State of Mississippi for monies due the Alabama Territory, and one which provided that a census be taken in the Territory. Walker also succeeded in having the legislature appoint a joint commission to locate "the most suitable route for a road from the falls of Tuscaloosa, to the Tennessee River."[17]

When the second session of the Alabama Territorial legislature convened in November 1818, the incumbent, Gabriel Moore, did not seek reelection as Speaker of the House because the legislature had granted his wife a divorce and granted a petition to resume her maiden name. Fearing repercussions from the highly publicized divorce, Moore decided to temporarily withdraw from politics. This decision allowed Walker to be unanimously elected as Speaker of the House in Moore's stead. In a letter to Senator Tait, Walker indicated that "this station relieves me from the labor of composition and drudgery of committee business." He thus had more time to focus on securing statehood for Alabama. Also, he turned to his good friend, Senator Charles Tait of Georgia, to aid him in this cause. Like Governor Bibb, Senator Tait had voted in favor of a bill to increase congressional salaries. As we have seen, Bibb resigned immediately when he failed to be reelected. Senator Tait thought about doing the same thing, but Walker urged him to stay so that he could shepherd an enabling act through Congress to secure statehood for Alabama. In this regard, Walker stated in response to a letter from Senator Tait in September 1818, "There is one suggestion in your letter which I do not like. You speak of your resignation of your seat in the Senate as a probable event. I am sorry for it . . . and shall deeply regret it." He continued, "But although you have done much for her [Alabama], your work is still incomplete. You have still the power & the means of heaping more favors on her; and I think you ought to crown your other labors of love and kindness by procuring the act of her admission into the Union. . . . Make Alabama, your future home, more dear to you by making yourself more dear to her."[18]

When Senator Tait decided to stay, Walker wrote him a long letter discussing the various issues of the day. Before this discussion, however, Walker remarked, "I regard you the Patron of Alabama, and should have felt your absence as a sinister omen. Now, I sanguinely hope for all the best." The first issue that Walker addressed was the population required to support admission into the Union. He asserted that 60,000 free inhabitants could demand admission, but Congress reserved the power of granting it earlier if they saw fit. In fact, Mississippi had just 47,000 inhabitants when admitted to the Union. The population at this time in the Alabama Territory, even with two counties not reporting, was 67,594, including 21,000 slaves. In any event, Walker believed that the Territory would have more than 60,000 white inhabitants by the time the next Congress met. Walker summed up this issue by telling Tait that, although not entitled to admission, Alabama had the right to expect it.[19]

Turning to the issue of apportionment, Walker informed Tait that he would send him a corrected copy of the census, which he felt would enable Senator Tait to make a fair and equal apportionment. Walker stressed that "I want nothing to Madison [County], but her rights," and trusted that attempts being made to deprive Madison of her rights would be defeated. He continued, "I am inclined to think that the apportionment will be made according to the ratio of one Representative for each thousand free inhabitants contained in each county—giving, however, to every County at least one Representative." Finally, regarding the location of the capital of the new state Walker advised Senator Tait, "The question of fixing on the site for the permanent seat of government will be hotly contested, and its issue is very doubtful." Walker closed this lengthy letter warning Tait that he would "pester [him] regularly every mail during my stay in this wretched little place [St. Stephens]."[20]

Two days later, Walker posted another letter to Senator Tait, enclosing a copy of the Joint Memorial of both houses of the legislature of the Alabama Territory, which prayed for its admission into the Union, and that the Territory be authorized to form a constitution and a state government. Walker again urged Senator Tait to support statehood, saying, "It is hoped that you will not only present these memorials to the Senate, but cheerfully lend your active aid and influence in their support." He also informed Tait that a "just and equal ratio" had been adopted by an overwhelming majority of the Committee of the Whole of the territorial legislature, and he had no doubt of its final passage.[21]

In yet another letter to Tait just a few days later, Walker informs Tait that the apportionment bill had been passed, but it was saddled with a rider which he had not expected, namely, the selection of the town of Cahaba as the permanent seat of the Territorial government. Walker let Senator Tait know that he objected to the method by which this had been accomplished. As we have seen, Governor Bibb used his Washington connections to pass a bill that gave Governor Bibb the authority to choose the location from land allotted by Congress to be utilized for the seat of government. Bibb knew that he had disappointed Walker and his constituents with his selection of Cahaba. He wrote to Senator Tait that he had "given much displeasure to the Madison folk and the people on the Warrior." However, that did not stop the governor from urging Senator Tait to ensure that the president did not yield on the issue or otherwise there would be "some collision" in the next legislative session in Alabama. This statement evidenced that Governor Bibb was determined to have Cahaba become the capital and used his influence as governor, the political superiority of south Alabama, and the Georgia faction to get the rider enacted.[22]

Historian William H. Brantley Jr.'s extensive study of the issue led him to conclude that there were two major reasons that Bibb was able to win approval for the Cahaba site. The first was the state's empty coffers that made free land very enticing; the second was the veto power held by Bibb over the apportionment bill desired by North Alabama. Because of his friendship with the governor, Walker reluctantly supported Cahaba, but voiced his displeasure at the high-handed way in which Bibb had handled the matter. Walker reluctantly supported Cahaba even though he claimed that he and his fellow northern representatives could have killed the rider. However, since four northern representatives were not present, Walker believed that only an impasse could have resulted. Walker told Tait that it was best overall to give effect to the will of the "accidental majority." Another sweetener in the pot to appease the northern representatives was the decision to make Huntsville the temporary capital until suitable buildings could be erected at Cahaba.[23]

As the second session of the territorial legislature was winding down, Walker urged Senator Tait not to wait too long to fix the time for holding the election of delegates to a constitutional convention. When the second session adjourned after two arduous eleven-hour days, Walker began his long trek home, covering 250 miles in six days. Once he arrived home at Oakland, Walker wrote Senator Tait yet again, exhorting him to fight for statehood. Senator Tait soon thereafter sent copies of the Enabling Act, which he had written, to Walker and others supporting statehood in Alabama. Most were pleased with the result. Walker had hoped that Tait could have procured two representatives for the new state, but he realized that such a request would have been unusual in that no other state had more than one. Tait, however, had been successful in securing a couple of unique provisions that other states did not enjoy. First, the act reserved two sections of land for the endowment of a state university to be opened "on the most liberal and satisfactory foundation." Second, over the objections of the state of Mississippi, Alabama's western boundary was left intact, allowing Alabama to claim most of the Tombigbee River.[24]

In correspondence with Tait in February 1819, Walker wrote, "I know you have done your duty and I hope to see you a popular man in Alabama." In April 1819, Walker sought to become popular himself when he threw his hat in the ring to become one of Madison County's delegates to the constitutional convention. Since he was supposedly repugnant to the "vulgarity of electioneering," Walker pledged to the voters that he would leave it to them "to decide for themselves without solicitation or tricks" as to whether he should "render the state some service." He obviously believed that if he did a good job at the constitutional convention that his colleagues would approach him, urging him to "accept some office of considerable trust in the state." Although it was generally accepted that he could be elected to the US House of Representatives, Walker preferred the US Senate. He thought the office of governor would tie him down too much to the "irksome routine of office." He hesitated on announcing his preference out of deference to William Wyatt Bibb, who he erroneously presumed preferred a Senate seat.

Finally, Walker let it be known that he would accept an offer from the legislature to serve in the Senate, so long as his health permitted. There was concern, though, among some of his friends about the state of his health—one of them even told him that it would be much preferable for him to be "a living Governor than a dead Senator." With that, Walker decided to wait until after the constitutional convention to decide exactly what office he would like to hold. Before the convention, however, President Monroe appointed Walker, with Senate approval, as United States Territorial Judge. This appointment was made without Walker's knowledge and, as Walker put it, was "in the teeth of my known wishes." But, he said, "I have been compelled, by a sense of public duty, to accept it for the short period which remains for our Territorial career." After the adoption of the Alabama Constitution, Walker in fact resigned his judgeship.[25]

Walker ran in a field of twenty-two to become one of Madison County's eight delegates to the constitutional convention. Finishing fifth out of the successful eight, Walker said, "I did succeed notwithstanding the usury law, the judgeship, my laziness, and my unfashionable non-electioneering course, and a thousand *et ceteras*." Readying for the convention, Walker informed Senator Tait that he was "cobbling up a Constitution for Alabama, such a one that I deem best for her." Unlike Tait, Walker anticipated sharp differences of principles among the delegates, particularly those pertaining to representation. Walker maintained that he was "no party man" and that he would be "moderate and cool myself and will attempt to infuse into the whole body of the spirit of conciliation . . . and moderation."[26]

Prior to the constitutional convention, Senator Tait visited Huntsville, where he was honored with a dinner presided over by Walker on April 21, 1819. There were many toasts, including one to the upcoming convention, praying that it "would be guided by an enlightened and disinterested patriotism, and terminate in a Constitution which shall secure to our latest posterity the blessings of liberty." After addressing the dinner, Senator Tait gave a closing toast to Alabama, imploring that "the wisdom of her Councils [may] equal those advantages which nature has bestowed upon her." Soon after Senator Tait left, Walker heard a rumor that President Monroe would be visiting in Nashville and Knoxville, but it was not certain he would come to Huntsville. The president indeed paid a surprise visit to Huntsville, arriving before the townspeople were aware of his presence. The president's party was put up in the Huntsville Inn by a quickly organized host committee headed by Clement Comer Clay, who invited the president for a formal dinner to be held the next afternoon. The dinner was presided over by LeRoy Pope and attended by 100 prominent Madison Countians. The day after the dinner the president and his party left for Nashville, but he stopped for two or three hours at Walker's cabin, Oakland, "where he was mustered by a mid-day rel-ish—sort of a second breakfast." Walker observed, "His extreme plainness, and the simplicity of his manners were matters of surprise to many. He was very affable . . . and decidedly a popular man."[27]

After the excitement of President Monroe's visit, Huntsville turned its attention to the upcoming constitutional convention, which was to convene on July 5, 1819. During the opening session, John Williams Walker was unan-imously elected president of the convention. One delegate observed that it was not going to be an easy task to agree on principles because the delegates were from many different states, bringing with them different prejudices. To min-imize these prejudices and bring more harmony to the task at hand, the con-vention resolved on July 6 that a Committee of Fifteen should be appointed by the president of the convention. Their duty would be to draft a skeleton consti-tution for the convention as a whole to consider. Walker was apparently given a free hand to select the committee and chose as its chairman his close friend from Huntsville, Clement Comer Clay. It is assumed that Walker handed over to the committee what he had been "cobbling" up as a constitution.[28]

On July 7, 1819, the convention adopted rules for its conduct of busi-ness, granting President Walker a great deal of power, including the abil-ity to speak and vote on all issues, the authority to maintain order, and the authority to compel delegates to attend. On July 13, 1819, Walker read the Committee of Fifteen's draft to the whole convention. Walker was influen-tial throughout the debates, particularly regarding the controversial issue of representation in the legislature. The original provision had provided that the federal ratio should be the basis of apportionment. But Walker shocked the Committee of the Whole when he proposed that none "but free white per-sons" should be counted in determining representation in the legislature.[29] Quite a few southern counties vigorously opposed the removal of the fed-eral three-fifths ratio since they stood to gain representation by it. Walker's amendment, however, carried the day, leaving the northern counties gener-ally pleased by this crucial change. Walker, in turn, defeated efforts to limit counties' representation—ideas promoted by southern Alabama leaders such as Henry Hitchcock, Judge Toulmin, William R. King, and Israel Pickens—to weaken the advantage North Alabama would gain if actual numbers of people were counted.[30]

In addition to representation issues, Walker had a keen interest regard-ing the militia and who chose its officers. In this regard, Walker was in favor of the militia being able to elect their own officers popularly. Thus, he used his influence to limit the number of legislative appointments to just two positions—adjutant general and quartermaster general. He later joined a minority that was unsuccessful in removing all legislative power to make

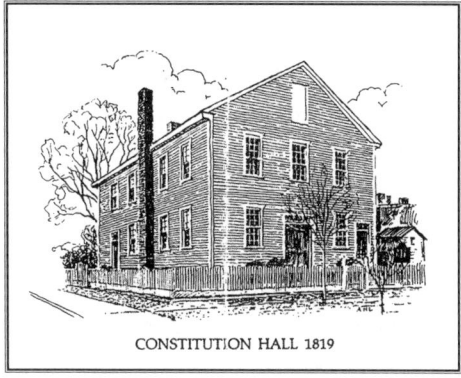

CONSTITUTION HALL 1819

Figure 6.2. Constitution Hall, site of the 1819 Constitutional Convention. Courtesy of Huntsville-Madison County Public Library.

appointments. As for the judiciary, Walker sided with the majority in voting against a six-year term limit for judges as opposed to holding office with no term limits, during periods of good behavior. A decade later, however, due to an increasing mistrust of the judiciary, the first amendment to the Alabama Constitution provided for a popular election of judges and six-year term limits. Walker also favored the establishment of a state bank and unsuccessfully supported a proposal reducing the number of legislative votes needed to establish a bank from two-thirds to one-half.[31]

After deliberations on these and other issues, the Alabama Constitution of 1819 was adopted and signed by the forty-four delegates to the convention on August 2, 1819. As soon as the signing was completed, Israel Pickens called for a resolution praising Walker for his efforts as president of the convention. The resolution, which was unanimously adopted, read: "Resolved, that the thanks of this convention be presented to John W. Walker, President, thereof, for the dignity, ability, and impartiality with which he has discharged the arduous duties of the Chair." In his response Walker said, "We have given to the state of Alabama a Constitution—not indeed perfect—not precisely such as any one individual of this community, would, unassisted, have framed in his closet." Yet it is "emphatically republican and such as gives us a clear and indisputable title, to admission into the great family of the Union." A few days after the convention, Walker wrote to Senator Tait that he was "nearly worn out and exhausted from the duties of President of the Convention." As for the work of the convention, however, he said, "Suffice it at present, to say that in general we got along harmoniously; and have framed a very good Constitution."[32]

A few years after the convention, Governor Bibb's brother, John D. Bibb, who was sometimes at odds with Walker, nevertheless wrote in his journal that Walker was "considered to be decidedly the most talented member of the Convention." He also observed that Walker was "much emaciated and his physical powers greatly weakened by consumption," but he "presided with dignity and impartiality and gave entire satisfaction to all parties." He further recognized his "refined manners," elocution skills, and his gracious and courteous manner. The convention's secretary, John Campbell, not as complimentary of Walker, wrote to his brother that Walker "knew little more of parliamentary proceedings than your boy, Richard, although an accomplished scholar and a man of smartness." He stated further that Walker was "amazingly spoilt by the flattery which is lavished upon him in our new country."[33]

Impressed with his service leading the constitutional convention, the Georgia faction made Walker part of their statewide strategy by offering him a US Senate seat. Since it turns out that Bibb was not interested in the position as Walker earlier had thought, Walker felt free to accept it. The Royalists, as the Georgians were sometimes referred to because of their stance on unlimited interest rates and the establishment of a state bank, sought to place Georgian Charles Tait in the second senatorship. Political expediency, however, dictated that the second seat be filled by someone from south Alabama. To get into position to assume his Senate seat, Walker resigned his position as federal territorial judge in September, using his poor health as his excuse. When the legislature convened in November 1819, representatives from south Alabama chose William Rufus King for the second seat, allowing him to accompany Walker to Washington to serve as Alabama's first US senators. Walker, as usual, was concerned about his health, but he hated most leaving his family, especially considering the arrival of his fourth son, who was named Charles in honor of Charles Tait. But Walker pushed forward, and when he arrived in Washington he presented his credentials on December 7, 1819, and took his seat in the Senate. The next day the resolution for the admission of Alabama into the Union passed both chambers and was sent to the president, who signed it on December 14, 1819.[34]

Tait was disappointed that he did not receive the second Senate seat, but he took it in stride, stating that he was content if it was not possible to present him as a candidate without "disturbing the harmony of our political leaders." Instead, Tait petitioned Walker and Secretary of the Treasury Crawford to support his selection for the federal judgeship for the Alabama District. Judge Harry Toulmin sought the position for himself and even solicited the support of Walker. However, when Walker arrived in Washington to serve in the Senate, he went straight to the White House and informed the president that he supported Tait for the judgeship. The support of Secretary Crawford and Secretary of War John C. Calhoun sealed the deal and the appointment of Tait was quickly made. The Senate unanimously confirmed the appointment on May 13, 1820.[35]

During the politicking for the second Senate seat and the federal judgeship, William Wyatt Bibb was elected the first governor of the state of Alabama. Bibb won a very narrow margin of victory over Tuscaloosa attorney Marmaduke Williams. Bibb won by only five votes out of 2,453 in Madison County, which was a sign of adverse things to come for the Broad River Georgians. Matters worsened for the Georgians when Governor Bibb died in July 1820 from injuries sustained when he was thrown from his horse. After a lackluster administration, Thomas Bibb decided not to seek reelection. In 1821, Israel Pickens announced for governor in opposition to the Georgians. Apparently feeling the need to mend fences back home, Walker volunteered to be the Georgia faction's candidate for governor. He was too late, however, as the faction had already settled on Dr. Henry Chambers of Madison County as their candidate. Looking upon the bright side, Henry Hitchcock told Walker that "we have at least acted safely and perhaps saved you from a mortification of defeat, and . . . I think you may well congratulate yourself on being released from the trouble of the contest." Historian Hugh C. Bailey posited that the real reason that Walker was not made a candidate was his prominent role in the 1818 passage of the Usury Law, his close association with the Planters' and Merchants' Bank, and the fear that Pickens would attack both vulnerable points with a vengeance. Walker indeed dodged a bullet, as Pickens was elected overwhelmingly, campaigning on the issues of currency, a state bank, and the domination of the Georgians.[36]

Upon assuming their Senate seats, Walker and King were at first faced with the controversy surrounding the admission of Missouri into the Union. However, the question was soon tentatively resolved in what became known as the Missouri Compromise. Walker expressed his naïve satisfaction for the compromise, indicating to Tait that "it was a wild and necessary occasion and has saved the Republic."[37] Walker also unrealistically supported the annexation of a portion of Florida. In this regard, he first urged the delegates to the constitutional convention to include a memorial in the Alabama Constitution which petitioned that after annexation of Florida from Spain, the portion of Florida lying west of the Apalachicola River be added to Alabama: "Our Geographical symmetry will be marred unless this annexation takes place." Unfortunately, Senator Walker was unable to muster the necessary votes for the proposed annexation. Other significant matters of interest during Walker's service in the Senate included his working to promote the interests of his conservative supporters in the banking and lending industries by opposing the passage of a bankruptcy bill that would have afforded more protections to debtors. Also, he and Senator King supplied the winning votes rejecting a proposed tariff, which Walker felt would harm southern agricultural interests. Although Walker opposed money for internal improvements elsewhere, he was pleased that the federal government set aside three percent of Alabama land sales for internal improvements. Walker was also pleased with his appointment to the Committee on the Militia and the Committee on Naval Affairs, which in 1820 left a million-dollar appropriation intact.[38]

According to Hugh C. Bailey, Walker's greatest contribution as senator was a successful campaign to secure the revision of the nation's land laws. His campaign was in response to a report from the United States Public Land Office in the summer of 1820 that fifty-three percent of the monies due from purchasers of public lands was due from Alabama. Walker thus gave his support to the Land Law of 1820, which reduced the price of land to $1.25 an acre and ended the credit system. Despite its implementation, it provided no substantial relief. Walker, therefore, introduced a bill that became the Land Law of 1821. It provided for the relinquishment of lands and resale by the government and return to the original owner of proceeds above $1.25 an acre, with discounts for prompt payments. This law became a model for land relief throughout the next decade. In the meanwhile, Alabama's debt was reduced in half by September 1821, making Senator Walker very popular back home.[39]

The Panic of 1819 affected Walker's business interests to a certain extent as cotton hit rock-bottom prices and torrential rains left cotton in the bolls. However, Walker instructed his agent, who was also his brother-in-law, to sell some of his slaves[40] and to collect debts owed to him. As a result, he was provided with a decent income through the economic downturn. With an improved income, Walker's wife, Matilda, and his newborn sixth son, William Memorable, could accompany Walker to Washington in late 1821. Two months after their arrival, the Walkers learned that their two-year-old son, Charles Henry, had died in Alabama.[41] When they came home, Walker's health continued to decline to such an extent that on November 21, 1822, he resigned from the Senate. In his letter of resignation to Governor Israel Pickens, Walker stated, "The state of my health has been so precarious, and so much worse than usual during the past summer as to render it for some time doubtful whether I shall be able to attend the approaching session of Congress. . . . I recognize the paramount claim of the State upon my services." William Kelly of the People's Party, led by Governor Pickens, was chosen by the legislature to take Walker's seat in the Senate over John McKinley, who was the Georgia faction's candidate.[42]

John Williams Walker died on April 23, 1823. He was survived by his wife, Matilda, and three sons—Percy, LeRoy, and Richard Wide. Percy Walker was a lawyer and served in the Alabama House of Representatives and the US House of Representatives. LeRoy Pope Walker served in the

Alabama House of Representatives and as the Confederate States of America's Secretary of War. Richard Wilde Walker served as an associate justice of the Alabama Supreme Court and was a senator in the Confederate Congress. The senior Walker was interred in the Maple Hill Cemetery of Huntsville along with many notable politicians of the era.[43]

The citizens of Huntsville adopted a resolution honoring Walker, which read in part, "*Resolved*, That this meeting deeply deplore, in common with their fellow-citizens, the loss of our country in general, and our infant state in particular, has sustained in the death of the late HON. JOHN WILLIAMS WALKER, whose unsullied virtue in private and distinguished services in public life, have secured to him the affections and confidence of his countrymen." The *National Intelligencer* said of Walker, "When first known in public life, he was already affected with the pulmonary complaint which terminated his mortal career." The *Intelligencer* opined that Walker "knew that he was doomed to an early grave," but pressed forward as if with a firmness that suggested that he was unaware of the deadly disease. As the *Intelligencer* said, "Perhaps no man was ever so short a time in the Councils of his country, who left behind him more friends or more enviable fame." Recognizing that Walker was instrumental in the founding of Alabama, on December 26, 1823, the Alabama legislature created a county in north Alabama and named it Walker County in his honor. Walker, like several of his protégés, was buried In Huntsville's Maple Hill Cemetery.[44]

7

JUDGE CHARLES TAIT

"Patron of Alabama" and Alabama's First Federal Judge

Figure 7.1. Charles Tait, the "Patron of Alabama." Courtesy of the Alabama Department of Archives and History.

As a US senator from Georgia, Charles Tait, along with the help of fellow Georgians and Secretary of the Treasury William H. Crawford, played the most significant roles in securing statehood for Alabama. For his efforts, Tait was referred to as the "Patron of Alabama," and was appointed Alabama's first federal district court judge after having served in the US Senate from 1809 to 1819 representing Georgia. Tait also played a significant role in Alabama's history as a lawyer, educator, legislator, jurist, scientist, and planter.

Born on February 1, 1768, in Louisa County, Virginia, Charles Tait was the oldest of ten children of James and Rebecca Hudson Tait, a cousin of the mother of Henry Clay. During his early childhood, Tait worked on his father's tobacco farm, but with decreasing yields and increasing costs of production, in 1783, Charles's father decided to pick up stakes and join the southwestward migration to the more fertile soil of the Georgia piedmont. With the help of his friend Governor George Mathews of Georgia, James Tait was granted more than three thousand acres of land in three different Georgia counties and was one of the first purchasers of lots in Petersburg, the center of the Broad River region. Charles Tait did not immediately follow his family to Petersburg; instead, he remained in Virginia to obtain a basic education. When he rejoined his family in 1785, most of James Tait's land was utilized for the cultivation of tobacco. Along with his brother, Charles assisted his father in tending to the tobacco crop. While hauling tobacco to market at some point during his youth, Charles severely injured his leg when he was thrown from his horse. Unfortunately, infection settled in the wound and his leg had to be amputated. He thereafter wore a wooden stump for the remainder of his life.[1]

At the age of eighteen, Tait entered the inaugural class of the Wilkes Academy in Washington, Georgia, where he studied the academy's traditional classical course during 1786 and 1787. Also attending the academy at this time was Sarah Williamson, who would become Tait's second wife years later. Many of the other students became friends, while others would become antagonists in the future. While studying at Wilkes Academy, Bishop Francis Asbury befriended Tait. Bishop Asbury had converted Tait's parents to Methodism before they left Virginia and founded the first Methodist conference in Georgia in 1788 after they arrived in Petersburg. The Taits' close relationship with Asbury influenced Charles Tait to enter Cokesbury College in Abingdon, Maryland—America's first Methodist college, founded in May 1788. Within a few months, Tait was appointed to the faculty as a French professor and put in charge of the college's charity students. Reading law at the same time, he remained at Cokesbury until 1794.[2]

While teaching at Cokesbury, Tait met and married Mrs. Anne Lucas, a widow from Baltimore, with whom he had two sons: James Asbury, born in 1791, and Charles Jefferson, born in 1794. Charles Jefferson died one month after his birth. During this period, James Tait was urging his son to come home to Georgia. Since Charles was discontented with his position at Cokesbury, he resigned and returned to Elbert County, where he was admitted to the Georgia bar on February 5, 1795. Tait, however, did not let his license to practice law interfere with his continuing interest in education, and in April 1795 he was installed as the fifth rector of the Richmond Academy at Augusta, Georgia. The following year, William H. Crawford, the future secretary of the treasury and presidential candidate, was appointed as head of the academy's English department. He and Tait thereafter formed a friendship that would last throughout their lives, and would prove valuable for Tait later in his life. They both were intensely interested in political affairs, and soon after Crawford came to the academy they established a public debating society, which attracted prominent Augustans as members. By 1797, the Richmond Academy was experiencing financial problems that necessitated a reduction of faculty salaries. Thus, Tait resigned his rectorship in 1798[3] and returned to his law practice at Elberton, where he also sought political office. He was succeeded at the Richmond Academy by Crawford, who served for a year as both rector and English teacher.[4]

In 1799, Tait, commencing his political career as a Jeffersonian Democrat, won election as a state senator from Elbert County. Serving in that capacity for only one year, Tait's primary focus was on the improvement of Broad River transportation facilities, despite the national party's opposition to internal improvements. Understanding the importance of the social and economic development of the frontier, Tait used his influence as chairman of the finance committee to pass a bill to improve navigation of the Broad and Savannah Rivers. Upon the expiration of his term, Tait established a law practice, working with Crawford, whose office was in Lexington in the neighboring county of Oglethorpe, until he was elected in November 1803 as a judge in the Superior Court of Georgia's Western Judicial Circuit. He served in that capacity until 1809.[5]

After his election, Tait came under attack from political opponents who were aligned with a faction in Georgia made up of settlers from North Carolina who had a long-standing feud with the Broad River Group. Elbert County was the center of the Virginia settlement in Georgia. Just to the south was the older Wilkes County, which became the center of a North Carolina settlement. There was much rivalry between these settlements, with the better-educated Virginia planters looking down their noses on their neighbors to the south. The rivalry was initiated due to the controversy surrounding the Yazoo land sales.[6] John Clark, the son of Revolutionary War general Elijah Clark, was the recognized leader of the North Carolina faction and participated in the Yazoo sales, whereas James Jackson of the Virginia settlement led the opposition to the sales. Jackson, who had been a member of the US Senate since 1793, resigned his seat, returned to Georgia, and won a seat in the state legislature so that he could personally organize an anti-Yazoo campaign.[7]

Jackson was successful in securing the repeal of the Yazoo law and organized the first political party in Georgia. The so-called Jackson party was composed primarily of the group of Virginia planters and professionals that had settled in the Broad River region, including Charles Tait, William H. Crawford, and William W. Bibb. The Clark faction, made up mostly of the North Carolinians settling in Wilkes County, claimed to speak for the small farmers and frontiersmen of the area. Historian Charles H. Moffat believes that the real difference between the factions was based on personalities rather than principle. Moffat quoted another as to the differences between the factions: "We know not what they differ about—but they do violently differ." The clash of personalities was such that in 1802, the Clark party enlisted a solicitor general of Oglethorpe County named Peter Lawrence Van Allen to harass and reticule Judge Tait. He did so by filing a petty lawsuit against Tait and, in a speech to the jury, assailed him with merciless satire. Tait finally had had enough and challenged Van Allen to a duel. At first Van Allen refused to accept the challenge, asserting that Tait was not worthy of a gentleman's acceptance, fully expecting that Crawford, as Tait's second, would take up the challenge himself. However, Crawford did not want to become involved in a fight not of his making. He changed his mind, however, when he chanced upon Van Allen in the lobby of a hotel in Washington, Georgia, whereupon Van Allen insulted Crawford in public and challenged him to a fight. Crawford was now compelled to accept so as not to be branded a coward. A duel followed, leaving Van Allen dead and Crawford unharmed.[8]

The rivalry continued between the two factions with John Clark's resentment of the growing legal reputation of Crawford and Crawford's encroachment upon territory that Clark considered his own. Matters worsened in 1803 when Tait defeated Clark's brother-in-law, John Griffin, for a judgeship of the Western Circuit of the Superior Court, which encompassed all of upper Georgia. Soon after Tait assumed office, John Clark opened the floodgates with a vicious, toxic attack on Judge Tait, accusing him of being "ill-tempered, immoral, corrupt, and dishonest, and generally incompetent." He specifically charged that Tait, while in the Georgia legislature, had passed a law overturning a court decision to benefit a client. Clark also charged that Tait, in his judicial capacity, rendered decisions that were consistently favorable to Crawford's clients, so much so that Clark alleged that parties who tried cases in the Western Circuit found it advantageous to employ Crawford as their attorney.[9]

Clark continued his attack on Judge Tait in 1806, when he learned that Judge Tait had been given a copy of an affidavit alleging that Clark had accepted $20,000 in counterfeit money for the sale of over 1,000 acres of land and then converted these funds to real money through the help of his brother-in-law who was state treasurer. Although Judge Tait decided not to act in response to the affidavit due to the untrustworthy reputation of the deponent, Clark insisted that Tait and Crawford were conspiring against him, and thus petitioned the legislature to impeach Tait on charges of conspiracy. Crawford vigorously came to the defense of Judge Tait, and after the examination of twenty-eight witnesses whose names were provided by Clark, Judge Tait was exonerated by a vote of 57 to 3. Having failed in his attempt to oust Tait, Clark turned his attention to Crawford, challenging him to a duel. Although Clark came through the duel without a scratch, Crawford's wrist was badly crushed.[10]

When Crawford refused to accept a renewal of the duel following recovery of his injured wrist, Clark decided to turn his attention back to Tait to settle accounts. But this time he decided to forgo a duel challenge and, instead, decided to beat him down in public. Thus, in the summer of 1807, Clark happened upon Tait riding on the streets of Milledgeville and publicly horsewhipped him with a cowhide lash, laying on some thirty strokes to Tait's back. According to Clark, "I applied the lash of my whip to his back and shoulders in such a manner as I thought his conduct deserved; and I presume . . . had his back been exhibited, it would have presented thirty or forty marks of my attention. After giving him this dressing, I told him he might go about his business as I now was done with him." Although Clark was indicted, tried, fined $2,000, and ordered to post a bond for good behavior for a period of five years, Governor Jared Irwin, a so-called Clarkeite, came to Clark's rescue by remitting the court sentence.[11]

Wearying of the rough and tumble of local politics as evidenced by the above incidents, as well others not reported here, Tait was eager to jump into national politics. The opportunity presented itself when John Milledge resigned his seat in the US Senate in 1809. Tait promptly threw his hat into the ring to fill the vacant seat. Undoubtedly to Tait's dismay, Maj. Elisha Clark, the brother of John Clark, ran in opposition to Tait. A fiercely fought contest in the Georgia legislature ensued, and Tait won on the third ballot by a majority of one vote. Tait took the oath of office on December 28, 1809, to serve the remainder of Milledge's unexpired term, and, in 1813, was reelected for the full term that would not expire until 1819. In 1812, Tait's Petersburg neighbor and future Alabama governor William Wyatt Bibb, joined him in the Senate, making Petersburg the only town in America to be home to two simultaneously serving US senators.[12]

When Tait took his seat in the US Senate, the United States was heading toward war again with Great Britain. Georgia's delegation to Congress at that time was composed of War Hawks.[13] Tait's friend and then Georgia's senior senator, William H. Crawford, believed that war was inevitable. Tait expressed his views of the potential for war in a letter to Georgia governor David B. Mitchell in February 1812: "If the O[rders] of C[ouncil][14] are not repealed War ought and I hope will be declared." When the United States declared war against Great Britain, Senator Tait was a member of the Senate Naval Affairs Committee and distinguished himself in using this position to bring about the enlargement and reorganization of the Navy. For example, in 1816 he sponsored and secured passage of a bill providing an annual naval appropriation of $1 million for a period of eight years, a vast sum of money for the time.[15]

Senator Tait corresponded regularly with such notables as US Secretary of War John C. Calhoun, Tait's cousin US Senator Henry Clay, US Senator and US Secretary of the Treasury William H. Crawford, US Senator John W. Walker, and Governor William Wyatt Bibb. Some of these letters reflect the angst produced by the war with Great Britain, such as one dated October 12, 1814, from Crawford to Senator Tait in which he wrote, "It is possible that the destruction of the capital will cause the present session of Congress to be held at Philadelphia or Lancaster." He went on to write that "the capture of Washington is thought by the True John Bulls to complete the conquest of the U.S. . . . I fear that there is but little patriotism in the nation." He further stated, "Party animosity in the eastern states has so deeply infected the minds of the leaders of the federal party in Massachusetts, that they would much rather fight the southern people than the enemy." Another letter dated October 25, 1814, from Henry Clay to Tait lamented, "The loss of our Capital filled me with grief, less for the loss of property than the loss of honor."[16]

Next in importance to Senator Tait's concerns regarding the war with Great Britain and his fervent support of the Navy was his interest in the creation of states on the southwestern frontier. In this regard, Senator Tait played a role in the admission of the states of Louisiana, Mississippi, and Alabama. Senator Tait was in favor of creating two states out of the Mississippi Territory, but he had to overcome the fact that in ceding their western lands to the federal government in 1802, Georgia had stipulated that they should be admitted as one state. Tait thus used his influence with his Georgia friends, and on January 4, 1813, he reported to the Senate that the state of Georgia had agreed to the creation of two states. With this finally agreed upon, the need for Congress to focus on problems associated with the War of 1812 outweighed its need take up the statehood issue for the time being.[17]

In 1816, another obstacle presented itself when, as related previously, Senator Bibb and numerous other legislators were forced to resign or were voted out of office after passing an act that effectively doubled the pay of all congressmen. Tait, who had also voted for the increase, initially planned to join the newly appointed territorial governor Bibb in Alabama to escape the storm of protest. But John W. Walker, Speaker of the House of Representatives in the Alabama territorial legislature, persuaded him to remain so that he could represent Alabama's interests. Walker had written to Tait, "I regard you the Patron of Alabama, and should have felt your absence as a sinister omen."[18] In January 1817, Tait, who was chairman of the committee to which the statehood legislation had been submitted, was finally able to obtain passage of a bill to enable the citizens of the western part of the Mississippi Territory to establish a state government, together with a separate bill providing for the organization of the eastern section as the Alabama Territory.[19]

Pushing for statehood for Alabama was the next step for Senator Tait. Many of Tait's friends and political associates from Georgia had rushed to Alabama with the opening of the Indian lands after the Creek War of 1813–1814. Since Tait was expected to join this group, he was also expected to assist them in securing statehood. His friend John Walker wrote to him: "But although you have done much for her [Alabama], your work is still incomplete. You still have the power and the means of heaping more favors on her; and I think you ought to crown your other labors."[20]

The completion of Senator Tait's work was in sight when, on December 11, 1818, he submitted a petition for Alabama's statehood to the US Senate. Working closely with the influential secretary of the treasury, William H. Crawford, Tait was soon made chairman of a committee to prepare an enabling act. In rapid fashion the committee formulated an act authorizing the framing of a state constitution for Alabama, which was signed by President James Monroe on March 2, 1819, just two days prior to the expiration of Tait's term in the Senate. Alabama's territorial leaders were generally pleased with the enabling act that Senator Tait was successful in getting through Congress. One favorable provision reserved two entire townships for the purchase of "a seminary of learning," or a state university. Another favorable provision reserved the sixteenth section of each township for the use of public schools. Additionally, the new state would be granted all the salt springs within its borders; and five percent of the net proceeds of the sale of lands by the United States within the new state were reserved for the construction of public roads and canals, as well as for the improvement of the navigation of rivers. The constitutional convention having completed its work, President Monroe signed a resolution of admission on December 14, 1819, making Alabama the nation's twenty-second state.[21]

Before leaving the Senate, Senator Tait was involved in the early stages of the debates concerning the admission of Missouri to the Union. In this regard, he was made chairman of the committee to which the Missouri question was referred in February 1819. Upon his recommendation, the Senate struck out the Tallmadge amendment that would have prohibited slavery in Missouri. He expressed his concern to Representative Thomas Cobb of Georgia that it was impossible not to connect the Missouri issue with "the momentous one of emancipation of slaves" and was prescient as to what would happen: "If Congress pursue[d] this question with a view to affect our right to own slaves . . . the slaveholding states must . . . form a separate Confederacy."[22]

Tait was living in Alabama by the time of its admittance into the Union in December 1814. As early as 1817, his son, James A. Tait, who had served in the Creek War in Alabama, returned to the area to scout out desirable lands

Figure 7.2. President James Monroe. Courtesy of the Library of Congress.

to which the entire Tait family might move. The elder Tait had dispatched his son on this trip in anticipation of his retiring from the Senate. His instructions as to what to look for included "on the summit of which a mansion house can be built in due time," a nearby stream for a mill and machinery, a spring, an extensive range for livestock, and other desirable land nearby, "where will settle a number of good neighbors." By the end of the year, James Tait had squatted on a tract of public land approximately 30 miles from Claiborne on the Alabama River in Monroe and Wilcox Counties. James built a cabin on the land and put in a crop in anticipation of the arrival of the rest of the Tait family. The elder Tait left Washington and proceeded directly to his new home in Alabama without going back to Georgia, his wife having died in 1818. Upon James's purchase of the land near Claiborne, the elder Tait arranged for the sale of his plantation back in Georgia.[23]

Resigning his Senate seat because of the lingering resentment of the Georgia electorate over his unpopular vote to increase congressional pay, Tait undoubtedly expected to be rewarded for his efforts in securing Alabama's statehood by being appointed as a senator from the new state. He quickly became involved in the political machinations of the Crawford machine that had come from Georgia to Alabama, including his friends William Wyatt Bibb and John W. Walker. Opposed to Crawford's Georgia faction was a group of settlers from Tennessee and North Carolina, who eventually lent their support to Andrew Jackson, but at this time they were more anti-Georgia than pro-Jackson. Many in the new state felt that Crawford and Tait considered Alabama as their political cash cow. Tait, however, met unexpected opposition from the anti-Georgia group in south Alabama. William Wyatt Bibb was elected governor under the new constitution and the Georgia faction endorsed Walker and Tait as candidates for the two Senate seats allotted by the US Constitution. Although Walker, a resident of Huntsville in north Alabama, faced little opposition, in south Alabama the anti-Georgia group supported William Rufus King, a former congressman from North Carolina, in opposition to Tait. Crawford, in an effort to get Tait selected, enticed King with an offer to be appointed as receiver of the General Land Office. King declined, causing some to view Crawford as an outside meddler. With a growing resentment against the Georgia faction, Tait withdrew his candidacy, stating, "I came to bring peace not a sword."[24]

While Tait would not serve in the US Senate from Alabama, he was determined to serve in some capacity because he saw public office as a sign of prestige, which he yearned for more than for material wealth. Fortunately for Tait, in April 1820, the federal judicial district of Alabama was created and, within a month, upon the recommendations of Crawford and Walker, President Monroe nominated Tait for the position. On May 13, 1820, the Senate unanimously confirmed Tait's nomination. After a delay completing the organization of the court, Tait took the oath of office in February 1821 in St. Stephens, the former territorial capital, and served as Alabama's only federal judge for the next five years. During his time of service on the bench, he established a reputation for a robust and courageous administration of justice despite the continuous efforts of political rivals and disgruntled lawyers to have him impeached and removed from office. For example, in 1822, a lawyer who had had been denied a license to practice in Tait's federal court, unsuccessfully petitioned the Alabama House of Representatives to bring impeachment charges against Judge Tait. The petitioner's notoriety in this regard was such that "some members of the Judiciary Committee . . . believed him to be insane." Understandably, the Committee on the Judiciary found "no regular or illegal proceedings" and instead praised Tait for refusing to relax the rules of the court in the face of threats of prosecution.[25]

Although he generally operated from his court offices in Mobile, Judge Tait occasionally held sessions of court in Huntsville and Cahaba, then the state capital. According to a biographer of Tait, he purportedly enjoyed most presiding in Cahaba where he relished the company of many of his former neighbors from Georgia, who had become state officials, as well as with leading members of the state bar and wealthy planters from the surrounding plantations. His domestic status when he was on the bench had improved in 1822 when he married Sarah Griffin, his first wife having died in 1818.

Ironically, Sarah Griffin was the widow of the man who had been his competitor for the Georgia judgeship in 1803 and sister-in-law of the man who had horsewhipped him in Milledgeville, Georgia, in 1807.[26]

Much of Judge Tait's cases, especially those brought in Mobile, involved such offenses as smuggling, the illicit slave trade, and piracy. Perhaps the most significant case heard by Judge Tait during his tenure on the federal bench involved three ships that were smuggling slaves into the United States in direct violation of federal law. In his decision, Tait declared all three vessels and their cargoes as forfeited to the United States, overturning an earlier decision by Alabama's territorial court, which had allowed the slaves to be turned over to the people to whom they were being shipped. The case was appealed to the US Supreme Court, which upheld Tait's main conclusions, thus setting a precedent for the further prosecution of slave smugglers.[27]

In addition to desiring to put an end to the international slave trade, Judge Tait was very interested in suppressing piracy on the high seas. He defined a pirate as "one who roves the sea in an armed vessel without commission or passport from any prince or sovereign state, . . . for the purpose of seizing by force and appropriating for himself, without discrimination, every vessel he may meet." He summed up acts of piracy occurring in 1822 in a charge to the grand jury as "an extraordinary spirit of rapine and plunder in the maritime class." He further noted that piracy was usually attended by "murder in its most frightful forms."[28]

In 1826, Tait resigned his federal judgeship to devote more time to running his plantation, to travel, and to pursue scientific interests. He and his wife set out on an extended tour of the northern states that took them up the Mississippi and Ohio Rivers to Pittsburgh, then via the Erie Canal and the Hudson River to New York City and New England. Traveling part-time by steamboat and part time by stage, they took their time visiting all the large cities and points of interest in their path. They spent nearly two weeks in New Haven, Connecticut, and attended commencement exercises at Yale University there. Also during their stay, Tait met Benjamin Silliman, the noted geologist and one of the first professors of Yale's science department, where he held the chair of Natural Science. Tait and Silliman thereafter exchanged correspondence. The Taits later moved on to Philadelphia, where they stayed for seven months. During this long stay, Tait attended the Academy of Natural Sciences of Philadelphia, where he made acquaintances with eminent scientists such as Isaac Lea, conchologist, and paleontologist; Charles A. Poulson, naturalist; and Samuel G. Morton, anthropologist. While at the academy he also read extensively from books on conchology and botany and examined specimens. On April 20, 1827, Tait was elected to membership in the American Philosophical Society. Tait was proud to have his name enrolled in such a prestigious society along with Benjamin Franklin, Thomas Jefferson, and David Rittenhouse.[29]

Finally pulling themselves away from Philadelphia, the Taits moved on to Virginia, where they visited numerous friends and relatives, including former President James Madison and Tait's former colleague in the Senate, James Barbour, who was now secretary of war. In the fall of 1827, the Taits finally returned to their home in Claiborne, where Charles Tait was to spend the rest of his life devoted to geological and agricultural interests. He began to study the vast deposits of fossils on his property along the bluffs of the Alabama River.[30] Referred to as the "Claiborne beds," these deposits contained the largest number of fossil Eocene shells known at the time, and Tait's investigation of them earned him election as a corresponding member of the Academy of Natural Sciences of Philadelphia in July 1832.

Tait spent the rest of his time managing his property, which included more than 4,000 acres and 115 slaves. Tait devoted most of these lands and resources to the production of cotton. He had learned from his experience in Georgia to pay close attention to the quality of his crop and its preparation for market. Thus, he usually got top dollar for his cotton, which was shipped to Mobile on steamboats by way of the Alabama River. In accordance with the business custom of his day, Tait sold his cotton and bought his supplies through a factor. For most of the time of his production of cotton, his accounts were handled by Jeremiah Austill, a prominent Mobile commission merchant, a cotton agent, and a participant in the legendary Canoe Fight during the Creek War of 1813–1814. In the early years, although his profits were rather meager, from 1824 until his death in 1835, his cotton production became more profitable. His largest crop occurred in 1831, when he produced 350 bales, which Austill sold for him for approximately nine cents a pound, or for a total of about $11,000 (over $300,000 in today's dollars). In 1834, Tait shipped 209 bales to Austill, which he sold for more than eighteen cents per pound, or a total of about $15,000 (over $400,000 in today's dollars).[31]

Purportedly, in Tait's later years he rather enjoyed staying home and attending enjoyable events, such as extravagant balls, parties, horse racing, and other social events with his wealthy planter neighbors. He was content to be out of politics and not holding public office, so much so that he even turned down an appointment in 1828 by President John Quincy Adams to serve as the US ambassador to Great Britain.[32]

The last few years of Tait's life were spent on his son's estate, Dry Fork, near Camden in Wilcox County, where he died on October 7, 1835, at the age of sixty-eight. He is buried in Dry Fork Cemetery in Wilcox County. Tait wrote the inscription on his tomb: "The deceased in the course of his pilgrimage through life, enjoyed much of public favor and patronage, for which

Figure 7.3. Dry Fork Plantation. Courtesy of the author.

he was grateful. He was for six years a Judge of the Supreme Court of the state of Georgia. The first Judge of the United States Court in the state of Alabama, and from the years 1809 to 1819, a Senator of the United States from the state of Georgia. May his posterity mark and emulate his example and greatly surpass him in good fortune."[33]

Legal historian Paul Pruitt Jr. summarized the worldview of Charles Tait, the Patron of Alabama, as follows: "During perhaps the most dynamic period in America's history, Charles Tait witnessed the early development of the United States from its revolutionary infancy to a nation that—by 1820—was able to establish its economic, political, diplomatic, and military independence from Europe. During the first two decades of the nineteenth century, the United States was attempting to legitimize itself both at home and abroad and Charles Tait played an active legislative and judicial role in the country's early development." During this period, American settlement was marching inevitably to the Pacific coast, while the so-called Monroe Doctrine was warning foreigners not to meddle in the affairs not only of North America, but the entire Western Hemisphere. Pruitt further described the lay of the land in which Tait functioned as follows: "During this vigorous period land was not only acquired but developed, and areas of the Old Southwest that had been wilderness territory a few years earlier were swiftly transformed from frontier to territory to cotton states."[34]

8

CLEMENT COMER CLAY

Delegate to the Constitutional Constitution of 1819, Key Drafter
of the Alabama Constitution, First Chief Justice of the Alabama
Supreme Court, US Senator, and the Seventh Alabama Governor

Figure 8.1. Clement C. Clay, Alabama's eighth governor and a US senator. Courtesy of the Alabama
Department of Archives and History.

Clement Comer Clay, although not from the Broad River region of
Georgia, initially allied himself with, and became a leading member of,
its powerful political machine when he arrived in Alabama from Tennessee in
1811. Eventually, he held himself out to the electorate as a Jacksonian Democrat
and was successful in securing office as a state legislator, a US congressman,
Alabama's eighth governor, and a US senator. As one of Alabama's founders,
Clay's resume was indeed impressive. In addition to the political offices to
which he was elected, he served in the Creek War of 1813–1814, was a delegate
to the Constitutional Convention of 1819, and was the state's first chief justice
of its supreme court.[1]

Born on December 17, 1789, in Halifax County, Virginia, Clement Comer Clay was the son of William Clay, a Revolutionary soldier, and his wife, Rebecca Comer. About 1795, the Clay family moved westward and settled in Grainger County, located in northeast Tennessee, where Clement and his seven brothers and sisters grew up. Clement's education began under his great uncle, Hopkins Muse, and continued at Blount College in Knoxville (now the University of Tennessee). After graduating in 1807, Clay read law under Hugh Lawson White of Knoxville, a trusted ally of Andrew Jackson. In December 1809, at the age of twenty, Clay was licensed to practice law. Then in November 1811, he moved to the new town of Huntsville in the Mississippi Territory and hung out his shingle to practice law.[2]

Ruth Ketring Nuermberger, biographer of the Clay family, described Clay's arrival in Huntsville as follows: "On a November day in 1811, young Clement Comer Clay rode into the rising frontier town of Huntsville. His visible resources were two horses, one slave, a few law books in his saddlebags, and a small amount of money." Nuermberger thought, "He was the typical early nineteenth-century young man 'on the make,' come to seek fame and fortune in the West." The Tennessee Valley, which attracted those seeking their fortune, was blessed with a mild climate and dark rich soil very conducive to the cultivation of cotton. Female journalist Anne Royall described the land in and around Huntsville as "rich and beautiful as you can imagine." As for Huntsville, Royall said, "It stands on elevated ground, and enjoys a beautiful prospect." She described the buildings and homes, most of which were built of brick, indicating that "the workmanship is the best I have seen in all of the states; and several of the houses are three stories high, and very large."[3]

Upon arriving in Huntsville, Clay soon aligned himself with the powerful Broad River faction, composed of wealthy planters and businessmen, who dominated Huntsville's economy. Huntsville Bank president LeRoy Pope and Pope's son-in-law, John W. Walker, led this group. Because the Georgia faction accepted Clay, he became a stockholder in, and director of, the Huntsville Bank. Just a couple of years after settling in Huntsville, and at the beginning of the Creek War in 1813, Clay volunteered as a private in a Madison County Battalion. He was soon promoted to Adjutant of the Regiment and assigned to the frontier, south of the Tennessee River, to assist in repelling the Indian attacks. After the war, in 1815, twenty-five-year-old Clement Comer Clay married sixteen-year-old Susanna Claiborne Withers. Susanna was born on July 23, 1798, in Dinwiddie County, Virginia, and was the daughter of John Withers and Mary Herbert Jones Withers. On December 13, 1816, their first child, Clement Claiborne Clay, was born. Two other sons came later—John Withers Clay and Hugh Lawson Clay.[4]

Commencing on January 9, 1818, Clay entered Alabama politics, when he was elected to the first legislature of the Alabama Territory. Serving with him in representing Madison County were Hugh McVay, John Williams Walker, and Gabriel Moore. Since the seven counties in the new territory had a total representation of twelve men, Madison County with four representatives held a dominant place. The twelve legislators, meeting in the frontier town of St. Stephens at its Douglas Hotel, created new counties and altered boundaries of those already established, incorporated an academy, formed two judicial districts, appointed an attorney general (district attorney) for each county, and made Clement Comer Clay one of five commissioners to select the best site for the territorial capital. The most important piece of legislation during that session was that of February 13, 1818, repealing all laws against usury, so that any interest rate adopted by written agreement was recoverable at law. This act, passed during a boom period, later had painful repercussions when the crash of 1819 brought Alabama back to earth and forced the act's repeal on November 22, 1819, together with relief measures. Those supporting the usury law, including Clay, would feel these repercussions for quite a while. As previously noted, Clay was also made one the commissioners on the selection of a site for the capital, and, unlike the rest of the commissioners, he supported Governor Bibb's choice of a site at the confluence of the Alabama and Cahaba Rivers. In both sessions of the territorial legislature, Clement Clay was exceedingly active. "He served on committees, he introduced bills, he was an active debater, and he kept business moving." In order to hasten home to tend to his cotton crop and law practice, he used his "utmost . . . exertions to bring the Session to a most speedy close," which he accomplished on November 21, 1818.[5]

In 1819, Clay was elected as a delegate from Madison County to the constitutional convention at Huntsville and was appointed chairman of the Committee of Fifteen to draft Alabama's first constitution, to be adopted by the convention as a whole. Within six days, Clay submitted the draft to the convention. It was debated for two weeks on the floor, with Clay taking an active and leading part in the debates as they progressed forward. Although the resulting constitution was considered liberal for its day, there were certainly conservative provisions. It was patterned partially after the Virginia constitution due to the origin of many of the delegates, nearly half of whom were from Virginia.[6]

When the constitutional convention adjourned on August 2, 1819, speculation quickly began as to who would fill the various state offices. Politicos meeting in Tuscaloosa nominated Clement Comer Clay for governor, but Clay had to decline because he would not reach the required age of thirty until after the election. He also turned down the opportunity to seek a seat in the legislature representing Madison County since the legislative session conflicted with the court terms where he practiced law and flourished with an accrual of business. In December 1819, the legislature elected Clay, without opposition, as one of the five circuit judges of the state. These five circuit justices together constituted the state's first Supreme Court. Although he was the youngest of his fellow judges, Clay was selected chief justice by his colleagues on the court. Clay held the highest judicial post in the state until 1823 when he resigned to resume private practice with James White McClung, who had taken over Clay's practice when he became chief justice. He probably resigned also because of the wear and tear of travel within the circuit, long stays away from his family, tiresome hours on the bench, and an annual salary of only $1,500.[7]

Soon after Clay resigned from the court, he got into a dispute that led to a duel with Dr. Waddy Tate of Limestone County. Both were reportedly injured, with some accounts indicating that Dr. Tate was shot in the leg. There is no record of what specifically was the root of the difficulty between the two. Dr. Tate was a prominent resident of Limestone County who, in 1818, partnered with Dr. Henry Chambers, William Adair, Thomas Bibb, and Thomas White to found a land company and to establish the town of Triana, just across the Limestone County line in Madison County. In 1825, Dr. Tate served in the Alabama legislature. After this duel, Clay took a temporary absence from public service and concentrated on the private practice of law. In addition to practicing law, Clement Clay was one of the original trustees of, as well as a stockholder in, the Planters' and Merchants' Bank of Huntsville, which was originally chartered on December 11, 1816, by the Mississippi Territorial Legislature. On June 23, 1820, the bank was forced to suspend specie payment. When efforts at resuming specie payments failed, Governor Israel Pickens forfeited the bank's charter. Thus, Clay saw the need to sell his stock at a loss and to resign from the board of directors so as not to be seen as a backer of the bank's policies. It was good for him that he did, as it had more enemies than friends as reflected in the Huntsville *Democrat's* "obituary": "The Huntsville bank, departed this life on the 5th instant, covered with Glory and dishonor—She died as she had lived, beloved by her friends, and detested by all the rest of the world. . . . She was venerated by the royal family as the very essence of all that was good or great." The editor then went on to exacerbate the war going on between the rich and the poor by labeling capitalists and their associates as belonging to the "Royal Party." He further stated that the bank "had been in the hands of a pack of shavers and extortioners, who have grown fat by grinding the face of the poor."[8]

In 1825, Clay decided to reenter politics and ran for a congressional seat against Gabriel Moore. Despite his attempts to distance himself from the Huntsville bank and the usury law, Clay was defeated. Moore's appeal to the so-called common man cost Clay the election. In his stump speeches, Moore emphasized that "he was not of the *Royal party*" and added that he was "supported principally by the poor, no friends save one or two of the rich have I." When Israel Pickens resigned from the US Senate in 1826, Clay threw his hat in the ring and vied against five candidates to fill the vacancy. Soon there were only two candidates—Clay and John McKinley, a future associate justice of the US Supreme Court. Clay lost by three votes in the legislature. McKinley's success had the blessing of Andrew Jackson, who believed that he was a better Jacksonian than Clay. In 1828, however, Clay successfully ran for a seat in the lower house of the Alabama legislature representing Madison County and was unanimously selected as Speaker of the House.[9]

From his position as Speaker, Clay promoted a series of anti-small-farm positions that were potentially a political time bomb. Alabama's small farmers, like other Jacksonian Democrats, were robustly anti-aristocrat, suspicious of the elite power structure of corporations, and on the lookout against any efforts to dilute their vote. Historian J. Mills Thornton III believes that "Clay made several political mistakes, which included pricing the Muscle Shoals Canal land grant out of the reach of poor squatters, requiring slave patrol duty from nonslaveholders, and opposing amending the state constitution. In other actions, he favored repealing the law that prohibited participants in duels from holding public office, opposed efforts to secure married women their separate estates, and voted to extend the state's jurisdiction over the Creek Indian territory."[10]

Apparently not contented with his position in the Alabama legislature, Clay ran for a seat in the US House of Representatives again in 1829, defeating Whig leader Captain Nicholas Davis of Limestone County in a closely fought race. The closeness of the election was due to Clay's previous opposition to low prices for the Muscle Shoals Canal land grant. Clay's opponent carried the counties of the western Tennessee Valley, due to his support of reduced prices and squatters' rights. Clay, however, defeated Davis by sweeping populous Madison County, where there was strong support for obtaining as much money from land grants to finance the construction of the proposed canal at the shoals. Thereafter, Clay eagerly supported the cause of squatters and public land debtors, at last separating himself from perceived aristocratic beliefs as evidenced by his reelection without opposition to the Twenty-second and Twenty-third Congresses from 1825 to 1831.[11]

During his last term in the US House, Clay became chairman of the Committee on Public Lands and pleased the Jacksonian farmers by becoming a strong advocate of the graduation and reduction of land prices and permanent preemptive rights for squatters. He apparently had made quite an impression for his talent and even former president John Quincy Adams said, "Clay is a man of talent and of much activity and perseverance, a fluent speaker, of very little power, but making up the deficiency of substance by the ardor of his zeal. So it is with almost all the Jackson leaders in the House." Regarding another important issue, Clay opposed the rechartering of the US Bank and supported Jackson's removal of its deposits to local banks. Clay concluded that state banks are fully capable of providing "a medium of exchange between remote parts of the country. . . . We are not dependent on a Bank of the United States; and God forbid we ever should find ourselves in a situation so humiliating."[12]

The Jackson administration greatly appreciated Clay's support of their removal of deposits from the Bank of the United States to state banks. Clay was complimented by a toast at a dinner in Columbia, Tennessee, honoring John Knox Polk as follows: "Hon. C. C. Clay, of Alabama—the firm, independent and unflinching supporter of the administration. When the hour of danger came, he did not court his political enemies, or wait in silence, which to see what the strong side was. With such men, the republic is safe." The Huntsville *Democrat* asserted that this toast was evidence that Clay "owes his political elevation not to his suavity of manners, or the personal predilection of friends but to his own intrinsic merit." The *Democrat* further stressed that Clay's inflexible honesty enabled him to "withstand the seductions, but also the menaces of the bank."[13]

In 1835, Clay won the Democratic nomination for governor of Alabama, and then defeated the Whig candidate, General Enoch Parsons, a prominent lawyer residing in Claiborne, by a margin of nearly two to one. This was the largest margin given any candidate for the office of governor up until that time. In his first message to the legislature, Clay focused on the danger presented by abolitionism and urged that northerners who had mailed abolitionist pamphlets to the South be subjected to criminal charges. He also pressed for strengthening laws against slave insurrections. On the positive side, he stressed education and internal improvements, but the Creek War of 1836 and the Panic of 1837 dominated events during his term. The Creek uprising was a result of desperate economic conditions among the Creeks and their impending removal from Alabama. This drove some 3,000 Creeks, under the leadership of Nea-mathla, into a rebellion against white communities in the eastern part of the state. By letter dated May 19, 1836, Major General Thomas A. Jessup informed Governor Clay that he would be in command of the soldiers enforcing the Creek Indian removal in Alabama, adding that the president "has authorized me to call on you for such volunteers of militia as I may consider necessary, in aid of the regular troops, to effect that object." Several units of the Alabama militia were called up by Governor Clay, of which he took personal command. In June 1836, Secretary of War Lewis Cass sent in Federal forces under General Jessup to assist the state militia.

Seven hundred friendly Creeks joined these combined forces. The war ended after the Creek's last stand at Hobdy's Bridge on the Pea River in Barbour County. After the battle, federal forces rounded up thousands of Creeks to send them on their way on the "Trail of Tears" to Oklahoma.[14]

The other major event occurring during Clay's term as governor was the Panic of 1837, which occurred when the land speculation bubble burst. It was caused in part by President Jackson's veto of the extension of the Bank of the United States, which deprived the country of a stable currency. Another factor was Jackson's executive order known as the Specie Circular, which required that the purchase of public lands be paid for in gold and silver. This had the effect of eventually diminishing the value of much of the nation's currency. As Alabama's banks suspended their specie payments, commerce and trade seriously declined and the price of land, cotton, and slaves were sent spiraling downward. The state's court dockets were filled with civil suits to recover debts owed creditors, and sheriffs were crying off property on the steps of courthouses. In response to this crisis, Governor Clay called a special session of the legislature and recommended radical legislation to ease the pain of Alabama's citizens burdened with debts. The legislature responded by enacting the Relief Act of 1837. In addition to sanctioning the suspension of specie payments by the banks, the Act authorized the state bank and its branches to immediately suspend the collection of debts and to provide their debtors with another three years to pay off their loans. It also required the selling of five million dollars of bonds by the branch banks so that even more money could be lent to the state's already strapped borrowers. These actions were popular with most of the electorate, but it left the state bank with an unmanageable indebtedness that would continue to plague the state and eventually lead to the bank's demise.[15]

Governor Clay, popular with state legislators who passed the Relief Act of 1837, was unanimously elected by them to the US Senate to replace John McKinley, who had been appointed by President Martin Van Buren to the US Supreme Court. With his election to the Senate, Clay resigned as Alabama's governor and took his Senate seat in September 1837. During his service in the Senate, Clay once again supported squatters' rights and the reduction of public land prices, called for the removal of the Cherokees to Oklahoma, and pushed for the adoption of President Van Buren's independent subtreasury scheme.[16] According to historian J. Mills Thornton III, Clay was forced to resign from the Senate in 1841 due to financial reasons related to the deepening depression. At least one other source indicates that the resignation was due to a family illness. However, by 1840 Clay was selling off slaves to meet his debts. During this period, Clay was also losing his popularity. In 1842, for example, Governor Benjamin Fitzpatrick appointed Clay to

Figure 8.2. Depiction of the Union's occupation of Huntsville.
Clay was arrested by Union soldiers in Huntsville in 1864.
Courtesy Huntsville-Madison County Public Library.

prepare a digest of the state's laws, but a growing number of political enemies in the legislature opposed its formal adoption.[17] Then in the summer of 1843, Governor Fitzpatrick appointed Clay to fill a vacancy on the state supreme court, but the following December, Whig and Calhounite Democrats joined forces to defeat Clay's election to a full term. Clay was slighted again when Governor Joshua L. Martin appointed Clay to the board that was supervising the liquidation of the Bank of Alabama in 1846, but in 1848 the legislature abolished the board, at least in part to rob Clay of the office.[18]

After these setbacks, Clay retired from public life and resumed the practice of law in Huntsville, in partnership with his sons—Clement Claiborne, Hugh Lawson, and John Withers. During the 1850s, Clay's economic condition began to improve such that by 1860 he owned eighty-four slaves, land worth $60,000, and personal property valued at $85,000 (in today's dollars, the land and personal property would have a value of approximately $3.8 million). Even though Clay had retired from public life for the most part, he continued his strong support of slavery and was still very vocal and public in his support of secession. During his congressional days, Clay had proposed very strong measures in favor of slavery, including one that would criminally prosecute northerners who mailed abolitionist pamphlets to the South. Because of his passionate stances on these issues, along with his son Clement Claiborne Clay's position in the Confederate government, the elder Clay was a target of Federal forces during the Civil War and was taken prisoner when federal troops occupied Huntsville in late 1864. His stay in prison wreaked havoc on his health to the point that he was an invalid by the summer of 1865 and died on September 6, 1866. His wife, Susanna, preceded him in death by a few months.[19]

Surviving Clay were his three sons—Clement Claiborne (December 13, 1816–January 3, 1882), John Withers (January 11, 1829–March 29, 1896), and Hugh Lawson (January 24, 1893–December 28, 1890). Clement Claiborne Clay graduated from the University of Alabama in 1837, served as private secretary to his father during his term as governor, later studied law at the University of Virginia, and was admitted to the Alabama bar in 1840. He also served three terms in the Alabama legislature, judge of the county court of Madison County, and in the US Senate for nine years until he resigned in January 1861 when Alabama seceded from the Union. Clay was then elected to the Confederacy's Senate. He later became head of the Confederate secret agents and, because they had previously paid John Wilkes Booth for services, there were suspicions that Clay was involved in the assassination plot of President Abraham Lincoln. Upon turning himself in to federal authorities in Macon, Georgia, Clay was arrested and ultimately imprisoned along with Jefferson Davis in Fortress Monroe in Hampton, Virginia, in 1865. He was held for twelve months without being brought to trial. He was finally released in May 1866 due to the efforts of his wife in meeting with President Andrew Johnson and the secretary of war. Upon his release, Clay practiced law until his death in 1882. He was buried in the Maple Hill Cemetery in Huntsville.[20]

John Withers Clay, like his brother, graduated from the University of Alabama and the University of Virginia. He practiced law with his father for two years and then took over as editor of the Huntsville *Democrat*, in which capacity he served for forty years. He later edited *Clay's Digest*, written by his father. Hugh Lawson Clay attended the University of Virginia in 1839–40 and was a lawyer in Huntsville. He also served as captain in the Mexican War and as adjutant general on the staff of General E. Kirby Smith of the Confederate States of America.[21]

Thornton submits that Clay "never genuinely accepted the pro-small farmer, anti-corporation heart of Jacksonian ideology" and "that he espoused Jacksonian ideals almost entirely to advance his political career."[22] Nonetheless, Clement Comer Clay's role in the state's formative period was momentous.

9

HENRY HITCHCOCK

Secretary of the Alabama Territory, Delegate to the Constitutional Convention of 1819, Alabama's First Attorney General, and Chief Justice of the Alabama Supreme Court

Figure 9.1. Henry Hitchcock, Secretary of the Alabama Territory and the State of Alabama's first attorney general. Courtesy of the Alabama Department of Archives and History.

Equally versatile as Clement Comer Clay was Henry Hitchcock, who migrated from Vermont to the Alabama Territory in 1817. Hitchcock, grandson of the Revolutionary War hero and Vermont founding father Ethan Allen, served as the first secretary of the Alabama Territory, was a delegate to the Alabama Constitutional Convention of 1819, won election as the state's first attorney general, wrote the first book published in Alabama, was appointed as a United States district attorney, and served on the Alabama supreme court, both as an associate justice and as chief justice. Hitchcock also found time to be a successful practicing attorney and businessman. Prior to the Panic of 1837, he was believed to be one of the wealthiest men in Alabama, with assets thought to be worth two million dollars.[1]

Henry Hitchcock was born in Burlington, Vermont, on September 11, 1792, to Samuel Hitchcock—a prominent attorney, district judge, attorney general, delegate to the Vermont Constitutional Convention of 1792, and patron of the University of Vermont—and Lucy Caroline Allen, daughter of Ethan Allen, leader of the Green Mountain Boys and hero of Fort Ticonderoga. Henry was the second of eight children, two of whom died in infancy. Henry had two brothers—Ethan Allen and Samuel. Ethan Allen Hancock became a career United States Army officer, and during the Civil War he served as a major general. His other brother, Samuel Hitchcock, attended the US Military Academy at West Point in 1822, and served about five years before resigning at the behest of his mother. After resigning from the army, Samuel became a student and spent several years in Europe. He died at sea at the age of forty-four while returning home to the United States. All three of his sisters—Lorraine, Mary Ann, and Caroline—died at relatively young ages as well. Lorraine, the eldest, died a few years after marrying a Major Peters of the US Army, leaving no children. Caroline died in early adulthood, having not married. Mary Ann married a Dr. Parkin, with whom she had a son. She died after a few years of residence in Alabama.[2]

Little is known of Henry Hitchcock's childhood in Vermont. His first recorded notable achievement was his brief attendance at Middlebury College before graduating with honors from the University of Vermont in 1811. Unfortunately, Henry's father died two years later, leaving Henry responsible for the support of his mother and younger brothers and sisters. To fulfill his responsibility, he ran a small farm while reading law in the office of local attorney Charles Adams and received admission to the bar of Vermont in 1815. After being licensed to practice law, Hitchcock engaged in "several important suits and would undoubtedly have soon been in a large and lucrative practice," but he was bitten by the bug of adventure and "sought a new and wider field in the South or West." Like his grandfather, he was "just the man for the pioneer life—resolute, sanguine, and thankful." Through the "professional aid of generous friends," he "left his family and native town on the 10th day of October, 1816," and set out for the Old Southwest.[3]

Hitchcock's journey to Mobile from Vermont was arduous and eventful. His first stop after leaving Burlington was New York City, which he found very attractive but, because of his limited means, he determined that he could not "indulge in any reflections calculated to weaken my faith in the advantages of the country where I am to establish myself." Having reluctantly left New York, Hitchcock moved on to Philadelphia, where he decided to attend

Figure 9.2. Statue of the legendary Ethan Allen
in Montpelier, Vermont. Hitchcock was Allen's
grandson. Courtesy of the Library of Congress.

sessions of the local court and reported to his lifelong friend, John N. Pomeroy, that these renowned attorneys were not as impressive as he had anticipated, and thus "there is not such a vast difference between what the world
calls great and little men." Hitchcock next set out down the Delaware River
to Newcastle, Delaware, and from there crossed over to Chesapeake Bay and
Baltimore. Then Hitchcock headed to Pittsburgh, where he booked passage
on a flatboat to travel down the Ohio and Mississippi Rivers. To help pay his
passage, Hitchcock often took to the oars to help row the flatboat. This was
work, according his friend Pomeroy, that "he as a Yankee was bound to know
how to handle." Hitchcock disembarked at Natchez on the Mississippi River,
and from there made his way to Mobile, where he finally arrived on January
22, 1817, basically broke and with very little luggage.[4]

At the age of twenty-five, Hitchcock was alone in what he described as "a
rude place—200 miles from civilization, surrounded by Indians. . . . Isolated
from the world, it was the logical refuge of rogues fleeing from justice." As to
his acceptance in general from the local inhabitants, he noted that "there is
very little affection for *us Yankeys* [sic], and they are ready to condemn us for
the same faults they themselves are guilty of." His location in such an isolated
spot and his status as a newcomer from New England were undoubtedly the
culprits in his having to wait a full two months for the first client, or even a

visitor, to walk through his door. It is apparent, however, that Hitchcock was confident that he would succeed in this new land as he attempted to compare it to New England in correspondence to Pomeroy. In a letter to Pomeroy dated April 12, 1817, Hitchcock stressed that the territory's population was rapidly increasing, most of those arriving had property, and some were considered wealthy. He went on to say that money was plentiful and that cotton was the staple crop, adding an enormous profit to the economy. He also stressed the mildness of the climate as compared to that of New England. Another definite plus for up and coming lawyers, as Hitchcock observed, was that the inhabitants were "extremely litigious." Hitchcock acknowledged that slaves added significantly to the profit of the owner, yet he described the institution of slavery as "odious and iniquitous."[5]

When clients finally started calling at his door, Hitchcock's practice began to strive, and he continually kept the courts busy. Also, within a year of his arrival, profits from his law practice enabled him to repay the funds advanced to him by friends, and to purchase a home in St. Stephens for his family—his mother, two sisters, a brother, and a cousin. Hitchcock had decided to purchase a home in St. Stephens rather than Mobile because, as the seat of the territorial government, St. Stephens presented a greater opportunity for young lawyers. Of St. Stephens, Hitchcock said, "I find more business there. It has more inhabitants of better character, is the seat of government, and has good lands in the vicinity." He further wrote, "There are many respectable, wealthy, and some literary men, a usual society of ladies, and is in many respects a pleasant place." Hitchcock noted that there was no preaching, but that since there were quite a few New Englanders, that situation was soon to be rectified with the arrival of a clergyman from Boston. Finally, Hitchcock noted that St. Stephens had an excellent academy for boys and girls headed by a master from Connecticut.[6]

Settling in at St. Stephens, Hitchcock took in William Crawford[7] as his law partner. Crawford was a receiver of public monies for land sales east of the Pearl River and an incorporator, and later president, of the Tombeckbe Bank at St. Stephens, which was chartered in February 1818. Crawford also served as the first US district attorney for the Alabama Territory, which did not prohibit him from the private practice of law so long as his practice did not interfere with his duties as attorney for the United States. Six months after the creation of the Alabama Territory, upon the recommendation of his law partner, on May 14, 1818, Hitchcock was appointed as the territory's first secretary by territorial governor William Wyatt Bibb. The job of secretary, which required Hitchcock to serve as acting governor in the absence of the governor, paid $1,200 per annum. During one such absence of the governor, Hitchcock found it necessary to call up the territorial militia to patrol Alabama's eastern border with the Creek Nation. While serving as secretary, Hitchcock also served as acting district attorney for a while, as well as district paymaster for the militia for services in the War of 1812. Obviously, with a shortage of public servants on the frontier, it was not surprising that Hitchcock had to double up on the offices he held. Hitchcock was asked to stand election for the US Congress, but respectfully declined because—as he told his friend Pomeroy—his inexperience "would place me in a situation which might render me if not ridiculous at least unpleasant." Also, he indicated that his financial situation was such that it would not allow him to leave his law practice.[8]

During his tenure as Alabama's territorial secretary, Hitchcock was thrust into performing several services that required him to be decisive in the absence of Governor Bibb. As noted, Hitchcock was called up to serve as acting governor in the summer of 1818, during which time Hitchcock called out the militia to guard the territory's eastern border from invasion by Creeks and Seminoles. Since it was his duty to maintain the militia, Hitchcock wrote to Secretary of War John C. Calhoun requesting federal assistance in paying his small contingent of militiamen for their service. As acting governor, in addition to military matters, Hitchcock was called upon to make appointments to fill various offices. His desk was so stacked with patronage requests that there was no shortage of candidates.[9]

Serving the territory in several capacities is evidence that Hitchcock was then one of St. Stephens's leading and most influential citizens. He also was an investor in the Tombeckbe Bank and became one of its directors. The esteem with which he was held in the community is reflected in his being asked to deliver the 1818 Fourth of July address at St. Stephens, an honor much sought after among prominent citizens. Due to his services to the people of the Alabama Territory, Hitchcock later emerged as a desirable candidate for delegate to the state's constitutional convention to be commenced on July 5, 1819, and was elected as a delegate from Washington County. He received ninety-three more votes than the other delegate from that county, Israel Pickens. In securing his election as a delegate to the constitutional convention, Hitchcock told Pomeroy that he made only one speech on the stump and the subject of that speech "was to convince the people that I am not *a monarchist!!* . . . Yes, a monarchist—and the reason was, because I came from the *north where all are monarchists.*"[10]

With statehood impending, Hitchcock observed, "We shall soon become a State and the advantage to a young man who now gets a standing will be greater than can be calculated." When Hitchcock, at age twenty-seven, assumed his role as a delegate to the state constitutional convention, he took advantage of gaining a "standing" by attending every session and actively participating in all the deliberations. Hitchcock was the only New

Englander among the delegates, and did not necessarily consider himself a defender of the planter interests as he was not a planter. But he also was not a champion of the yeoman class. Fifteen of the forty-four delegates to the convention, including Hitchcock and Israel Pickens, were appointed to the powerful committee (Committee of Fifteen) to prepare a draft of the constitution. All the members of this committee, except for Hitchcock, definitively represented planter interests. Clement Comer Clay of Huntsville prepared an outline of the proposed constitution, but Hitchcock, along with William Rufus King of Dallas County and John M. Taylor of Wilcox County, did the yeoman's work of reducing Clay's outline to a final form, which was adopted by the convention on August 2, 1819. The constitution that the planters and yeomen of the convention unanimously adopted was considered liberal for its time, primarily because of universal white male suffrage that barred requirements for ownership of property, paying taxes, or serving in the militia. Also, it prohibited imprisonment for debt and harsh treatment of slaves.[11]

Alabama became a state on December 14, 1819, and during the first session of the state's General Assembly, Henry Hitchcock won election as Alabama's first attorney general, receiving forty-five votes to his two opponents' combined total of twenty-four votes. He thereafter moved to the new state capital in Cahaba to take the office to which he had been elected. At that time, Hitchcock was practicing law with William Crawford in six Alabama counties and one Mississippi county, consisting of a circuit of over 800 miles that had to be traversed twice a year over dreadful roads. They had amassed clients in 1,300 cases and, in 1819, they took in 300 new cases. It was a necessity that they center their business in Cahaba as the Circuit Court, the Supreme Court, and the US District Court all met in Cahaba.[12]

After settling in to his new home in Cahaba in August 1819, Hitchcock embarked on a trip to seek out Colonel Andrew Erwin, a reputable planter in Tennessee, against whom he had a large claim. On this trip, Hitchcock reportedly spent two days visiting with Andrew Jackson at the Hermitage near Nashville. When he arrived in Bedford, Tennessee, he had the occasion to meet Colonel Erwin's sixteen-year-old daughter. They both were enamored with each other, but Hitchcock was not ready to take on the responsibility of a spouse. It was not until October 1821 that he and Ann Erwin got married at the mansion belonging to the bride's father. Ann's sister was the wife of Tennessean John Bell, a future candidate for president of the United States, and her brother married the daughter of Henry Clay.[13]

While he was attorney general, Hitchcock was honored with being named to deliver the eulogy in memory of Alabama's first governor, William Wyatt Bibb. In this eulogy, Hitchcock said, "The sovereignty of the people, the accountability and responsibility of officers, and the supremacy of the laws, expressions common and much discussed, had been with him themes of deep and solemn reflection." Hitchcock continued, "He did not, however, consider that the important secret of political science consists so much in inventing new systems of government, as in the application of known and tried principles to the habits, feelings, and dispositions of the community for which they are intended."[14]

Hitchcock also earned the distinction of writing the first book published in Alabama—*The Alabama Justice of the Peace: Containing All the Duties, Powers and Authorities of That Office as Regulated by the Laws Now in Effect in This State*. The book, which was published in Cahaba in 1822, was used by attorneys and justices of the peace as a manual and was "a combination digest of the laws and a comprehensive guide to legal and judicial procedure." Although the cost of publishing the book was more than $5,000, Hitchcock paid for it himself because he believed that previous digests and manuals for the Mississippi Territory had become inadequate for those now practicing within the new state of Alabama. According to author Phillip Beidler, this first book published in Alabama fit the needs of a frontier population: "To put it simply, in its disparate need to implement the role of law and order in arguably some of the most lawless precincts in the English-speaking world, Alabama had a justice system that needed a jump start as far as some guide to basic operations were concerned."[15]

On November 7, 1821, Israel Pickens of Washington County was elected as Alabama's third governor. He and Hitchcock had served together representing Washington County in the constitutional convention in Huntsville. Historian William Brantley Jr. maintains that Pickens and Hitchcock were enemies before and after Pickens became governor, but that the gap between them expanded after Pickens announced his candidacy for that office. According to Brantley, during the campaign Pickens and Hitchcock had a "violent disagreement." In a letter to Alabama Senator John W. Walker, Hitchcock let his feelings be known of how he felt about Pickens: "I trust that the good sense of the State has not been so far destroyed as to give Mr. Pickens the majority, tho' he has not hesitated to resort to any vile and dishonorable means to affect that object." After Pickens's election, Hitchcock wrote to Senator Walker complaining that Pickens had a "capacity for low intrigue" that would "enable him to keep the popular vein on his side." The precise cause of their intense disagreement is not known, but it was such that Hitchcock reported that "you know we do not speak to each other." Despite their animosity toward one another, Governor Pickens overlooked their differences and appointed Hitchcock to complete the index for Toulmin's *Digest of the Laws of Alabama* and to supervise the printing of the digest in New York. Since Judge Toulmin was too ill to complete these responsibilities, Pickens sought to appoint Hitchcock solely because of his competency. Hitchcock, in the spirit of cooperation, accepted the appointment because the state needed his services.[16]

While in New York supervising the printing of Alabama's new digest of laws, Hitchcock took the opportunity to visit many friends and relatives in his hometown of Burlington, Vermont, as well as in Vergennes, Vermont. From there, Hitchcock returned to New York where he finished his work regarding the printing of the digest and designed a family monument to be built near the grave of his father, Samuel Hitchcock. When he arrived back in Alabama, he was anxious to be relieved of his public responsibilities as attorney general, but waited until after Pickens's reelection as governor and the organization of a general assembly to resign his office on December 16, 1823.[17]

After stepping down as attorney general, Hitchcock continued to practice law with William Crawford. According to William Brantley Jr., between the organization of the Supreme Court in May 1819 and the beginning of January 1826, Hitchcock appeared in only five cases in which he represented the state; in the remaining forty-four cases, he appeared on the behalf of clients of his and Crawford's private law firm. This was possible because there was no prohibition against those in the public sector to represent private clients. There was even a significant case involving the Tombeckbe Bank in which Hitchcock represented the state's interest in a suit against the bank for failure to pay taxes, while his law partner, William Crawford, represented the bank and himself. That would be impossible today under much stricter ethical standards. In any event, as we have seen, Hitchcock resigned in December 1823 and limited himself to the private practice of law.[18]

In the spring of 1825, Hitchcock helped to welcome the Marquis de Lafayette to Cahaba. When Lafayette's boat docked at Cahaba, there was a large crowd to greet him. Waiting for Lafayette was a flowered arch and an American flag upon the bluff, at the foot of Second Street where Hitchcock delivered a welcoming address to Lafayette. Afterward, Lafayette paid a personal call on Hitchcock upon learning that he was the grandson of one of his friends from the revolution, General Ethan Allen, who had led his Green Mountain Boys in taking Fort Ticonderoga. As the excitement of Lafayette's visit died down, attention quickly turned to removing the capital from Cahaba to Tuscaloosa, which was approved by the General Assembly on December 13, 1825. Hitchcock believed that this move would cause Cahaba to go into a decline, and thus he decided to take his family to Mobile, where he had first settled when he migrated to Alabama in 1817. By 1825, Mobile was heavily involved in the cotton trade and was developing into a seaport of significant importance. Hitchcock thus wisely dissolved his partnership with Crawford and moved on to Mobile in November 1825.[19]

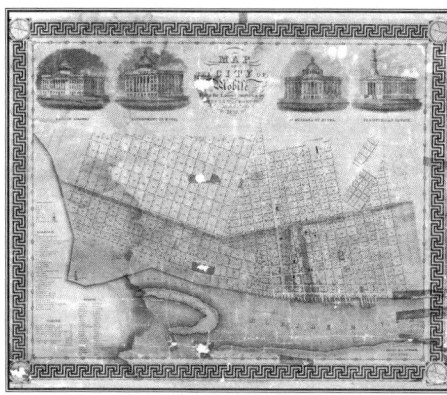

Figure 9.3. Map of Mobile, 1838. Hitchcock was a real estate developer in Mobile and at one time was considered the wealthiest man in Alabama. Courtesy of the Alabama Department of Archives and History.

Shortly after arriving in Mobile, Hitchcock returned to public service when he was appointed US district attorney in 1825 by President John Quincy Adams. Charles Tait, then the federal district court judge in Mobile, had recommended Hitchcock for this position to Senator Henry Clay. Hitchcock held this position until 1830, during which time and thereafter he began to devote more time to business interests and less to the practice of law, to such an extent that he became the leading commercial developer of Mobile. In the mid-1830s, Hitchcock collaborated with William Phineas Browne, also from Vermont, in the acquisition of prime real estate in Mobile. Browne later was credited with operating the state's first regular systematic underground coal mines near Montevallo in Shelby County. Hitchcock was also involved in the construction of several notable structures, including the New Government Street Hotel, worth $200,000 upon completion; the Barton Academy, the first public school in Alabama; and the Government Street Presbyterian Church, which Hitchcock paid for the most part out his own pocket.[20]

Hitchcock had always wanted to serve on the state supreme court of Alabama, but he shied away from such service because of the financial strains he was under in providing for his mother, sisters, brother, and other kin in Vermont. He and his wife also led a very expensive lifestyle as among Mobile's leading citizens. Since the capital was then located in Tuscaloosa, he could not afford to be away from his lucrative law practice. By 1835, however, Hitchcock determined that he could attend court in Tuscaloosa and maintain his Mobile residence. An opportunity to serve soon became attainable when Chief Justice Abner S. Lipscomb resigned. On January 9, 1835, the legislature elected Reuben Saffold as the new chief justice, Hitchcock to take Saffold's position as an associate justice, and Harry J. Thornton as another associate justice. Hitchcock had won the position over a powerful attorney from Tuscaloosa who was a future governor of Alabama, Henry W. Collier. During his tenure as an associate justice, Hitchcock wrote a total of sixty-five opinions, only two of which invited dissenting opinions from his colleagues on the court.[21]

In June 1836, Hitchcock was elected to succeed Chief Justice Reuben Saffold, serving with associate justices Arthur F. Hopkins and Henry W. Collier. In a few short months, however, Hitchcock resigned as chief justice in January 1837 to pay full attention to his many business interests and to stave off the effects of the Panic of 1837 as best he could. Although reputed to be the wealthiest man in Alabama at one time, Hitchcock struggled financially for the rest of his life, primarily pertaining to a large loan he had obtained from Mobile's branch of Nicholas Biddle's United States Bank of Pennsylvania. In the midst of dealing with these financial issues, Hitchcock was elected to represent Mobile in the Alabama House of Representatives on August 5, 1839. He would never take office, as six days later, on August 11, 1839, at the age of forty-seven, Hitchcock died of yellow fever during one of the worst epidemics in Mobile's history.[22]

After Hitchcock's death, his wife moved back to Tennessee to be near her relatives. Of the eight children of Henry and Ann Hitchcock's marriage, only three survived Henry's death—Caroline, Henry Jr., and Ethan Allen. Henry Jr. attended the University of Nashville, obtaining a degree in 1846. He then went to Yale, where he earned another degree in 1848. After reading law in Nashville, in 1851 Henry Jr. settled in St. Louis, Missouri, where he was admitted to the bar. The younger Hitchcock was opposed to slavery and in 1860 was a pro-Lincoln Republican. During the Civil War, the young Hitchcock rode with General Sherman in his famous march through Georgia to South Carolina. Later, he was involved in the founding of Washington University School of Law in St. Louis, Missouri. Caroline was married to Samuel Gradin Johnston DeCamp, who was a surgeon in the US Army. She died in 1863 in St. Louis, Missouri. Ethan Allen Hitchcock served as ambassador to Russia under President William McKinley and as US secretary of the interior under Presidents McKinley and Theodore Roosevelt.[23]

10

ISRAEL PICKENS

Delegate to the Constitutional Convention of
1819 and Alabama's Third Governor

Figure 10.1. Israel Pickens, Alabama's third governor, whose election broke the back of the Georgia
machine. Courtesy of the Alabama Department of
Archives and History.

Israel Pickens immigrated to the Alabama Territory from North Carolina
in 1817, about the same time as his political nemesis, Henry Hitchcock,
emigrated from Vermont. Pickens was already politically experienced in that
he had served in the North Carolina state senate from 1808 to 1810, and as
a representative from North Carolina in the US Congress from 1811 to 1817.
At first, Pickens aligned himself with Governor William Wyatt Bibb and the
powerful Georgia faction. But in 1820, he began to distance himself from the
Georgians as he began to sense that the poorer yeoman farmers would win
the day. Pickens thus successfully mounted a populist challenge to Bibb and
his political machine.

Born in Mecklenburg (now Cabarrus) County, North Carolina, on

January 30, 1780, Israel Pickens was the son of Captain Samuel and Jane Carrigan Pickens. Captain Pickens served in the American Revolution and was a descendant of French Huguenot settlers. Israel was educated in a private school under the tutelage of Reverend John Robinson. He thereafter studied law at Washington College located in Washington, Pennsylvania. In 1802, Pickens settled in Burke County in western North Carolina, where he began to practice law. His election to the North Carolina state senate in 1808 started him on the road to a political career that next took him to the US House of Representatives, where he became a staunch supporter of President James Madison and was one of the so-called War Hawks in Congress. This was a group of southern and western politicians who pushed for war with England in 1812. During his time in Congress, Pickens befriended William Rufus King—also of North Carolina and a future settler in Alabama—with whom he boarded in Washington at Claxton's Hotel on Capitol Hill. Pickens and King voted with the narrow majority of the US House and of the North Carolina delegation for an internal improvements bill passed in late 1816. Earlier, Pickens had supported the rechartering of the Bank of the United States. In the final session of the Fourteenth Congress, he was chairman of the committee on public expenditures.[1]

While Pickens was moving up the political ladder, he also courted and married Martha Lenoir, one of nine children born to General William and Ann Ballard Lenoir, on June 4, 1814. As was true of most of Alabama's settlers during this period, Pickens was soon struck by "Alabama Fever," which was the result of soaring cotton prices and the opening of fertile lands from the cessions of the Creek War of 1813–1814. Foregoing a run for a fourth term in Congress from North Carolina, in the spring of 1817 Pickens instead moved to St. Stephens, soon to be the capital of the Alabama Territory, where he took the job as register of the land office for Washington County. Because she was pregnant, Pickens's wife, Martha, remained in North Carolina until the fall of 1817. Pickens, on the other hand, immediately took over his responsibilities as land agent. He soon found that the land surveys were inadequate and that many private claims were not properly designated, causing Pickens to predict that this would result in many tracts being sold with adverse titles. He also believed that due to the inadequate surveys, quite a few tracts could not be offered for sale.[2]

While performing his duties as land agent, Pickens went about strengthening his private affairs by purchasing approximately 3,300 acres of public land in southwest Alabama, periodically from July 31, 1817, until February 18, 1818. His experiences as a government official and as a man who was quickly amassing wealth brought him into the confidence of the business leaders in the St. Stephens area. As a result, he was named the first president of the Tombeckbe Bank, which was the first bank to be chartered in Alabama by the territorial legislature. Because of Pickens's management abilities, the Tombeckbe Bank—unlike the unpopular Planters' and Merchants' Bank of Huntsville—did not have to suspend specie and was a success. To maintain solvency and keep providing specie, Pickens astutely arranged to have one of the Tombeckbe bank's agents serve as the cotton factor for three-fourths of the cotton cultivated in the surrounding area.[3]

During his service as president of the Tombeckbe Bank, Pickens became increasingly caught up in Alabama politics. He represented Washington County, along with Henry Hitchcock, in the Constitutional Convention of 1819, and was selected to serve on the powerful Committee of Fifteen. At this time, he aligned himself with Governor William Wyatt Bibb and the powerful Broad River faction of Georgians. It was not long, however, before Pickens realized that the Georgia faction was losing its power due to being regarded as a party of the privileged classes, or the "Royal Party," which alienated many of the state's voters. Closely associated with the so-called Royal Party in north Alabama was the Planters' and Merchants' Bank of Huntsville. When the Panic of 1819 hit, the Huntsville Bank speculated with government specie, exchanged its own devalued notes at par for government specie, overextended its outstanding loans, and finally suspended specie payments. Bank president LeRoy Pope was a lightning rod for complaints from many Alabamians who were grasping for air in a sea of debt. Also, many Alabama voters feared that the actions of most of the Georgia faction were motivated only by concern for the bank in which they were a stakeholder.[4]

After Governor William Bibb's death, Pickens began to distance himself from the Georgia faction and, when Governor Thomas Bibb decided not to seek reelection, Pickens announced his candidacy for governor in opposition to the Georgians. Pickens let it be known that he was in favor of the chartering of a state bank, which would transfer fiscal control away from private banks dominated by the wealthy planter class. Seen as the "champion of the people," and on the right side of the banking issue, as well as with a more engaging personality, Pickens defeated the Georgia faction's candidate, Dr. Henry Chambers, a prominent physician who had emigrated from Virginia to Huntsville in 1815. The final tally of votes was 9,616 for Pickens to 7,129 for Chambers. Most of Chambers's support was limited to a small number of counties in north Alabama, which was perhaps the last stronghold for the Broad River faction from Georgia.[5]

Pickens took the oath of office on November 9, 1821, and delivered his inaugural address to a joint session of the legislature in which he remarked on the incredible quickness of Alabama's emergence from the wilderness: "The fairest portion of our territory, and even the spot where we are assembled, was but yesterday unknown as the residence of civilized man." He continued, "The prospects which nature alone presented have successfully invited a respectable order of emigration, and filled our forests with the improvements of good society." He then focused on the need for further developments of the state's navigable waterways and overland transportation methods. He also opined to those assembled that the constitution unquestionably required the reapportionment of one or both houses of the legislature. He next asserted that the speculation in public land sales had contributed to the state's fiscal problems and to "the suppression of vigorous industry." He stated further, however, that the state could overcome its financial issues because of more than two million dollars being pumped into the economy by the annual production of cotton within the state.[6]

In 1821, the Huntsville bank's supporters obtained the passage of a bill erecting a state bank, to which the state would contribute two-fifths of the capital and have two-fifths of the control. The ominous features of this legislation were that existing private banks could become branches of the state bank and control it during its formative period, well before the state would be authorized to exercise the control commensurate with its capital contribution. Due to these anticipated results, Governor Pickens vetoed the bill. The legislature sustained his veto, thus stopping the private bank supporters in their tracks. Not surprisingly, the focus of Pickens's two terms as governor was the establishment of a state bank, which would dominate already existing private banks controlled by the planter class. Pickens, in laying out his proposals to the legislature, called for the yet unconstructed University of Alabama to be allowed to invest an amount not exceeding $100,000 in stock of a state bank. To ensure that the university would not need such funds for construction right away, Pickens deftly managed to delay debate of the location of the university to future sessions of the legislature, while at the same time pressing for the incorporation of the university and allowing its trustees to sell land and invest the proceeds from this sale.[7]

Pickens decided to let the dust settle a bit before pushing for a banking bill more in line with what he and his common folk electorate had in mind. Then in 1823, Pickens was reelected as governor, again defeating Chambers, this time by a vote of 6,942 to 4,604. With his reelection and with a more favorable pro-People's Party legislature, Governor Pickens immediately began to push the legislature to establish a state bank that would ensure a sound currency. The legislature responded by presenting the governor a banking bill that he could accept. The bill provided for an initial capitalization of a little more than $200,000. The trustees of the University of Alabama, just as Governor Pickens had so deftly maneuvered to arrange, subscribed approximately half of that amount. The remainder of the capital came from state bonds sold on the New York market and from the sale of federal land grants reserved for financing transportation improvements in Alabama. The State Bank of Alabama opened in Cahaba in 1824 and was directed by a president and a board of directors to be elected annually by both houses of the legislature. The first president of the bank was none other than Andrew Pickens, the governor's brother.[8]

The State Bank of Alabama was the first major institution that required the oversight of the legislature. Unfortunately, as noted by historian Leah Rawls Atkins, members of the legislature "viewed the bank as an immense pork barrel waiting for their eager spoons." To make sure that they could get to the trough, the Senate rejected an amendment to the bank bill that would have prevented legislators from doing business with the bank. Politics would dominate the election of bank officers and directors as evidenced by the election of the governor's brother as the bank's first president. For many years, however, the bank's profits paid the costs of administering Alabama's state government. The bank eventually collapsed after losing the confidence of the public and being charged with mismanagement during the Panic of 1837.[9]

While Governor Pickens was pushing for his bank bill, he was grieving over the loss of his wife, who had died soon after his reelection. To make matters worse, his infant son, William James, followed his mother in death soon thereafter. Pickens dealt with his loss by immersing himself in carrying out his agenda for his second administration. As we have seen, Pickens got his way in establishing the State Bank of Alabama, but he could not push through the legislature a measure providing that Alabama's presidential electors be chosen by districts rather than on a statewide basis. His intent was to prevent Andrew Jackson from getting all of Alabama's allotted electors since he was supporting John Quincy Adams for president in 1824. As Pickens had expected, Jackson received all the state's electoral votes. Additionally, when the legislature passed a resolution supporting Jackson's bid for the presidency, Governor Pickens vetoed the resolution because he did not see it as a proper subject for legislation. Pickens, however, was politically adroit enough not to ignore the popularity of Jackson within the state, and he praised Jackson's military feats in the veto message: "Indeed our language is wanting in richness to furnish adequate terms of commendation of the military services of our hero." In further praise, Pickens said, "His signal gallantry has not merely given him a rank among the conquerors of modern times, but his uniform and eminent usefulness in the protection of our southern frontier has enlisted his name among the saviors of his country and to none is the recollection of his important services more dear than to the people of Alabama."[10]

No doubt the most exciting event during Pickens's service as governor was the Marquis de Lafayette's visit to Alabama in 1825. Pickens played host to the French hero of the American Revolution and was given carte blanche by the legislature to lavishly entertain the aging general. Pickens went so far as to hire a band from New Orleans to play at a ball in Montgomery for Lafayette. When Lafayette arrived in Montgomery, a crowd of three thousand greeted him on Goat Hill, the future site of the capitol building in Montgomery. After being serenaded with French horns and bugles and a band playing "Hail to the Chief," Lafayette was formerly introduced to Governor Pickens, who was reportedly awed and left speechless. According to one account, Pickens was so overcome by excitement that he was unable to deliver his planned address to the assembled crowd. Other accounts, however, indicate that the governor quickly recovered and made an excellent speech. Lafayette continued and made stops in Selma, Cahaba, Claiborne, and Mobile. The visit, while very exciting and historic, practically cleaned out the state's treasury—the visit's total expenditures amounted to almost $17,000, or approximately $350,000 in today's dollars.[11]

Dr. Henry Chambers, whom Pickens had defeated twice in elections for governor, died on January 25, 1825, on the way to Washington to assume his seat in the US Senate, to which he had been elected in the latter part of 1824. He had defeated William Kelly by a vote of 41–36 after distancing himself from the Georgia faction and becoming a Jackson supporter. Pickens used his influence with Governor John Murphy, whom Pickens had selected to succeed him, to receive the interim appointment to Chambers's vacant seat. This appointment, however, disregarded the long-standing gentleman's agreement that the state's US Senate seats would be filled with one candidate from north Alabama and one from south Alabama.[12]

Unfortunately, Pickens came down with tuberculosis and he spent most of the 1826 Senate session confined to bed. He did not get any better and felt obligated to resign. He then went to Cuba in March 1827 with the hopes that warmer weather and the sea air would ease his miseries. To the contrary, his condition worsened and he died on April 24, 1827, in Matanzas, Cuba, leaving behind a daughter and two sons. Pickens's nephew, Samuel, who had accompanied him to Cuba, buried Pickens in Lemonar and erected a monument over his grave. Samuel then returned to Alabama and served as executor of his uncle's estate and made sure that his children were well cared for. A little over three years after Pickens's death, the Alabama legislature appropriated money to return his body for burial in the family cemetery near Greensboro, Alabama. In 1830, the Greensboro Guards militia unit marched in a procession carrying Pickens's body to the Greensboro cemetery for interment. Israel Pickens was finally back at home.[13]

Historian Hugh C. Bailey best summed up the influence that Israel Pickens had in the founding of Alabama: "He was a superb politician, one

Figure 10.2. Marquis de Lafayette. Governor Pickens
welcomed Lafayette to Alabama in 1825. Courtesy of
the Alabama Department of Archives and History.

who fought for his convictions, but one who knew the value of patience, compromise, and opportunism. His greatest fame flows from the death blow he and his friends gave to the 'Georgia Machine.'" Bailey also observed that his "shrewd calculations in establishing and nurturing the state bank were major political achievements which had a long-range influence for all Alabama."[14] While Israel Pickens did not hold as many offices as did some of the founders of the state, his accomplishments had a wide-ranging effect during the formative period of Alabama.

REUBEN SAFFOLD II

Soldier in the Creek Indian War, Member of the Territorial Legislature, Delegate to the Constitutional Convention of 1819, and Associate Justice and Chief Justice of the Alabama Supreme Court

Figure 11.1. Reuben Saffold II. Courtesy of Mark Dauber.

Like many of Alabama's founders and early settlers, Rueben Saffold II caught the "Alabama Fever," and, in 1813, he and his family emigrated from Georgia, to a point approximately sixty-seven miles north of Mobile. He was a soldier in the Creek War of 1813–1814, and later served in the territorial legislature in 1818. He was also a member of the Constitutional Convention of 1819, and that same year became one of the circuit judges of the new state. Saffold continued as a circuit judge until 1832 when he became one of the three justices chosen to serve on the newly created Supreme Court. He succeeded Abner Lipscomb as chief justice in 1835.

Reuben Saffold II was born on July 15, 1788, in Wilkes County, Georgia.

He was the son of Reuben and Sarah (nee Bird). The elder Saffold was a veteran minuteman of the American Revolution, who received a grant for land in Washington County, Georgia, as a bounty for his services during the war. He owned 700 acres of land and three slaves in Wilkes County in 1785, and bought 200 more acres and ten slaves in 1794. The elder Reuben died in 1817 in Wilkes County about four years after Reuben II had moved to southwest Alabama. Sarah Saffold died in Wilkes County sometime around 1827.[1]

Not much is known of Reuben II's early years other than the fact that he read law in the office of Major Edward Payne and practiced law in Watkinsville until 1813. In 1811 he married Mary Phillips, daughter of Colonel Joseph and Jane (Walker) Phillips of Morgan County. In June of 1813, Reuben and his wife and two young sons emigrated to the Tombigbee settlement of Pine Level, located in Clarke County, later renamed Jackson in honor of Andrew Jackson. They traveled there as part of a wagon train led by the legendary frontiersman Sam Dale down the newly opened Old Federal Road.[2]

Upon his arrival, Saffold soon joined the local militia holding the rank of private. His unit joined several other units in the area planning to intercept a group of Creek warriors returning to south Alabama from Spanish Pensacola where they had obtained gunpowder and supplies from the Spanish government. On July 27, 1813, these units attacked the returning Creeks at the village of Burnt Corn, not far from present-day Monroeville. The American militiamen gained the early advantage with a surprise attack on the Indians who were peacefully eating lunch, but they lost their advantage when they recklessly ransacked the Indians' pack horses, which allowed the warriors to regroup and launch a surprise counterattack. This counterattack sent the Americans into retreat, so much so that they mustered themselves out of service. Reportedly, Saffold was among the last to retreat. In any event, the men were ridiculed and their leader, Colonel Caller, was humiliated further when he became lost in the woods for over two weeks. Although wounded in the skirmish, Samuel Dale did not let the ridicule bother him because, as previously mentioned, he soon became legendary for his prowess in the so-called Canoe Fight. Neither did Saffold, who was promoted to the rank of lieutenant colonel and given command of a company reconnoitering along the Perdido River. After his service there, Saffold was promoted again to colonel in the militia of the Mississippi Territory.[3]

After peace had been achieved, Saffold resumed the practice of law in Jackson, which was near St. Stephens, the site of the future capital of the Alabama Territory. While in Jackson, Saffold was on the board of trustees of the Jackson Academy. In 1813, Saffold entered politics when he was elected as a territorial legislator in the Mississippi Territory, representing Clarke County. He served in that capacity until Alabama became a state in 1819. Perhaps anticipating the potential for the Alabama River basin, between 1814 and 1817, Saffold bought land and slaves in Dallas County. On January 8, 1817, Saffold was one of the signatories to a memorial to the US Congress asking for statehood for the Mississippi Territory. Of course, Congress would eventually grant statehood to both Mississippi and Alabama. Saffold's emergence as a prominent citizen of the area was further demonstrated by his being elected by the shareholders of the Tombeckbe Bank in the town of St. Stephens to its board of directors. Even more demonstrative of his public standing was his election as a delegate to the Constitutional Convention of 1819, representing Clarke County along with James Magoffin. Saffold was chosen for the all-important Committee of Fifteen, which was tasked with writing an original draft to be considered by the convention as a whole. Based upon his rapid rise in political prominence, an antebellum Democratic Party newspaper years later said the Saffold name was "the very synonym of Democracy in Alabama."[4]

After the completion of the constitutional convention, Saffold and his family moved to Dallas County in December 1819. There, Saffold began construction of a large hewn house sixteen miles south of Selma near Pleasant Hill. Named Belvoir, meaning "beautiful view," it was completed in 1825 and became the hub of a very large cotton plantation with a significant number of slaves. Sometime between 1838 and 1842, a statelier Greek Revival style plantation mansion replaced the original hewn house. It is known that the hewn house was still there in 1838 when English naturalist Philip Henry Gosse was serving as a teacher for Saffold's children, as well as other children in the area. It is also known that it had been completed before Saffold's death in 1847.[5]

On December 16, 1819, two days after Alabama was admitted to the Union, Saffold was elected by the legislature as one of the state's first five circuit judges—the others being Abner Smith Lipscomb, Henry Y. Webb, Richard Ellis, and Clement Comer Clay. Between 1819 and 1831, individual circuit court judges, when convened as a whole body, constituted the Alabama Supreme Court. In their capacity as individual circuit court judges, they were required to travel at least twice a year, usually in the fall and spring, to each court in their respective circuits. The circuit judges sat as the Alabama Supreme Court for the first time in May 1820 in a private residence in Cahaba. Before settling down to deciding cases, the judges' first acts of business were to adopt the court's rules of procedure and elect Clement Comer Clay as chief justice. Saffold served as a circuit judge until 1832, when a separate supreme court was established with its own associate justices rather than circuit court judges filling two roles. Saffold was elected by the legislature as one of the three justices on the new supreme court in 1832, and in 1835 he became the chief justice when Abner Lipscomb stepped down from that position.[6]

Even though Saffold resigned as chief justice after only a year in that

Figure 11.2. Belvoir Plantation, the home of Reuben Saffold II. Courtesy of the Alabama Department of Archives and History.

position, that year was one of the most eventful years in the supreme court's history up until that time. There was a popular revolt against the supreme court because of a decision it had rendered regarding the usury laws of Alabama. A law passed by the territorial legislature in 1818 had taken away all restrictions on interest rates. As interest rates skyrocketed, the state's first legislature quickly repealed the law in 1819. Interest rates in turn were limited to eight percent. In response, William Kelly, Speaker of the House of Representatives and a member of the so-called People's Party, sought to make things even more favorable to debtors by seeking to repeal the statute of limitations pertaining to the recovery of excessive interest rates. His attempt failed in the legislature in 1825, and in 1827 the supreme court dealt Kelly and his party another blow when it ruled that the statute of limitations prevented the recovery of excessive interest already paid out under contracts negotiated under the 1818 law.[7]

This decision sent Kelly and his followers into a tailspin, making it the focus of the election of 1828 within the Tennessee Valley, where they ranted against the court and the creditor class. When Kelly was reelected, he brought charges against the three justices of the supreme court—Chief Justice Saffold, along with Associate Justices John White and Anderson Crenshaw—under a provision of the constitution that allowed for the removal of judges for "willful neglect of duty or other reasonable cause, which would not be sufficient ground for impeachment." This led to the so-called Trial of the Judges, which was conducted before the Alabama Senate, with William Kelly serving as the prosecutor. The prosecution was weakly based upon broad allegations of improper rulings and decisions of the court, particularly regarding cases pertaining to the usury laws. After four days of testimony educed by the leading lawyers in Alabama, the senate voted unanimously to acquit Chief Justice Saffold, and the other justices were exonerated by a large margin. Although Saffold was soundly vindicated, Kelly rode an anti-court sentiment to obtain a six-year term limit amendment that was adopted as the state's first constitutional amendment in 1830.[8]

It is possible that Saffold resigned from the court after just one year because the trial left a bad taste in his mouth. He was presumably not in financial straits as he had acquired two other plantations in Dallas County. He also was effective in his role as chief justice. Alabama's first historian, Albert James Pickett, said of him, "The reports of the Supreme Court of Alabama are enduring memorials of his strength of mind, patient investigation, deep research, and profound learning." In any event, after resigning in 1836, he lived in Mobile while he helped establish a public warehouse for the government. It was not too long, however, before he returned to Belvoir to resume the practice of law out of an office on his own grounds. It is apparent that Saffold was content being back at Belvoir practicing law and running his plantations as he turned down an offer from Governor Benjamin Fitzpatrick in 1843 to fill an opening on the supreme court when Justice Henry Goldthwaite resigned. Saffold, however, did accept an appointment by Governor Fitzpatrick to a commission established by the legislature to collect unpaid loans and otherwise wind up the affairs of the Planters' and Merchants' Bank. Unlike serving as a justice of the supreme court, as a bank commissioner Saffold could still practice law and obtain a significant income from that practice.[9]

Because Saffold was a solid Democrat devoted to the cause of the South and a firm supporter of Texas independence, in April 1844 he was being hyped by state Democratic newspapers as a qualified replacement for Senator William Rufus King, who had accepted an appointment from President John Tyler to be Minister Plenipotentiary to France. While the vacant Senate seat was one appointment Saffold would probably have accepted, Governor Fitzpatrick predictably chose his brother-in-law, Congressman Dixon Hall Lewis, to fill King's position. Lewis was not only the governor's brother-in-law, but also a zealous supporter of the influential US secretary of state John C. Calhoun.[10]

Saffold continued to practice law out of his plantation office at Pleasant Hill while his sons, Benjamin and Milton, read law under his supervision. In early February 1847, however, Saffold became severely ill. His son Benjamin wrote to his sister, Mary Anne Bolling, in Lowndes County, informing her of "Pa's sudden and severe sickness," which the family physician had diagnosed as "apoplexy." Reuben Saffold II died on February 15, 1847, at the age of fifty-eight and was interred at Belvoir. He left behind his wife and twelve children, three of whom were also notable attorneys—Benjamin Franklin, William Byrd, and Milton Jefferson.[11] There were many press accounts of Reuben Saffold's passing, including one from the *Mobile Register*, which was full of praise for Saffold's character and ability: "The Hon. Reuben Saffold died at his residence in Dallas County on the 15th instant, of a paralysis under which he had lingered for about a week. Judge Saffold was one of the prominent men of the State. He was formerly, and for many years, on the bench of the Supreme Court—a position which he sustained with dignity and ability, and in which he was highly respected for his legal learning. On leaving the bench he removed to this city, where he resided some two or three years, when he returned to Dallas and resumed the practice of the law. He continued in the active duties of his profession up to the end of his life, respected and esteemed wherever he was known."[12]

Reuben Saffold II played a very important role in the founding of Alabama as well as during its formative period. Like others, he sought to enrich himself by accumulating rich fertile lands in what would become Alabama, but he arrived at a time of instability when there was an emerging civil war between factions of the Creek Nation. Unlike most other founders, Saffold joined the local militia and put himself in harm's way to help defend his new homeland. When peace was finally achieved after the Creek War, Saffold embarked upon a career of service to his state.

12

GABRIEL MOORE

First Speaker of the House of Alabama's Territorial Legislature, Delegate to the Constitutional Convention of 1819, US Senator, US Congressman, and Alabama's Fifth Governor

Figure 12.1. Gabriel Moore, Alabama's fifth governor and a US senator and US congressman. Courtesy of Alabama Department of Archives and History.

Perhaps the most interesting of Alabama's founders was Gabriel Moore, one of Madison County's earliest settlers. Moore arrived in Huntsville in 1810 and was soon representing Madison County in the Mississippi Territorial Legislature. In 1817, he became the Speaker of the House of Representatives of the Alabama Territorial Legislature. A nasty divorce and Moore's participation in a duel caused him to resign from the legislature. However, these adversities did not hold him back, and he went on to become one of Madison County's delegates to the Constitutional Convention of 1819, serve as a senator in the Alabama legislature in 1820, win election to the US Congress for several terms commencing in 1822, win election as Alabama's fifth governor in 1829, and serve in the US Senate from 1831 to 1837.

Gabriel Moore, a son of Matthew and Letitia Moore, was born circa 1785 in Surry (later Stokes) County, North Carolina. His parents had emigrated from Louisa County, Virginia, circa 1774. Upon their arrival in North Carolina, the Moore family purchased land and took up grants at the foot of Sauratown Mountain on the Dan River. A year after the birth of their eighth child, Gabriel, the Moores completed a brick dwelling that came to be known as Moore's Castle. This home was purportedly the finest private residence built in the Dan River valley at this early date. When the elder Moore died in 1801, his will directed that the proceeds from the sale of his iron works be applied for the education of his three youngest sons—Gabriel, Tucker Woodson, and Matthew Redd. According to one source, Gabriel was educated in Greensboro at David Caldwell's Academy, then known as the "Log College," which would later expand and become the University of North Carolina. Another source indicates that "part of Gabriel's education must have been under Edward Hickman, who operated a school in the area. . . . However, there is no documentation of his graduation from the University of North Carolina, as tradition maintains." There is no doubt though that he read law in North Carolina before migrating to Huntsville in 1810.[1]

When Moore arrived in Huntsville he was immediately appointed as tax assessor and collector for Madison County. In that position, in addition to the administration of the revenue laws, he was tasked with the duty to supervise the census for Madison County in 1810. He had been commissioned an attorney on May 12, 1808, by Governor Robert Williams of the Mississippi Territory. Moore also became heavily involved in land speculation, beginning at the federal land sale at Nashville on December 18, 1808, where he joined wealthy speculators from Georgia and Virginia. During this period, he also served as an aide-de-camp to General Ferdinand L. Claiborne of the Mississippi Territorial militia.[2]

In 1811, Moore was elected to the House of Representatives of the Mississippi Territory representing Madison County, and continued in this office until Mississippi became a state and Madison County became a part of the Alabama Territory. Moore's political career was centered around appealing to the small yeomen farmers rather than the wealthy planter class. He was renowned among the common folks for stump speeches he delivered to them in which he asserted that he "came not from the 'Royal Party' but from the poor." Despite this assertion, he was certainly not dirt poor as he owned almost five hundred acres of land and four slaves. He was also "an affluent attorney as well as small farmer." As an example of his support for the average man, Moore introduced a bill to have the name of the town of Twickenham changed to Huntsville. As mentioned previously, LeRoy Pope had dictated that the town be named Twickenham in honor of the estate of the English poet Alexander Pope. The small farmers were so incensed at what they perceived as aristocratic arrogance that they made the town's name an issue in the next year's election to the territorial legislature. They were successful in defeating two out of the three candidates put up by Pope's Georgia faction, and Moore was then successful in having his bill changing the name to Huntsville enacted into law.[3]

Moore represented Madison County in the Mississippi Territorial Assembly from 1811 to 1817, and served as the assembly's speaker from 1815 to 1817. When Alabama became a separate territory in 1817, Moore continued to represent Madison County and served as speaker in the new Alabama Territorial Assembly in January and February 1818. The General Assembly's second session in November 1818 was its last before Alabama became a state. Early in that session, the assembly was stunned when Speaker Moore's wife petitioned it for a divorce, as well as permission to revert to her maiden name, Mary Parham Caller. Her petition for divorce followed a marriage doomed from the beginning because of meddling by Mary's father, militia colonel James Caller of Washington County, who had promoted the union with the hopes of uniting his family—politically influential in the southern part of the territory—with that of an emerging prominent politician in the northern portion of the territory. The marriage quickly fell apart because Mary probably had only married Moore to appease her father even though she was apparently in love with someone else. This highly publicized divorce caused Moore to resign as Speaker and remove himself from politics for a while. Adding insult to injury, Moore later engaged in a duel with his ex-wife's brother, fortunately resulting in no serious injuries to either party. As will be seen, however, neither the divorce nor the duel put a permanent end to Moore's political career.[4]

Moore, in fact, quickly landed on his feet, becoming one of Madison County's eight delegates to the state constitutional convention meeting in Huntsville in the summer of 1819. Some of the positions he took during the convention demonstrate his liberal leanings. In this regard, he moved that senators serve for two-year terms rather than three, was in favor of reducing the minimum age for representatives from twenty-three to twenty-one, and supported the election of judges for six-year terms instead of on good behavior. Moore continued his comeback from personal difficulties when he was elected as the first state senator from Madison County, and in 1820 he became president of the Alabama Senate. A year later, Moore resigned from the Alabama Senate to run for a seat in the US Congress.[5]

At that time, Alabama had but one seat in the US House of Representatives. In 1821, the candidates against whom Moore ran for this single seat were George W. Owen of Monroe County and Silas Dinsmore, a former US agent to the Cherokee and Choctaw Indians. Owen carried some south

Alabama counties, but Moore's popularity in North Alabama was such that he was able to win by an overwhelming margin. Moore carried Madison County by a four-to-one margin, and in Jackson County he received 999 of the 1,006 votes cast. Moore ran for a seat in the US House of Representatives three more times and only once did he receive opposition.[6]

In his first term, Moore was Alabama's solitary congressman and thus served as the state's representative at large. During his next three terms, however, he represented only the northern part of the state, as the state was now divided into three separate districts. During his time in Congress, Moore pursued surveys of possible routes to connect the Alabama River and Tennessee River systems, and a means by which to facilitate navigation on the Tennessee River. Moore was eventually successful in acquiring federal aid for navigation improvements around Muscle Shoals. This was undoubtedly achieved due to Moore's acquaintance with John C. Calhoun, who, as US secretary of war, placed a high priority on the Muscle Shoals canal. Moore's support of this project was the beginning of a friendship between the two.[7]

Other matters addressed by Moore in his first term in Congress included raising Alabama's ratio for reapportionment from one representative for each 50,000 rather than one for each 40,000. Moore also authored two resolutions to protect prospective landholders, both of which were later defeated. In one of these, he moved that the Committee on Public Lands be instructed to inquire into "the expediency of authorizing the sale of public lands by entry, in lots of forty acres." He explained that such an arrangement would make possible the sale of land which would not ordinarily be sold, and would "enable honest but poor men to become proprietors." In the other resolution, he proposed that the Committee on Public Lands inquire into "the expediency of granting pre-emption rights to settlers on the public lands," those who had settled prior to a date in 1819 not yet determined. In the following session, Moore introduced yet another resolution on land policy. This resolution instructed the Committee on Public Lands to consider a bill to prohibit land office receivers from purchasing lands at either public or private sales in order to prevent government money being used by receivers to bid against immigrants to the state. This resolution prevailed.[8]

Moore was reelected to Congress in 1823 without opposition. During this term, Moore took part in the debates over the Tariff of 1824, a protective tariff designed to protect American industry from cheaper British commodities, especially iron products, wool and cotton textiles, and agricultural goods. Moore along with his friend, John C. Calhoun, considered the tariff a device that benefited the North at the expense of the South. Moore was particularly opposed to a high duty on cotton bagging, arguing that the tax on cotton bagging was not passed along to the consumer because it was not the product sold to the consumer as merchandise; rather, it was an article that envelops the cotton. In addition to the tariff, Moore joined with others calling for surveys of routes to link the Alabama and Tennessee River systems and to permit navigation at Muscle Shoals. Due to his efforts, Muscle Shoals would eventually receive significant improvements.[9]

Moore hesitantly endorsed his acquaintance, Andrew Jackson, in the 1824 presidential election. According to John McKinley, future justice of the US Supreme Court, in a letter he wrote to Speaker of US House of Representatives Henry Clay in September 1823, Moore had first declared support for John C. Calhoun and then for John Quincy Adams. Finding "neither suited for his constituents," he finally threw his support to Jackson. According to John M. Martin, a biographer of Moore, it was not clear whether Moore sided with Jackson because of "conviction or expediency." In any event, Martin asserted that Jackson "was the distinct favorite of northern Alabama and was supported by the majority of Alabamians." It appears, however, that Moore's support of Jackson was based upon expediency, since, although he was an acquaintance of Jackson, he only reluctantly supported him. He was also a friend of Calhoun but did not lend him his support. The fact that northern Alabama was heavily in Jackson's camp probably was the deciding factor for Moore to support Jackson. Moore's support notwithstanding, candidate Henry Clay threw his support to John Quincy Adams, who won the presidency by a vote of the House of Representatives. In later years, Moore would take a maverick position that would invoke the wrath and opposition of then President Jackson.[10]

In 1825, Gabriel Moore finally faced formidable opposition for his seat in Congress in the person of Clement Comer Clay. As Moore had done in the past, he presented himself as a candidate of the common man. He made sure that everyone understood that he had no connection whatsoever to the Royal Party or the Bank of Huntsville. In fact, according to one Clay supporter, he ended his speeches by asserting, "I am supported principally by the poor. No friend saving one or two of the rich have I." A supporter of Clay warned him that Moore was winning over voters, especially since he had "frequented evry [sic] grog shop and visited every old woman." To further ensure the support of common folk Jackson admirers, Moore waffled on the tariff question that he had once opposed. When all was said and done, Moore won reelection to his seat in the US Congress over Clay. The next year, Moore refused to support Clay's pursuit of a Senate seat, which ensured Clay's defeat. From this point forward Clay despised Moore to such an extent that, years later, the two coincidentally rode the same stagecoach for 170 miles without speaking to each other.[11]

When Moore returned to Congress in 1825, he continued to seek benefits for holders of relinquished lands. He called on the secretary of the treasury for information needed to guard the public from "fraudulent practices and combinations of individuals in the sale of relinquished lands." He also wished to ascertain whether the public interest would not best be served if former owners were given the right to repurchase relinquished land at some proportion of its original sale price. In the following session of Congress, Moore fought for a resolution instructing the Committee of Public Lands to determine the usefulness of allowing settlers on relinquished lands to live on these lands until sold and to harvest the crops growing at the time of sale.[12]

In 1827, Moore introduced a resolution seeking authorization of a survey of Muscle Shoals to determine the practicality of constructing a canal around the shoals. During the next session in 1828, he helped push through a bill granting over 400,000 acres of land to Alabama to be used for improving navigation on the Tennessee River. Moore's support of internal improvements and education was summed up in a toast to those who had secured the grant: "The citizens of Alabama—may they speedily realize and enjoy the benefits and advantages tendered them by the liberality of the General Government for the encouragement of Education and the Internal improvement." In one of his last legislative proposals, Moore introduced a resolution calling on the Committee on Public Lands to consider granting Alabama 97,129 acres for the improvement of the Black Warrior, the Cahaba, the Coosa, and the Tennessee Rivers. In his last session in 1828, Moore again opposed high duties, particularly on cotton bagging, as he had done in 1824 and 1827. Moore's opposition was to no avail as the Southern representatives were unable to prevent a law that exacted high tariffs on their goods.[13]

On February 7, 1829, Moore announced that he would be a candidate for governor of Alabama rather than for his seat in Congress. It turned out that he was unopposed for governor and assumed office on November 25, 1829. In his inaugural address, Moore requested the legislature follow a policy of "harmony, liberality, forbearance and toleration." Moore once again pushed for his long-time priorities, such as internal improvements and land debt relief for Alabamians financially strapped by the Panic of 1819. In 1830, as the navigational improvements commenced at Muscle Shoals, Governor Moore brought before the legislature his old project of linking the Alabama and Tennessee Rivers. Appealing to the small farmers in the state, Governor Moore advocated "a better and more equitable system of disposing of the public lands." In this regard, he promoted making lands available in smaller parcels and at graduated prices based on the fertility of the soil. Moore stressed to the legislators that without such changes the small farmers could not afford the high prices and would migrate westward away from Alabama.[14]

Governor Moore, a strong proponent of education during his administration, stated that "the increase of knowledge is the best security for sound public morality." He was also excited about the eminent opening of the University of Alabama, which he believed would extend "the benefits of education to even the humblest of our citizens." He also was an advocate for penal and judicial reform. He was unsuccessful, however, in getting the legislature to establish a centralized penitentiary system, which would have provided rehabilitation for the prisoners. Moore wanted an enlightened criminal justice system and reminded the legislature that the Alabama constitution provided for "a penal code founded on principles of reformation, and not of vindictive justice." Moore was successful in having the legislature establish a three-man supreme court to replace the existing system of five circuit court judges sitting as a supreme court when needed. This legislation was enacted on January 14, 1832, after Moore resigned as governor, and included a provision whereby supreme court justices were elected for six-year terms rather than for good behavior.[15]

Opposed to the Bank of the United States, Moore described it as a "mammoth institution" with power "over our State institutions, not only unfriendly to their healthy existence, but our state sovereignty itself." Moore, however, praised the Bank of Alabama and called for the legislature to establish branches of the bank in both the Tennessee Valley and south Alabama, so as to provide more efficient service to those areas. Legislators, however, refused to do so during Moore's term as governor. Moore still counseled Alabama's congressional delegation to vote against rechartering of the Bank of the United States, and, if so rechartered, Moore recommended that the state delegation seek restrictions on its operations within the state.[16]

Before Governor Moore had delivered his final message to the state legislature, he was purportedly involved in an effort to remove McKinley from his seat in the US Senate. Moore, who was pro-Jackson and anti-Bank of the United States, spread rumors about McKinley's loyalty to Jackson. Charges of secret coalitions and behind-the-scenes maneuvering were making the rounds as the Huntsville *Democrat* then questioned Moore's commitment to Jackson. Moore, however, won McKinley's seat after the latter resigned unexpectedly, with Moore then taking office in the Senate in March 1831. In so doing, he turned his duties as governor over to Samuel B. Moore, who was of no kin. When Moore took off for Washington, he almost immediately became entrapped in the factional discord in Jackson's first administration. Although Moore held himself out as a Jackson supporter, he nevertheless allied himself in 1832 with Vice President John C. Calhoun and voted against Senate confirmation of Martin Van Buren, Jackson's nominee as American minister to Great Britain. When Calhoun cast the tie-breaking vote against him, Van Buren lost the position. Obviously, this incurred the wrath of Jackson, prompting him to ask his friend John Coffee to help

Figure 12.2. Martin Van Buren. Moore's vote against Van Buren for Minister to Great Britain infuriated President Jackson and essentially ended Moore's political career. Courtesy of the Library of Congress.

garner popular opposition to Moore. Public meetings held in north Alabama in February and March of 1832 clamored for Moore's resignation. Soon the state legislature followed suit and also called for Moore's resignation. Moore refused and instead served out the remainder of his term until 1837. In the interim, realizing that he would not be given a second term as senator by the legislature, Moore decided to run for his old seat in the US House of Representatives. For the first time in his political career, however, Moore was defeated. He was decisively beaten by Reuben Chapman, who later became Alabama's thirteenth governor. Undoubtedly, Moore was distressed that it was Clement Comer Clay who took his seat in the Senate.[17]

At last Moore had finally stumbled and was involuntarily retired from public office. His much earlier scandalous divorce did not stop him, but his defiance of President Jackson did. Not only was he down and out politically, he was in financial straits partly because of the Panic of 1837 but more so because his nephew who handled his business interests while he was in Washington duped him out of most of his property. Between 1841 and 1843, the Circuit Court of Madison County placed liens in favor of his creditors on more than two thousand acres of land and sixty slaves. Despite his circumstances, Moore turned to the Whig Party seeking appointments to several patronage jobs such as collector of customs at Mobile, consul at Havana, US Marshal of northern Alabama, and chargé d'affairs in Texas. Unable to secure any of these appointments, in 1843 Moore set out with eight of his slaves north to Cincinnati, Ohio, where he purportedly executed deeds of emancipation for them. He then went briefly with his emancipated slaves to a rented plantation in Panola County, Mississippi. After a brief stop there, Moore moved on to the Republic of Texas in 1844. Shortly after his arrival, he died on August 6, 1844, near Caddo Lake in Harrison County. After his death, it was revealed that he had fathered a child by one of his slaves, for which he had executed a deed of manumission on September 27, 1842.[18]

Historian Harriet Amos Doss best summed up Moore's contribution as a founding father of Alabama as follows: "Moore's death in relative obscurity and poverty contrasted sharply with the prominence he had enjoyed as a gifted politician who served the state for more than twenty years. He helped to shape Alabama's first constitution and influenced the early form and structure of the government of the new state. His greatest political successes came when he championed the concerns of the common people and professed Jacksonian rhetoric. When he challenged Jackson, even selectively, his popular following eroded."[19]

13

WILLIAM RUFUS KING

US Senator and Thirteenth Vice President of the United States

Figure 13.1. William Rufus King, thirteenth vice
president of the United States. Courtesy of the
Alabama Department of Archives and History.

William Rufus Devane King, congressman, diplomat, US senator, and vice president of the United States, is the only American executive official ever to be sworn into office on foreign soil. At the time of his inauguration, he was in Cuba on the advice of his physician in the hopes of a warmer climate fending off worsening tuberculosis. Unfortunately, he only lived another twenty-five days, and just two days after returning to his home in Alabama.

King was born on April 7, 1786, in Sampson County, North Carolina. He was the second son of William and Margaret Devane King. William King was described as "a gentleman of fortune and character." Of Irish ancestry, he was a wealthy planter and a justice of the peace. At the time of his son's birth, he owned more than twenty-four slaves. He had fought in the Revolutionary War, served as a delegate to the North Carolina convention called to ratify the US Constitution in 1789, and was a frequent member of the North Carolina House of Commons. His mother was a descendant of a prominent Huguenot family.[1]

The younger King attended Grove Academy near Kenansville, Fayetteville Academy, and the Preparatory School at the University of North Carolina, where he became a member of the Philanthropic Society. He studied at the university from 1801 until 1804 when he left at the end of his junior year to study law under William Duffy—one of the state's leading lawyers—at Fayetteville. In late 1805, King obtained a license to practice law and set up an office in Clinton, which was the county seat of Sampson County where he had been born.[2]

In 1808, King sought a seat in the North Carolina House of Commons and was elected as a Jeffersonian-Republican. As a new member of the House of Commons, King defended resolutions to support measures taken by the Jefferson administration against the aggressive actions of France and Great Britain. A productive member of the house, he was reelected in 1809 but resigned before the end of the session to become solicitor of the First Circuit of the state court, which met in Wilmington. He must have impressed the electorate, because in 1810, just a few months shy of the constitutionally mandated age of twenty-five, he won the Wilmington District's seat in the US House of Representatives. By the time he was sworn in, however, he had reached the required age.[3]

Upon taking his seat in 1811 in the Twelfth Congress, he joined with young "War Hawks" John C. Calhoun and Henry Clay to support measures to strengthen the military power of the United States and to push for war against Great Britain. Successful in these endeavors, King was reelected to Congress without opposition in 1813 and 1815, but in April 1816 he resigned his congressional seat to serve as legation secretary under William Pinkney, recently appointed US Minister to Russia. As reflected in his journal, King had always wanted to visit Europe: "Actuated by a desire to visit the continent of Europe, which I had fostered from a very early period of my life . . . I determined to resign my situation and request the appointment of Secretary of Legation. . . . My wish when made known, was promptly met by the government and I received the President's commission bearing the date, the 23rd, April 1816." Pinckney and King first went on a special mission to the King of Naples, where they were unsuccessful in obtaining reimbursement for seized American ships. In January 1817, they arrived in St. Petersburg, where they served for about a year. Before returning home, King traveled as a

Figure 13.2. Chestnut Hill, King's plantation on King's Bend. Courtesy of the Alabama Department of Archives and History.

tourist throughout the European continent. In February 1818, Pinkney and King returned to the United States.[4]

While King was abroad in Europe, "Alabama Fever" had broken out as settlers converged on the Alabama Territory's rich and fertile lands. King's older brother, Thomas Devane King, took advantage of available lands and located his family on the banks of the Black Warrior River in what is now Tuscaloosa County. The younger King wrote to his brother to advise him of the raging land fever in the Alabama Territory and of the richness of the fertile soils. After a short stay in North Carolina upon his return from Europe, William Rufus King followed his brother to the Alabama Territory, and in October 1818 he purchased 750 acres of land within a large bend on the Alabama River in Dallas County. There he soon built his home, Chestnut Hill, and established a plantation. The residence was situated on a small knoll surrounded by chestnut trees only five and a half miles from Cahaba, the new state capital. In March 1819, King, along with several others, formed a land company and founded the town of Selma approximately nine miles upstream from Cahaba.[5]

King quickly became involved in Alabama politics in 1819. King's achievements in North Carolina undoubtedly enticed the Dallas County electorate to send him to the Alabama Constitutional Convention of 1819 in Huntsville as their only delegate. King's North Carolina experience also led him to be appointed to the powerful subcommittee, which was tasked to come up with a draft of the constitution. On this subcommittee, he worked alongside Henry Hitchcock of Washington County and John M. Taylor of Madison County. As soon as the constitution was adopted, King left Huntsville to travel to North Carolina on business. While he was away in North Carolina, the first Alabama state general assembly met and he was chosen almost unanimously as one of the US senators to which the state was entitled under the federal constitution. Upon learning of his election to the Senate while he was on his way home, he reversed his course and headed directly to Washington to assume his new duties.[6]

John Campbell, former secretary of the constitutional convention, said of the new senator from south Alabama: "He is about thirty-three years of age, a very gay, elegant looking fellow—a fluent speaker and a man of respectable talents." Another contemporary of the day, however, aware of King's practice of wearing a wig long out of fashion, dismissed him as a "tall, prim, wig topped mediocrity." A more favorable description came from novelist John Updike, who described King's face as "darkly handsome and smolderingly receptive." Senate historian Mark O. Hatfield stated, "He was distinguished by the scrupulous correctness of his conduct. He was remarkable for his quiet and unobtrusive, but active, practical usefulness as a legislator. . . . This honor be it spoken, he never vexed the ear of the Senate with ill-timed, tedious, or unnecessary debate."[7]

When King got to the Senate, he favored the Missouri Compromise, assumed leadership in the fight for generous land legislation, and became an opponent of protective tariffs. He also exerted a powerful influence in support of the Land Act of 1820. When he was initially elected to the Senate there were short-term and long-term seats—King was elected to the short-term seat, and thus he had to seek reelection in 1822. He won that race over William Crawford by a narrow margin of 38–35 votes. Crawford was the president of the Tombecbe Bank and was the dispenser of patronage in Alabama under the influence of Secretary of War William H. Crawford, who bore the name of the Alabama Crawford but was of no kin.[8]

King was now on his way to serve for twenty-nine years in the US Senate representing the State of Alabama. In 1828, he was reelected to the Senate without opposition as a moderate Jacksonian Democrat. Although he supported John Quincy Adams for president in 1824, he later became disenchanted with Adams's policies and joined the ranks of many other Alabamians in endorsing Andrew Jackson. King opposed the tariff acts of 1824 and 1828 and had a special interest in Indian removal and public land policies. Due in large part to King's efforts, Alabama cast all its electoral votes for Jackson in the 1828 presidential election. After Jackson's election in 1828, King became one of the foremost allies of the Jackson administration in the Senate. Although King generally supported the Jackson administration throughout its term, he did associate himself with the so-called little Senate group that was loyal to South Carolina's John C. Calhoun—Jackson's first vice president and later antagonist. King, however, still shared Jackson's fierce opposition to Henry Clay's "accursed American System" of protective tariffs against foreign competition, a central banking system, and a public works

Figure 13.3. President James Buchanan.
Courtesy of the Library of Congress.

program involving internal improvements such as canal and road-building.[9]

At some point during his 1828 term in the Senate, supposedly in the early 1830s, King became involved in "an affair of honor" with Major Michael Kenan, a Dallas County planter who had emigrated from North Carolina. Kenan allegedly accosted King with disrespectful language on the streets of Cahaba—the exact nature of which is not known, although it is possible that it was related to King's sexual orientation. King resented this verbal attack and retaliated by drawing his sword-cane and running it crosswise over Kenan's chest. King then refused to accept a challenge from Kenan because of the nature of Kenan's insult. The note of challenge had been delivered by a neighbor of Kenan, John C. Perry, who was unaware of its import. However, when it was declined, he delivered another one with knowledge of its import. When this one was declined, Perry challenged King on his own behalf, and a duel was arranged to take place out of state. Perry then let discretion take the better part of valor and refused to attend the meeting because the matter was too frivolous to warrant his engaging in deadly combat with a friend who had done him no wrong.[10]

King's private life has long been the subject of speculation by historians with respect to his sexual orientation, which was also publicly questioned during his lifetime. Rumors circulating in Washington were that President Jackson called him "Miss Nancy" (a nineteenth-century euphemism for an effeminate man) and "Aunt Fancy." Rumors expanded as King, who never married, roomed with Senator James Buchanan, who also never married, for a period of some fifteen years. Newspapers of the time speculated as to their relationship, and the postmaster general supposedly called them "Buchanan and wife." Others used the term "Siamese twins." Despite the jokes and innuendos, historian Daniel Brooks has stated that "any negative reactions to their relationship appear to have had little effect, and the men continued with their living arrangements and their work as legislators." Of course, Buchanan went on to be elected as the nation's fifteenth president and King the thirteenth vice president.[11]

Getting back to politics and legislation, King utilized his chairmanship of the Senate Committee on Public Lands in 1831 and 1832 to promote President Jackson's land policies. In this regard, he disagreed that lands should be priced primarily to bring large amounts of revenue into the federal coffers. He also believed that public lands should only be made available for sale to those who planned to settle them. He believed further that a reduction in land prices would stimulate both territorial settlement and national economic growth. Although he joined in with his region's antagonism to high protective tariffs, he opposed John C. Calhoun's position that the South had the right to nullify odious laws, such as the 1828 "Tariff of Abominations." King stated that he viewed nullification "as neither peaceful nor constitutional, but revolutionary in its character, and if persevered it must, in the nature of things, result in the severance of the Union." When Henry Clay introduced a compromise tariff bill in early 1833 that would reduce the tension between the federal and state forces, King, in comport with his moderate nature, quickly offered his support for the bill. His backing of this compromise bill pleased neither President Jackson nor Southern firebrands, who did not believe that he had worked hard enough for his region's interests. However, King undoubtedly managed to please the president when he and Senator Thomas Hart Benton led a vigorous and ultimately successful campaign to expunge from the record a censure that had been handed down by the Senate when Jackson refused to furnish a document to the Senate relating to Jackson's order to remove federal funds from the Bank of the United States.[12]

In 1832, King served as a delegate to the Democratic convention in Baltimore and was appointed to the Committee on Rules. He reported on behalf of the committee a rule requiring a two-thirds vote for the selection of a nominee. Although he opposed the nomination of Martin Van Buren for the vice presidency, King dutifully supported the party ticket. Despite severe criticism offered by the advocates of nullification because of King's moderate stand at the time of the crisis, King was reelected to the Senate in 1834 with only slight opposition. Although he still had reservations about Van Buren, he dutifully supported him for the presidency in 1836. Deeply concerned about the Panic of 1837 because it affected him personally and threatened to split the Democratic

Party, he supported repeal of the Distribution Act of 1836 and creation of the Independent Treasury System to help alleviate existing problems.[13]

As the 1830s were coming to end, King, a moderate and long-serving Southern senator, caught the fancy of leaders in the Democratic Party as a possible vice presidential candidate for the 1840 election. President Van Buren's vice president was then Richard M. Johnson, who was disfavored because he had had a negative impact on the ticket in the 1836 election due to a scandalous personal life. As a result, party leaders began a search for a strong second-term running mate for Van Buren. King was a logical choice because he had been in the national limelight for a quarter of a century and he had substituted for Vice President Johnson during his many absences from the Senate. Also, because of his close relationship with James Buchanan, he hoped to obtain significant support in electorally rich Pennsylvania, Buchanan's home state. Buchanan wanted to impede the presidential ambitions of both Senator Thomas Hart Benton and Secretary of State John Forsyth by blocking their paths to the vice presidency in 1840. King stepped to the plate and offered to his friend Buchanan that in return for Pennsylvania's help in securing the vice presidency in 1840, he would refuse to run for president in 1844 so that Buchanan would have a straight path to winning the presidency. Although Buchanan agreed to this proposal, the whole plan fell apart because King failed to gain support from Democratic leaders in influential states, including Pennsylvania. Although the Democrats indeed dropped Richard M. Johnson, they chose not to nominate King and instead left it up to the state electoral delegates to select a candidate. The electors divided their votes between Littleton W. Tazewell of Virginia and James Knox Polk of Tennessee. These machinations became moot, however, because William Henry Harrison defeated Van Buren in the election.[14]

King's often-belligerent relationship with Henry Clay was demonstrated by a purported confrontation between the senators in March 1841 when there was a Whig majority in the chamber for the first time. Soon a fight broke out over Senate printing patronage, as Clay proposed to dismiss Democrat Francis P. Blair, editor of the *Washington Globe*, as official printer for the Senate; Clay "believed the *Globe* to be an infamous paper, and its chief editor to be an infamous man." King retorted that Blair's character would "compare gloriously" to that of Clay. That remark sent Clay to his feet, shouting, "That is false, it is a slanderous base and cowardly declaration and the senator knows it to be so." King responded, "Mr. President, I have no reply to make—none whatever." King next wrote out a challenge to a duel and had another senator deliver it to Clay, who was slowly realizing that he had been perhaps too quick in the choice of his words. Nevertheless, both Clay and King chose seconds and prepared for their duel. Their preparations were interrupted, however, when the

Senate sergeant-at-arms arrested both men and turned them over to the civil authorities. King insisted upon an apology from Clay. On March 14, 1841, Clay delivered one and indicated that he would have been better keeping to himself the intensity of his feelings. This prompted King to deliver his own apology in the Senate chamber, after which Clay supposedly walked over to King's desk; there the men shook hands to the applause of the chamber.[15]

Despite this ugly incident, in 1842 King's name was once again being tossed about as a possible vice presidential candidate for the 1844 Democratic ticket. John C. Calhoun, who was contemplating a run for the presidency in 1844, tried to persuade King not to seek the vice presidency, as there was not room for another Southerner on a national ticket. Calhoun's candidacy, however, was overwhelmed by a resurgent Van Buren candidacy in late 1843. The names most frequently mentioned for Van Buren's running mate were King and Polk. King's supporters again touted that King was from a Southern state loyal to the Democratic Party, as opposed to Polk's Whig-leaning Tennessee. Once again, however, King was unable to nail down significant support in the electorally rich eastern states, which caused his candidacy to lose its momentum by the time of the 1844 Democratic convention in Baltimore. Van Buren himself ruined his own chances of becoming the presidential nominee when he declared his opposition to the annexation of Texas. King, however, hoped that the party leaders would turn to Buchanan to take Van Buren's place, and that he would again offer to serve as his running mate, arguing that his presence on the ticket would help secure electoral votes from North Carolina.[16]

President Tyler put an end to King's hopes on April 9, 1844, by appointing him minister to France. King was readily confirmed to this post, which had been vacant for some eighteen months. In June, King, at the age of fifty-eight, left for Paris to pursue his top priority as minister, which was to keep France from interfering with the US plan to annex Texas. Accompanying King on his journey to Paris were several of his family members, including his widowed niece Catherine Ellis, age twenty-nine; his nephew Alfred Beck, twenty-six, of Camden; his nephew William Thomas, fifteen; and his body servant, John Bell. Shortly after arriving in Paris, King presented his credentials to King Louis Philippe. It was reported that the French monarch, who had visited Mobile while in exile in the United States, greeted the American minister in part as follows: "Mr. King, I am not unacquainted with your eminence in the American Republic; I know with how much ability you have filled many posts of honor, and I am now really rejoiced that a man of so much experience and so much fame as a statesman represents that great republic of yours at this Court."[17]

As American minister to France, King contributed greatly regarding the success of three measures important to the United States: the annexation of Texas, the settlement of the Oregon boundary, and the Mexican War. According to early Alabama historian A. J. Pickett, because King was unable to establish a rapport with the French foreign minister, Louis Philippe consented to allow King to discuss the subjects of his mission with him, rather than having him go through the foreign office. King was able to convince Louis Philippe that France would be ill advised to join England in its proposed plan of intervention in Texas, thus permitting the United States to annex Texas without fear of foreign interference. He also obtained assurances that the French would not intervene against the United States on England's behalf during the Oregon controversy, nor would they oppose the United States during the Mexican War.[18]

In the fall of 1846, having determined that his mission to France had been a success, King asked President Polk to accept his resignation. At home, back in Alabama, King did not seek election as governor in 1847 and instead began a campaign to unseat Dixon Hall Lewis, who had been elected to his old seat in the US Senate. Opposed by both the Whigs and the Lewis element of the Democratic Party in the 1847 contest, King was unable to secure a majority in the legislature and suffered his only defeat at the state level. Shortly after King's defeat, he was nominated yet again for the vice presidency by the Alabama Democratic Party, but he received only scattered support at the National Convention. In just seven months Alabama's other Senate seat became open when Arthur P. Bagby resigned in June 1848 to accept appointment as foreign minister to Russia. Governor Reuben Chapman appointed King to fill the remainder of Bagby's term. After making concessions to the states' rights wing of the Democratic Party, King was able to defeat Arthur Hopkins and win election to a full term in 1849.[19]

With the death of President Zachary Taylor in the summer of 1850, King was selected as president pro tempore when Vice President Millard Fillmore was sworn in as president, leaving the vice presidency vacant and the Senate without a presiding officer. King, because of his prowess with respect to Senate rules and procedures, had previously held this position from 1836 to 1841. As a moderate, King used his position as presiding officer in the Senate to promote decorum and calmness as tensions increased over the volatile issue of slavery and statehood. He urged Northern senators not to give in to intensifying pressures to introduce anti-slavery petitions. Meanwhile, King was a member of the committee—including Senators Henry Clay and Daniel Webster—that drafted the Compromise of 1850. King's philosophy was that Congress had "about as much constitutional power to prohibit slavery from going into the Territories of the United States as we have power to pass an act carrying slavery there." Although he believed that abolishing slavery in

Figure 13.4. Pierce and King political poster.
Courtesy of the Library of Congress.

the District of Columbia would be unfair to the slaveholders in the adjacent states, he nevertheless supported abolition of the slave trade there. Back in Alabama, King met hostile opposition from a faction of "Southern Rights" secessionists, led by William Lowndes Yancey,[20] who complained that King's voting record better reflected the interests of Massachusetts. King, who was still a Union man, had just as large a group of supporters who applauded his support for compromise, union, and peace. Conceding that Southerners had just cause to complain about the compromise, he nevertheless advised acquiescence and spoke against taking steps that might threaten the Union.[21]

In January 1852, through the efforts of Senator King, the Alabama Democratic convention endorsed the Compromise of 1850. The convention also instructed the state's national convention delegates to support King for either the presidency or vice presidency. At the national convention in Baltimore, the delegates selected Franklin Pierce of New Hampshire as president on the forty-ninth ballot. To appease the Buchanan wing of the party, Pierce's supporters allowed Buchanan's followers to fill the second position on the ticket, knowing full well that they would choose King. Thus, on the second ballot, with little opposition, King was easily nominated as candidate for the vice presidency of the United States after many years in pursuit of this goal. Pierce and King easily defeated the Whig Party ticket of Winfield Scott and William A. Graham in the election of 1852.[22]

However, during this campaign, King, who was developing a bad cough and said to look like a skeleton, was diagnosed with tuberculosis and followed his doctor's advice to seek refuge in a warmer climate. He thus resigned his Senate seat and his position as president pro tempore in December 1852. In resigning his position as president pro tempore, he asked his fellow senators to permit him "to express my grateful acknowledgement for your uniform personal kindness and the general support you have never failed to give me in my efforts to preserve order and enforce parliamentary law." On January 17, 1853, King set sail for the moderate climate of Cuba, via Key West, Florida. After landing in Havana, he moved eastward to Matanzas and settled on a palatial sugar plantation at Ariadne. As the inauguration date approached, King realized that he would not be able to return to Washington in time to take his oath of office as vice president. On March 2, 1853, Congress quickly enacted a bill authorizing the US Consul in Havana to administer the oath of office to King. Thus, King became the first and only executive official of the United States to be sworn in on foreign soil when the oath of US vice president was administered to him by US Counsel William L. Sharkey on March 24, 1853. He was so feeble at the time that he had to be helped to his feet by two American soldiers so that he could have the oath administered to him and so that he could see the beauty of the 300-foot peak overlooking Ariadne plantation where this unique inauguration was being held.[23]

Many newspapers throughout the country carried excerpts from a letter from Cuba describing the inauguration, which was initially published in the New Orleans *Picayune*. One of these was the *Mountain Sentinel* (Ebensburg, Pennsylvania). The letter first emphasized, "For the first time in the history of the Republic, has the man chosen by the people for the second post of honor, taken the oath of office in a foreign land." After describing the beautiful setting for the inauguration, particularly "the clear blue sky of the tropics over our heads," the writer took on the reality of the situation, stating, "His health is very poor, and no one accustomed to seeing patients with pulmonary disease in this climate, but knows he cannot survive very long." The writer further stated, "The old statesman views his coming fate with calmness, as one who has fought the good fight and will lay hold of eternal life."[24]

As time wore on, King's condition worsened until he desperately wanted to return home to Chestnut Hill prior to his death. To facilitate matters, US Counsel Sharkey wrote a letter dated March 26, 1853, to Secretary of State William Marcy regarding King's health: "He is very feeble and thus would seem to be but little ground to hope for a recovery. He proposes to leave the Island on the 6th of April." Thus, King was given the go ahead to set sail for Mobile on the USS *Fulton*. Although not yet home, King needed to rest a few days after the tiring voyage from Cuba to Mobile. After a few nights' rest at the Battle House Hotel in Mobile, King boarded a steamboat to head up the Alabama River to King's Landing. Running full steam ahead, the boat purportedly broke several speed records on the Alabama River. On April 18, 1853, the very next evening after arriving at King's landing, William Rufus King died in the front room of his Chestnut Hill mansion, surrounded by family members and loyal servants. Having never married, he was survived only by his nephew and namesake, Captain William R. King of Dallas County, who was also his adopted son. Captain King was later killed in the Civil War at the Battle of Sharpsburg.[25]

On April 20, 1853, President Franklin Pierce ordered that the work of all governmental departments be suspended "in testimony of respect for eminent station, exalted character, and, higher and above all station, for a career of public service and devotion to this Union which for duration and usefulness is almost without parallel in the history of the Republic." Jefferson Davis, who was then secretary of war, ordered flags to be displayed at half-staff in addition to other methods of honors involving gun salutes and parades of military personnel. A joint committee of the Alabama legislature resolved, "Be It Resolved by the Senate and House of Representatives in General Assembly convened, That while the State of Alabama deplores the death of the Hon. William Rufus King, Vice-President of the United States, she will ever cherish, with emotions of gratitude, his memory as one of her earliest devoted friends and worthiest patriotic sons."[26]

After the departure of icons such as Henry Clay from the Senate, King had become known as "the father of the American Senate." After King's death, it was no surprise that so many of his colleagues eulogized him with praise. Senator Robert M. T. Hunter of Virginia said, "Of all the public men whom I have known, there are none whose lives teach more impressively the great moral of the strength which public virtues gives than that of Colonel King." Senator Edward Everett of Massachusetts praised his service as presiding officer in the Senate: "He possessed an eminent degree, that quickness of perception and promptness of decision, that familiarity with the now somewhat complicated rules of congressional proceedings, and that urbanity of manner, which are required in a presiding officer." Senator Lewis Cass of Michigan also praised King: "While loving the state in which he so long resided, and which had given him so many proofs of confidence and affection, he loved also our common country, and at home and abroad proved himself the true patriot, the able and faithful citizen." Renowned Senator Stephen A. Douglas of Illinois said of his Southern colleague, "For forty-five years he devoted his energies and talents to the performance of arduous public duties—always performing his trust with fidelity and ability, and never failing to command the confidence, admiration and gratitude of an enlightened constituency."[27]

A memorable eulogy for Senator King was delivered by Congressman

Milton S. Latham of California: "He was from principle a States' Rights man; but he did not love the Union less because he loved Alabama more. While he was serving his own State with fidelity and honor, he was not remiss in his duties to the Whole American Confederacy." Congressman Philip Phillips of Alabama said, "A great man has fallen, and it is fit that we mourn him! Dying, as he lived, with a full knowledge of the past, and a just appreciation of the future, may I not indulge in the hope, that the light of his example may long continue to illuminate the path of the future Representatives of the State which holds his remains and cherishes his memory!" Other eulogies were delivered by Senator Thomas Hart Benton of Missouri, Senator John M. Clayton of Delaware, Congressman Sampson Willis Harris of Alabama, Congressman Joseph Chandler of Pennsylvania, Congressman John L. Taylor of Ohio, and Congressman William S. Ashe of North Carolina.[28]

William Rufus King not only was central to the shaping of the Alabama Constitution in 1819, he was perhaps the most preeminent political figure during the state of Alabama's formative years, having served for almost thirty years in the US Senate representing the interests of his fellow Alabamians. Despite all his achievements and service, however, he will forever be remembered for the speculation concerning his private life and the uniqueness of his having been sworn in as vice president on foreign soil just twenty-five days prior to his death. However, not only was King a prominent founder of Alabama who helped shaped its course during its formative years, he was also a voice of reason regarding the ominous clouds on the national horizon who nonetheless would not live to continue his support of the Union.

CONCLUSION

The founders of Alabama were a very resourceful and resolute group of people. Of the fourteen founders featured in this book,[1] eight were born in the commonwealth of Virginia, five of whom migrated to the Broad River region of Georgia before settling in Alabama. Most of these migrated to Alabama with their family in response to the raging "Alabama Fever" to take advantage of the fertile soil to plant cotton, since their own fields were worn out and they wanted to escape a poor economy back home. Of the remainder of these founders, three were born in North Carolina, and one each in Georgia, Pennsylvania, Vermont, and England. Harry Toulmin, the one born in England who was a Dissenting minister, left to escape religious persecution rather than a poor economy.

These Alabama founders were not that far removed in the context of time and generation from the founding fathers of the United States who struggled for their independence from Great Britain. One Alabama founder discussed here fought in the American Revolutionary War, while five were sons of men who fought in that war and one a grandson. Alabama founder LeRoy Pope purportedly served in the colonial army at the age of fifteen during the Revolutionary War. According to one unconfirmed account, he was a courier for General Washington during the Battle of Yorktown in 1780. Henry Hitchcock's grandfather Ethan Allen, along with Benedict Arnold, led the legendary Green Mountain Boys in the capture of Fort Ticonderoga in 1775.

Another four of Alabama's founders fought in the Creek War of 1813–1814. Alabama founder Samuel Dale was seriously wounded at the battle of Burnt Corn Creek, but later he earned the title of the "Daniel Boone of Alabama" for his successful participation in the legendary Canoe Fight. Alabama founder Reuben Saffold fought as a private in the militia at Burnt Corn Creek, along with Sam Dale. Later Saffold was promoted to the rank of lieutenant colonel and given command of a company reconnoitering along the Perdido River. After his service Saffold was promoted again to colonel in the militia of the Mississippi Territory. At the beginning of the war, Clement Comer Clay volunteered as a private in a Madison County Battalion. He was soon promoted to Adjutant of the Regiment and assigned to the frontier south of the Tennessee River to assist in repelling the Indian attacks. Alabama founder General John Coffee fought in the Creek War as General Andrew Jackson's right-hand man, gaining his first fame in the war during the Battle of Tallushatchee. General Jackson was jubilant over Coffee's victory, writing to Governor Blount in Tennessee, "We have retaliated for the destruction of Fort Mims."

Some Alabama founders had already ably served in important positions in other states before arriving in Alabama. For example, Samuel Dale, then living in Georgia, was in the business of contracting to transport families in the Mississippi Territory, including Judge Reuben Saffold's family. Judge Harry Toulmin had served as the president of Transylvania Seminary, as well as the Kentucky secretary of state, before leaving Kentucky for Alabama. LeRoy Pope was appointed one of the commissioners to govern Petersburg, Georgia, in the Broad River region. William Wyatt Bibb, a physician, had served in the Georgia house of representatives and as a senator from Georgia in the US Senate. Befriended by Bishop Francis Asbury, who founded the first Methodist conference in Georgia in 1788, Charles Tait became the rector of the Richmond Academy at Augusta. In 1799, Tait won election as a state senator from Elbert County in the Georgia state senate. In November 1803, Tait was elected as a judge in the superior court of Georgia's Western Judicial Circuit. In 1809, Tait reached the pinnacle of his political career in Georgia when he was elected to represent Georgia in the US Senate. Commencing in 1808, Alabama founder Israel Pickens served in the North Carolina state senate. He later served for three terms in the US House of Representatives before catching "Alabama Fever" and moving to St. Stephens. Another Alabama founder from North Carolina, William Rufus King, was elected to the North Carolina House of Commons in 1808 and then to the US House of Representatives in 1811, where he served along with Israel Pickens. King was reelected for two more terms before resigning and serving as legation secretary under William Pinkney, who had recently been appointed US Minister to Russia.

Nearly all the founders examined in this work held prominent positions after settling in Alabama. Two served as territorial judges, one served in the territorial legislature, one served as secretary of the Alabama Territory, one as Speaker of the House of the Alabama Territorial Legislature, one as governor of the Alabama Territory, one as surveyor general of Public Lands, nine as delegates to the Constitutional Convention of 1819, one as state attorney general, five as governor of Alabama, one as federal judge, four as US senators, one as US congressman, three as chief justice of the Alabama Supreme Court, and one as US vice president. Four others served in the Alabama General Assembly. As to political affiliations, six of these Alabama founders were members of the powerful Broad River Group who dominated the first few years of the territorial and statehood periods, and who played a key role in getting Alabama admitted to the Union. In opposition to this group were founders who had come from North Carolina. They liked to be referred to as the party of the common people, as opposed to the title they placed upon the Georgians—the "Royal Party." The Broad River Group began to gradually lose its dominance after statehood had been obtained.

No matter what political affiliation they may or may not have had, many of Alabama's founders had close ties to national political figures and well-connected dignitaries, including several of America's founding fathers. When Harry Toulmin left England in 1793, he was armed with letters of introduction from Joseph Priestly to Thomas Jefferson and James Madison. Soon after he arrived in America, Toulmin visited Madison at his Virginia home, Montpelier. He later visited with Jefferson and James Monroe. At some point during his early years, John Coffee met and became the loyal friend of future president Andrew Jackson, and remained so until his death. Like a son to Jackson, Coffee was in the mercantile business with Jackson for a while; he married Mary Donelson, the niece of Rachel Jackson (Andrew Jackson's wife); he was Jackson's trusted aide-de-camp during the Creek War of 1813–1814; and he was a fellow investor with Jackson, particularly in the Cypress Land Company, which bought the land on which they established the city of Florence. Members of the Broad River Group from Georgia—particularly William Wyatt Bibb, John W. Williams, and Charles Tait—benefited from the influence of William H. Crawford, who was secretary of the treasury under Presidents Madison and Monroe, and who ran unsuccessfully for president in 1824. William Rufus King obviously had a close relationship with future president James Buchanan, as the two men lived together in a Washington boardinghouse for approximately fifteen years before Buchanan became president.

Alabama's founders were generally reflective of the times in which they lived and were not always without controversy. Like the general population, some owned slaves and most were supportive of the South's "peculiar institution." Nevertheless, two of those who owned slaves eventually emancipated them. In his will, Judge Harry Toulmin made provision for the emancipation of his loyal slave, Tony, directing that he be allowed to go to any state where he could obtain freedom and stating that he felt "towards him almost as one of my family rather than as a slave." Gabriel Moore likewise is believed to have taken his slaves to Cincinnati, where he executed deeds of emancipation for them. After his death, it was revealed that he had fathered a child by one of his slaves and for whom he had executed a deed of manumission on September 27, 1842. Alabama founder Henry Hitchcock acknowledged that slaves added significantly to the profit of the owner, yet he described the institution of slavery as "odious and iniquitous." Hitchcock would come to change his original position that there was nothing that could persuade him to purchase a slave. He justified his change of position on the basis that he, as a lawyer, would only use slaves for domestic work and would not increase their number nor abuse them. Alabama founders John Williams Walker and Charles Tait inherited slaves from their wealthy fathers. During the Panic of 1819, Walker sold some of his slaves to make ends meet. However, Clement Comer Clay's economic situation was such that by 1860 he owned eighty-four slaves.

A few of the Alabama founders examined herein resorted to the Code Duello, which despite being outlawed by the General Assembly was still used to settle differences and to retaliate for insults. As an example, John Coffee participated in a duel with a man who had allegedly made derogatory comments about his long-time friend, Andrew Jackson. Coffee was slightly wounded when his challenger fired prematurely. Before Alabama's first federal judge Charles Tait immigrated to Alabama, he became involved in a nasty dispute among political rivals in Georgia. Eventually, his rival horse-whipped Tait on the streets of Milledgeville, Georgia. Soon after Clement Comer Clay resigned from the Alabama Supreme Court, he got into a dispute that led to a duel with a physician from Limestone County. Both were reportedly injured, with some accounts indicating that Dr. Tate was shot in the leg. There is no record of what specifically was the root of the difficulty between the two. Senator William Rufus King issued a challenge to a duel to none other than Senator Henry Clay, who had criticized the Senate's official printer, Francis P. Blair. Both Clay and King chose seconds and prepared for their duel. Their preparations were interrupted, however, when the Senate sergeant-at-arms arrested both men and turned them over to the civil authorities. This forced the parties to issue apologies to each other in order to bring the matter to a close. Because of an embarrassing divorce granted by the territorial legislature to Speaker of the House Gabriel Moore's wife, Moore resigned as Speaker. Adding insult to injury, Moore later engaged in a duel with his ex-wife's brother, fortunately resulting in no serious injuries to either party. Despite these problems, Moore went on to become a US congressman, a US senator, and Alabama's fifth governor.

Notwithstanding the flaws and shortcomings of Alabama's founders, they were a remarkable and resolute group of people who left their everlasting mark in the founding and the shaping of the state of Alabama. Alabama's bicentennial in 2019 is certainly a great time to learn more about these distinctive individuals.

APPENDIX

Delegates to the Alabama Constitutional Convention of 1819
Listed below are the convention delegates from each of the counties. A brief biographical sketch is included, except for those where little or no biographical information is available in the traditional sources of biographies of Alabama notables, such as Thomas McAdory Owen's *History of Alabama and Dictionary of Alabama Biography* and Willis Brewer's *Alabama: Her History, Resources, War Record, and Public Men, From 1540 to 1872*. Additionally, a search was made of the search tools provided online of by the Alabama Department of Archives and History as well as a general Internet search. In some cases, although Owen and Brewer listed them in their biographies, no information was given except to state that these individuals had served their county at the Constitutional Convention of 1819.

Autauga:
James Jackson (1773–1832). State of birth: Georgia. Member of the state of Alabama House of Representatives, 1820; member of the state of Alabama Senate, 1825.

Baldwin:
Harry Toulmin (1766–1823). Country of birth: England. Federal Judge in Tombigbee District. See Chapter 1 for a detailed biography.

Blount:
Isaac Brown (?–?). Served in the Alabama House of Representatives, representing Blount County in 1819–1820.
John Brown (?–?). State of birth: believed to be South Carolina. Served in the Alabama House of Representatives, representing Blount County in 1819–1820 before Jefferson County was cut off from it. In 1832, he served as the judge of the Jefferson County Court. In 1834, he moved to Tuscaloosa, where he became a steward of the University of Alabama.
Gabriel Hanby (1786–1826). State of birth: Virginia. In 1815 and 1816, represented Surry County in the North Carolina House of Commons. Also, served as a brigadier general in the Alabama militia, attached to the Second Division, Third Brigade, Sixth Regiment, State Militia for Blount County. Served in the Alabama Senate in 1819, representing Blount County. Established a three-story log cabin and inn at a strategic location on the Warrior River near Locust Fork.

Cahawba (now Bibb):
Littlepage Sims (circa 1765–1830). State of birth: Virginia. Member of the

Alabama Territorial legislature and a senator in the Alabama General Assembly in 1819. A surveyor by trade.

Clarke:

Reuben Saffold (1788–1847). State of birth: Georgia. Soldier in Creek Indian War, Member of Territorial Legislature, Chief Justice of the Alabama Supreme Court. See Chapter 11 for a detailed biography.

James Magoffin (1799–1868). State of birth: Pennsylvania. Served in Alabama House of Representatives in 1821. Register of Land Office in St. Stephens for more than thirty years.

Conecuh:

Samuel Cook (1757–1825). State of birth: possibly Kentucky. A veteran of the Revolutionary War and a member of the Mississippi Territorial Legislature. Also, served in the Alabama House of Representatives in 1820.

Cotaco (now Morgan):

Melkijah Vaughn (1797–1871). State of birth: Georgia. A member of the Alabama Territorial General Assembly. Served very briefly in Captain Thomas Eldridge's Company of Mounted Men of the Mississippi Militia. A merchant by trade.

Thomas D. Crabb (1792–1829). State of Birth: Maryland. Served in Alabama Senate in 1822 and 1825.

Dallas:

William Rufus King (1786–1853). State of birth: North Carolina. Congressman from North Carolina, one of Alabama's first US Senators, diplomat, and thirteenth vice president of the United States. See Chapter 13 for a detailed biography.

Franklin:

Richard Ellis (1781–1846). State of birth: Virginia. Served as one of the first associate justices of the Alabama Supreme Court. Later President of Convention of 1836 that declared Texas's independence from Mexico. Served in the Republic of Texas legislature.

William Metcalf (1764–circa 1835). State of birth: Virginia. Served in Alabama Senate in 1819 and 1822.

Lauderdale:

Hugh McVay (1766–1851). State of birth: South Carolina. Served briefly as Alabama's ninth governor when Governor Clement Comer Clay (1835–1837) was appointed to a seat in the US Senate. Since he was Speaker of the House, McVay served as acting governor from July 17, 1837, until November 30, 1837, when Governor Arthur P. Bagby assumed office. McVay served in the Alabama House of Representatives from 1820 to 1825. He then served in the Alabama Senate from 1837 to 1844.

Lawrence:

Arthur Francis Hopkins (1794–1866). State of birth: Virginia. Served as Lawrence County's delegate to the state senate (1822–1824). After practicing law in Huntsville for several years, Hopkins returned to the legislature in 1833, this time as a representative of Madison County. He was elected associate justice of the Alabama Supreme Court in 1836, and in 1837 he was chosen to succeed Henry Hitchcock as chief justice.

Daniel Wright (1759–1838). State of birth: Virginia. Moved to Mississippi shortly after the constitutional convention and was elected a judge of the circuit court in that state.

Limestone:

Thomas Bibb (1783–1839). State of birth: Virginia. The first president of the Alabama Senate. Served as Alabama's second governor, succeeding his brother William Wyatt Bibb, who died in office. See Chapter 5 for a detailed biography.

Beverly Hughes (?–?). Served as a trustee of the Athens Female Academy (only information found for this delegate).

Nicholas Davis (1781–1856). State of birth: Virginia. Served as a US Marshal in Virginia. Served as a captain in the War of 1812. Purportedly he was a political and personal ally of Henry Clay. Twice was a candidate for governor on the Whig ticket, and served as president of the Alabama Senate for five terms.

Madison:

Clement Comer Clay (1789–1866). State of birth: Virginia. Served as first chief justice of the Alabama Supreme Court, US senator, and eighth governor of Alabama. See Chapter 8 for a detailed biography.

John Leigh Townes (1774–1846). State of birth: Virginia. Admitted to Virginia bar in 1806. Served as a captain of a volunteer company during the War of 1812. Served as a legislator in Virginia in 1815. In 1824, he was ordained as a Presbyterian minister.

Dr. Henry Chambers (1790–1826). State of birth: Virginia. Obtained a medical degree from the University of Pennsylvania. Served on General Andrew Jackson's staff as a surgeon during the Creek War of 1813–14. In 1820, Chambers was elected to the Alabama House of Representatives. Chambers, a member of the Broad River Group, ran against Israel Pickens for governor, losing both times. Chambers sought to broaden his political base by serving as an elector for Andrew Jackson in the presidential election of 1824. This strategy proved effective, and in 1825 he defeated incumbent William Kelly in a close vote by the Alabama legislature for a seat in the US Senate. He never took his seat, however, as he died en route to Washington.

Lemuel Mead (?–?). The Mead family was from Virginia. Lemuel Mead served on the Circuit Court of Madison County. His nephew was Lemuel G. Mead, who raised an infantry regiment during the Civil War which fought at Shiloh.

Henry Minor (1783–1839). State of birth: Virginia. Served as a circuit court judge, a supreme court associate justice, and as a reporter of decisions for the

Alabama Supreme Court and as Clerk of the Supreme Court.

Gabriel Moore (circa 1785–1844). State of birth: North Carolina. Served as first Speaker of the House of the Alabama Territorial legislature, elected to represent Alabama in the US Congress, elected as Alabama's fifth governor, and served in the US Senate. See Chapter 12 for a detailed biography.

John Williams Walker (1783–1823). State of birth: Virginia. Served as president of the Constitutional Convention of 1819 and was appointed Alabama's first US Senator. See Chapter 6 for a detailed biography.

John M. Taylor (circa 1788–circa 1860). State of birth: Virginia. Served as circuit court judge and associate justice of the Alabama Supreme Court.

Marengo:

Washington Thompson (?–1824). Died in Greene County in the spring of 1824. Only information found for this delegate.

Marion:

John D. Terrell (1775–1850). State of birth: Virginia. Served as a state senator from Marion County in the first session of the Alabama General Assembly in 1819, and in 1822 served as state representative in the General Assembly, again representing Marion County. He worked as a surveyor of Chickasaw Indian lands in what are now the states of Alabama and Mississippi, as well as served as US Government Chickasaw Indian Agent for the region of the state where these lands were located.

Mobile:

Samuel H. Garrow (1780–1850). Birthplace: France. In the days before Mobile had a mayor, Garrow was the last of what was called the President of Mobile, an office in which he served between 1818 and 1819. Years later, he went on to serve as the fifth mayor of Mobile from 1824 to 1827, and again from 1829 to 1831. He also represented Mobile County in the state senate in 1819 and in the state house in 1820. Also, he served as a captain in the War of 1812.

Monroe:

John Murphy (circa 1785–1841). Birthplace: North Carolina. Served in the first session of the Alabama House of Representatives, was a state senator, served Alabama in the US Congress, and was elected in 1825 and 1827 as Alabama's fourth governor.

John Watkins (circa 1785–1853). State of birth: Virginia. Received a medical degree from the University of Pennsylvania. Purportedly he provided medical care to the victims of the massacre at Fort Mims as he was the only physician in that part of the state. Served in both the Alabama Senate and House of Representatives.

James Pickens (?–?). No information found for this delegate.

Thomas Wiggins (?–?). Served on arrangements committee for the visit of the Marquis de Lafayette to Alabama.

Montgomery:

John Dandridge Bibb (1788–1848). State of birth: Virginia. He was the brother of the first two governors of Alabama, William Wyatt Bibb and Thomas Bibb. In addition to being a planter, he served on the territorial court and later served as state senator from Montgomery County in 1822.

James W. Armstrong (circa 1781–1835). State of birth: South Carolina. Only information found for this delegate.

St. Clair:

David Conner (?–?). Served four terms as a state senator representing St. Clair County (1819–1822).

Shelby:

George Phillips (1769–1835). State of Birth: North Carolina. A physician by trade, he presided as chief justice of the Shelby County Court.

Thomas A. Rodgers (1792–1821). State of birth: Tennessee. Served as secretary of the senate and secretary of state (1819–1821), serving in that capacity at the time of his death in Cahaba.

Tuscaloosa:

Marmaduke Williams (1754–1850). State of birth: North Carolina. Williams was an unsuccessful candidate to be Alabama's first governor, losing to William Wyatt Bibb; he was a member of the Alabama House of Representatives, 1821–1839; and judge of the Tuscaloosa County Court, 1832–1842. His brother was Robert Williams, who had been governor of the Mississippi Territory.

John L. Tindall (1784–1864). State of birth: Georgia. A member of the building committee in charge of the construction of the state capitol building, a member of the state House of Representatives, president of the State of Alabama Bank, and a practicing physician.

Washington:

Israel Pickens (1780–1827). State of birth: North Carolina. President of the Bank of Tombecbe; Alabama's third governor. See Chapter 10 for a detailed biography.

Henry Hitchcock (1792–1839). State of birth: Vermont. Served as secretary of the Alabama Territory, Alabama's first attorney general, and chief justice of the Alabama Supreme Court. See Chapter 9 for a detailed biography.

NOTES

Introduction

1. R. B. Bernstein, *The Founding Fathers Reconsidered* (Oxford: Oxford University Press, 2009).

2. This term will be utilized herein, along with the term "Georgia faction" or "Georgians," to refer to this group.

3. In addition to the extensive biographies of the above key founders of the state, there is an appendix containing very brief biographies of most of the delegates to the Alabama Constitutional Convention of 1819.

4. The Tombigbee District, also known as the Bigbee settlements, was in what is now southwest Alabama near the forks of the Tombigbee and Alabama Rivers.

5. J. Mills Thornton III referred to Toulmin as "Czar of the Tombigbee District." Thornton, *Politics and Power in a Slave Society* (Baton Rouge: Louisiana State University Press, 1978), 7.

6. *The Creek War of 1813–1814.*

7. Edward Chambers Betts, *Early History of Huntsville Alabama, 1804–1870*, rev. ed. (Montgomery: The Brown Printing Co., 1916), 23.

8. Moore's political career, however, was far from over, as he served as a delegate to the constitutional convention, and was elected to the state senate, the US Congress, the governorship, and the US Senate.

9. In addition to serving in the Constitutional Convention of 1819, William Rufus King served for many years in the US Senate and very briefly served as the thirteenth vice president before his death twenty-five days after being sworn in.

10. James Benson Sellers, *Slavery in Alabama* (Tuscaloosa: University of Alabama Press, 1950), 232, quoting from *Martin v. Reed*, 37 *Alabama* 198.

11. So-called free persons of color, although free, were still second-class citizens without the right to vote and with many constraints placed upon them. Many of these constraints were related to their interaction with those still under bondage. The Alabama Constitution of 1819 authorized the General Assembly to provide for slaves by requiring owners to treat them "with humanity, to provide for them necessary food and clothing, to abstain from all injuries to them extending to life or limb, and, in case of their neglect, or refusal to comply with the directions of such laws, to have such slave or slaves sold for the benefit of the owner or owners." Ala. Const. of 1819, Art. VI.

Chapter 1

1. Charles D. Lowery, "The Great Migration to the Mississippi Territory,

1798–1819," *Journal of Mississippi History* (August 1968): 175–79; Herbert James Lewis, *Clearing the Thickets: A History of Antebellum Alabama (New Orleans: Quid Pro Books)*, 45.

2. James F. Doster, "Early Settlers on the Tombigbee and Tensaw Rivers," *Alabama Review* 12 (April 1959): 84–85; Robert Haynes, "Early Washington County, Alabama," *Alabama Review* 20 (July 1965): 183–87; Albert B. Moore, *History of Alabama*, 1934, Reprint (Tuscaloosa: Alabama Book Store, 1951), 67.

3. Haynes, "Early Washington County," 31; Theodore Bowling Pearson, "Early Settlement around McIntosh Bluff: Alabama's First County Seat," *Alabama Review* 20 (October 1978): 243; Lewis, *Clearing the Thickets*, 59.

4. Jacqueline Anderson Matte, *The History of Washington County First County in Alabama* (Chatom, AL: Washington County Historical Society, 1982), 22–23; Haynes, "Early Washington County," 32–33; Alan V. Briceland, "Ephraim Kirby, Mr. Jefferson's Emissary on the Tombigbee-Mobile Frontier in 1804," *Alabama Review* 24 (April 1971): 89–90.

5. Briceland, "Ephraim Kirby," 83–98; Lewis, *Clearing the Thickets*, 60–62.

6. Lewis, *Clearing the Thickets*, 62–63; Briceland, "Ephraim Kirby," 104–13.

7. "To Thomas Jefferson from Rodominick H. Gilmer, 8 November 1804," Founders Online, National Archives (http://founders.archives.gov/documents/Jefferson/99-01-02-0611 [last update: March 20, 2015]). This is an Early Access document from *The Papers of Thomas Jefferson*. It is not an authoritative final version. "To James Madison from Harry Toulmin, 1 May 1804 (Abstract)," Founders Online, National Archives (http://founders.archives.gov/documents/Madison/02-07-02-0142 [last update: March 20, 2015]). *The Papers of James Madison*, Secretary of State Series, vol. 7, April 2–August 31, 1804, ed. David B. Mattern, J. C. A. Stagg, Ellen J. Barber, Anne Mandeville Colony, Angela Kreider, and Jeanne Kerr Cross (Charlottesville: University of Virginia Press, 2005), 128–29. See Briceland, "Ephraim Kirby," 110–13.

8. English Dissenters were Christians who separated themselves from the Church of England during the sixteenth through eighteenth centuries. They abhorred state interference with religion and founded their own churches and established their own communities. Many Dissenters, including Harry Toulmin, migrated to America.

9. From the biography of Harry Toulmin written by Clara Keyes in the Dictionary of Unitarian and Universalist Biography, an online resource of the Unitarian Universalist History & Heritage Society. Keyes, "Harry Toulmin," http://uudb.org/articles/harrytoulmin.html (last accessed October 23, 2016).

10. Keyes, "Harry Toulmin"; Paul M. Pruitt Jr., *Taming Alabama: Lawyers and Reformers, 1804–1929* (Tuscaloosa: University of Alabama Press, 2010), 2.

11. Keyes, "Harry Toulmin."

12. Marion Tinling and Godfrey Davies, eds., *The Western Country in*

1793: Reports on Kentucky and Virginia by Harry Toulmin (San Marino, CA: 1948), vii, xv, 3; "Comments on America and Kentucky, 1793–1802," *Register of the Kentucky Historical Society* 47 [1949]: 9.

13. Pruitt, *Taming Alabama*, 3. When Transylvania Seminary was first established in 1780, Kentucky was still part of Virginia. Time Line, Transylvania University (http://www.transy.edu/about/timeline.htm?mi=history; accessed May 29, 2015).

14. Pruitt, *Taming Alabama*, 3.

15. Ibid.; Keyes, "Harry Toulmin."

16. Pruitt, *Taming Alabama*, 3–4; Lewis, *Clearing the Thickets*, 63.

17. "To James Madison from Harry Toulmin, 1 May 1804 (Abstract)," Founders Online, National Archives; "To James Madison from Caleb Wallace, 20 April 1804 (Abstract)," Founders Online, National Archives, http://founders.archives.gov/documents/Madison/02-07-02-0087 (last update: March 20, 2015). Source: *The Papers of James Madison, Secretary of State Series*, vol. 7, 2 April–31 August 1804, 92–93; Robert V. Haynes, *The Mississippi Territory and the Southwest Frontier, 1795–1817* (Lexington: University Press of Kentucky, 2010), 264.

18. According to Jefferson's list of appointments, Toulmin also had been "appointed Receiver of public monies for Lands at Hobuhentoopa or St Stephens —dated 5 Octr." "List of Appointments, with Jefferson's Notes, 9 November 1804," Founders Online, National Archives, http://founders.archives.gov/documents/Jefferson/99-01-02-0614 (last update: March 20, 2015). This is an Early Access document from *The Papers of Thomas Jefferson*. It is not an authoritative final version.

19. Pruitt, *Taming Alabama*, 5.

20. "To James Madison from Harry Toulmin, 5 November 1804," Founders Online, National Archives, http://founders.archives.gov/documents/Madison/02-08-02-0262 (last update: 2015-03-20). *The Papers of James Madison*, Secretary of State Series, vol. 8, September 1, 1804–January 31, 1805, and supplement 1776–June 23, 1804, ed. Mary A. Hackett, J. C. A. Stagg, Mary Parke Johnson, Anne Mandeville Colony, Angela Kreider, Jeanne Kerr Cross, and Wendy Ellen Perry (Charlottesville: University of Virginia Press, 2007), 259–60.

21. Pruitt, *Taming Alabama*, 5; Thomas McAdory Owen, *History of Alabama and Dictionary of Alabama Biography* (Chicago: S. J. Publishing Company, 1921), 676.

22. Appendix, "Mississippi Territorial Register of Appointments, Civil and Military. 1805–1817," cited in Matte, *History of Washington County*, 29; Pruitt, *Taming Alabama*, 5–6; "Portrait of Judge Toulmin Presented," *Alabama Lawyer* (April 1950): 157; Owen, *History of Alabama*, 676; Dunbar Roland, ed., *Courts, Judges, and Lawyers of Mississippi*, 1798–1935 (Jackson: State Department of Archives and History and the Mississippi Historical Society, 1935), 21; John D. W. Guice, "The Cement of Society: Law in the Mississippi Territory," *Gulf Coast Historical Review* 1 (Spring 1986): 84–85.

23. Doster, "Early Settlers," 89.

24. Lewis, *Clearing the Thickets*, 65; Briceland, "Ephraim Kirby," 92–98. Kirby had earlier said of the frontier settlers that they were "generally without integrity, morality, industry or any other good quality."

25. Lewis, *Clearing the Thickets*, 65–66; Larry Lewis, *Slave Narratives: A Folk History of Slavery*, Volume 1, *Alabama Narratives* (1938; reprint, Phnom Penh, Cambodia: Keith W. Brooks Publishing, 2013), 247. In an interview conducted in 1884, Tony indicated that he knew Andrew Jackson and had seen George Washington. As to Jackson, he explained that he accompanied General Jackson as a waggoner when the general led his forces from Mobile to Pensacola in 1814. He also claimed to have witnessed a shell exploding near Jackson during the battle. Tony probably had been loaned by Judge Toulmin to the American Army. As for General Washington, he said he saw him when he delivered an address on a visit to Frankfort, Kentucky, where Harry Toulmin and Tony were living at the time.

26. Pruitt, *Taming Alabama*, 6.

27. Ibid., 7–8; Keyes, "Harry Toulmin"; Thomas Perkins Abernethy, "Aaron Burr in Mississippi," *Journal of Southern History* 15 (February 1949): 15.

28. Abernethy, "Aaron Burr in Mississippi," 9–11.

29. Ibid., 11–12, 16–18; Stuart O. Stumpf, ed., "The Arrest of Aaron Burr: A Documentary Record," *Alabama Historical Quarterly* 42 (Fall and Winter 1980): 113–23; Roger G. Kennedy, *Burr, Hamilton, and Jefferson: A Study in Character* (New York: Oxford University Press, 2000), 328, 333–38; William Baskerville Hamilton, *Anglo-American on the Frontier: Thomas Rodney and His Territorial Cases* (Durham, NC: Duke University Press, 1953); Albert James Pickett, *History of Alabama, and Incidentally of Georgia and Mississippi, from the Earliest Period* (1851; reprint, Birmingham, AL: Birmingham Book and Magazine Co., 1962), 490–94.

30. Lewis, *Clearing the Thickets*, 66–67; Pruitt, *Taming Alabama,* 8; Harry Toulmin to Secretary of State, July 6, 1805, "General Correspondence, 1795–1815," *Mississippi Territorial Transcripts*, 58-A.

31. Robert V. Haynes, "Law Enforcement in Frontier History," *Journal of Mississippi History* 22 (January 1960) 35; Matte, *History of Washington County*, 33; Pruitt, *Taming Alabama*, 33; Isaac J. Cox, *The West Florida Controversy, 1798–1813: A Study in American Diplomacy* (Baltimore: Johns Hopkins University Press, 1918), 176–87.

32. Pruitt, *Taming Alabama*, 8–9; Lewis, *Clearing the Thickets*, 67–68.

33. Leland L. Lengel, "The Road to Fort Mims: Judge Harry Toulmin's Observations on the Creek War, 1811–1813," *Alabama Review* 29 (January 1976): 18–21; Gary Burton, "Pintlala's Cold Murder Case: The Death of Thomas Meredith in 1812," *Alabama Review* 63 (July 2010): 163–91; "Crawley Deposition," in *Correspondence of Andrew Jackson*, ed. John Spencer Bassett (Washington, DC: Carnegie Institution, 1926–1935), 1:225–26n.1.

34. A little over two weeks later, on July 23, 1813, Toulmin, who was at Fort Stoddert, wrote to Brigadier General Ferdinand Claiborne, who was

on the road from Baton Rouge. In this letter Toulmin discusses an uprising of Creek Indians in Pensacola. He said that there were even reports that they planned to assassinate several of their own chiefs. There were further reports that the Creeks were preparing to attack white settlers in Alabama, so Toulmin urged General Claiborne to get there quickly, saying, "I pray you to hasten your approach. Should our militia be defeated; our settlement will probably fall a sacrifice." Toulmin to Claiborne, Harry Toulmin Letters, SPR234, Folder 2, Alabama Department of Archives and History (henceforth ADAH), Montgomery, Alabama.

35. Lengel, "Road to Fort Mims," 26–32; Eron Rowland, *Mississippi Territory in the War of 1812* (1921; reprint, Baltimore: Genealogical Publishing Company, 1968), 31; Henry Halbert and T. J. Ball, *The Creek War of 1813 and 1814* (1895; reprint, Tuscaloosa: University of Alabama Press, 1995), 279.

36. Malcom Cook McMillan, *Constitutional Development in Alabama, 1798–1901: A Study in Politics, the Negro, and Sectionalism* (Chapel Hill: University of North Carolina Press, 1955), 19–22; Richard A. McLemore, "Division of the Mississippi Territory," *Journal of Mississippi History* 5 (1943): 79–82; Moore, *History of Alabama*, 93–95.

37. McMillan, *Constitutional Development in Alabama*, 20–22; McLemore, "Division of the Mississippi Territory," 81; Moore, *History of Alabama*, 95.

38. McLemore, "Division of the Mississippi Territory," 82; McMillan, *Constitutional Development in Alabama*, 23–24; *U.S. Statutes at Large*, volume 3, 371–73.

39. Pruitt, *Taming Alabama*, 11.

40. Ibid., 12.

41. Thornton dubbed Toulmin the "Czar of the Tombigbee District."

42. Ibid.

43. Lewis, *Clearing the Thickets*, 76.

Chapter 2

1. J. F. H. Claiborne, *Life and Times of Gen. Sam. Dale, the Mississippi Partisan* (New York: Harper & Brothers Publishers, 1860), 15–16.

2. Samuel Dale's biographer, J. F. H. Claiborne, along with two others, personally interviewed Dale and put his thoughts to paper. To what extent their notes from the interview are accurate is not known, but they are purported to come straight from the source.

3. Claiborne, *Life and Times of Gen. Sam. Dale*, 25–28, 31.

4. Ibid., 36–44.

5. Herbert J. "Jim" Lewis, "Samuel Dale," *Encyclopedia of Alabama* http://www.encyclopediaofalabama.org/article/h-2460 (accessed June 15, 2015); Claiborne, *Life and Times of Gen. Sam. Dale*, 44–49.

6. Claiborne, *Life and Times of Gen. Sam. Dale*, 50–55.

7. Ibid., 50–56. Regarding Tecumseh's statement—"Slay the women and children!"—it is asserted in H. S. Halbert and T. H. Ball's work on the

Creek War that such statement was in error, because "at no period in his life, in none of his war speeches, did Tecumseh ever give vent to such a sentiment." Halbert and Ball, *The Creek War*, 50. It also appears that Agent Hawkins thought there was a more peaceful tone to the speech in which Tecumseh told the audience not to harm Americans. Benjamin W. Griffith Jr., *McIntosh and Weatherford: Creek Indian Leaders* (Tuscaloosa: University of Alabama Press, 1988), 75–76n.25.

8. Dale reported such to Agent Hawkins, but Hawkins was convinced that the Creeks were only fighting each other in a civil war with Peter Mc-Queen leading the traditionalists and Big Warrior leading the accommodationists. Claiborne, *Life and Times of Gen. Sam. Dale*, 65–72.

9. Ibid., 68–71.

10. Pickett, *History of Alabama*, 521–25; Claiborne, *Life and Times of Gen. Sam. Dale*, 72–77.

11. It was here that Dale would be when Creeks led by William Weatherford attacked Fort Mims on August 30, 1813.

12. Lewis, "Samuel Dale," *Encyclopedia of Alabama*; Claiborne, *Life and Times of Gen. Sam. Dale*, 84.

13. Two of the warriors had jumped out of the canoe when it was first fired upon from the shore. Claiborne, *Life and Times of Gen. Sam. Dale*, 122.

14. Pickett, *History of Alabama*, 561–65; Claiborne, *Life and Times of Gen. Sam. Dale*, 122–26. Jerimiah Austill's account of the Canoe Fight can be found in the *Alabama Historical Quarterly* 6, no. 1 (Spring 1944).

15. Lewis, *Clearing the Thickets*, 92; Joel Campbell Du Bose, *Sketches of Alabama History* (Philadelphia: Eldridge and Brothers, 1901), 47.

16. Frank Lawrence Owsley Jr., *Struggle for the Gulf Borderlands: The Creek War and the Battle of New Orleans* (Gainesville: University Press of Florida, 1981), 47.

17. Gregory A. Waselkov, *A Conquering Spirit: Fort Mims and the Red Stick War of 1813–1814* (Tuscaloosa: University of Alabama Press, 2006), 164–65; Griffith Jr., *McIntosh and Weatherford*, 127–31; Halbert and Ball, *Creek War*, 244–46, 249–56.

18. Claiborne, *Life and Times of Gen. Sam. Dale*, 140–42.

19. Ibid., 150–52.

20. Ibid., 168–71; Dale to Governor William Wyatt Bibb, September 23, 1818, *Creek War Military Records Collection*, SPR359, ADAH, Montgomery, Alabama.

21. William H. Brantley, *Three Capitals, A Book about the First Three Capitals: St. Stephens, Huntsville & Cahawba, 1818–26* (1947; reprint, Tuscaloosa: University of Alabama Press, 1976), 101–2, 116–17, 134; *Ala. Acts* (1821), 53, 60–61, 115–16; *Ala. Acts* (1822), 138; *Ala. Acts* (1823), 115; *Dale vs. the Governor*, 3 Stewart 387.

22. Claiborne, *Life and Times of Gen. Sam. Dale*, 171–72; Herbert J. Lewis, "Lafayette's Visit to Alabama," *Encyclopedia of Alabama*, http://www.encyclopediaofalabama.org/article/h-2152 (accessed June 22, 2015).

23. Richelle Putnam, *Lauderdale County, Mississippi: A Brief History* (Charleston, SC: History Press, 2011), 21; Claiborne, *Life and Times of Gen. Sam. Dale*, 173–76.

24. Claiborne, *Life and Times of Gen. Sam. Dale*, 177–78, 212.

25. *http://thecoleplantation.blogspot.com/p/sam-dale-daleville-ms.html*.

26. Ibid., 232.

27. Lewis, "Samuel Dale," *Encyclopedia of Alabama*.

Chapter 3

1. Jerry Coffee, "Coffees of Gravesend, Kent," Roots Web, http://archiver.rootsweb.ancestry.com/th/read/COFFEE/2009-07/1247520022 (accessed June 24, 2015); Herbert J. (Jim) Lewis, "John Coffee," *Encyclopedia of Alabama*, http://www.encyclopediaofalabama.org/article/h-3041 (accessed June 24, 2015); Paulin Wilcox Burke, *Emily Donelson of Tennessee* (Knoxville: University of Tennessee Press, 2001), 56.

2. Jan Grant, transcriber, "Letters of John Coffee," *Tennessee Historical Magazine* 2 (December 1916); online version, http://genealogytrails.com/ala/history_jcoffee1.html (accessed June 24, 2015).

3. Ibid.

4. Mark R. Cheatham, *Andrew Jackson, Southerner* (Baton Rouge: Louisiana State University Press, 2013), 42. Coffee was later with Jackson when he fought in a Nashville street brawl against the Benton brothers, Jesse and Thomas Hart Benton. There Jackson took a bullet that nearly cost him an arm. If it had not been for Coffee's charge in Jackson's defense, the Bentons would have probably killed Jackson. Marquis James, *The Life of Andrew Jackson* (New York: Bobbs-Merrill Company, 1938).

5. James, *Life of Andrew Jackson*, 39–42; Grant, "Letters of John Coffee."

6. Grant, "Letters of John Coffee."

7. Waselkov, *Conquering Spirit*, 153; 163; Griffith Jr., *McIntosh and Weatherford*, 111–13.

8. John Coffee to Mary Coffee, from Camp Batey near Huntsville [undated], "Letters of John Coffee."

9. Mrs. Crawley was Martha Crawley, who was kidnapped in May 1813 by a party of Creek Indians returning from a visit with Tecumseh and the Shawnees. Mrs. Crawley was taken to several Creek towns as a hostage and was held in captivity in Black Warriors Town for several months. She eventually was able to escape. Herbert James Lewis, *Lost Capitals of Alabama* (Charleston, SC: History Press, 2014), 101; Griffith Jr., *McIntosh and Weatherford*, 81–82.

10. Crockett was known in his lifetime as "David." "Davy" was a name attributed to him by writers and the 1950s Hollywood producers.

11. John Coffee to Mary Coffee, from Headquarters 24 miles south from Ditto's Landing, October 24, 1813, "Letters of John Coffee"; Lewis, *Lost Capitals*, 101–2.

12. John Buchanan, *Jackson's Way: Andrew Jackson and the People of the*

Western Waters (Edison, NJ: Castle Books, 2005), 235–37; John Coffee to Mary Coffee from Ten Islands, Coosey [*sic*] River, November 4, 1813, in Grant, "Letters of John Coffee"; Lewis, "John Coffee," *Encyclopedia of Alabama*.

13. Griffith Jr., *McIntosh and Weatherford*, 119–22; Buchanan, *Jackson's Way*, 235–38, 241; Walter R. Borneman, *1812: The War That Forged a Nation* (New York: HarperCollins Publishers, 2004), 146–48.

14. Owsley, *Struggle for the Gulf Borderlands*, 68–73, 75–76; Pickett, *Alabama*, 579–87; Buchanan, *Jackson's Way*; Griffith, *McIntosh and Weatherford*, 138–43.

15. Griffith Jr., *McIntosh and Weatherford*, 144–48; Owsley, *Struggle for the Gulf Borderlands*, 79–81.

16. Lewis, *Clearing the Thickets*, 101–4.

17. Anne Royall, considered by some as the first female journalist in America, was visiting Huntsville at this time and was duly impressed with General Coffee: "General Coffee is upwards of six feet in height and proportionally made. Nor did I ever see so fine a figure. He is 35 or 36 of age. His face is round and full and features handsome. His complexion is ruddy, though sunburnt. His hair and eyes black, and a soft serenity diffuses his countenance." Nancy Rohr, "Jackson's Victorious Return to Huntsville: One Fine Day," *Huntsville Historical Review* 27 (Summer-Fall 2000): 12–13.

18. Ibid., 1, 17–20.

19. Fredriksen Johnson, *American Military Leaders: A-L* vol. 2 (Santa Barbara, CA: ABC-CLIO, 1999), 161.

20. Burke, *Emily Donelson*, 161. In January 1818, Anne Royall met General John Coffee, describing him this time in her journal as "upwards of six feet in height, and proportionally made." She went on to say that she had not ever seen "so fine a figure." At that time, Coffee was 35 or 36 years with "features handsome." She described his complexion as "ruddy, though sunburnt." She indicated that she had expected "to see a stern, haughty, fierce, warrior," but saw "no such thing." Instead, he was as "mild as the dew drop, but deep in his soul you see very plain that deliberate, firm, cool, and manly courage, which has covered him with glory."

21. Ibid., 50. Anne Royall, *Letters from Alabama on Various Subjects* (Washington, DC: 1830), 45.

22. In a letter to his fellow commissioners responsible "for marking the boundary lines of the ter. ceded by the Creek nation," Coffee admonishes them for being negligent in responding to his suggestions for the survey. He also mentions discussions with leaders of the Indian nations and Gen. Andrew Jackson's order for a volunteer guard to protect the surveyors while the lines are marked. Coffee to Commissioners, February 14, 1816, John Coffee Papers, LPR27, Box 1, ADAH, Montgomery, Alabama.

23. Lewis, "John Coffee," *Encyclopedia of Alabama*; Hugh C. Bailey, *John Williams Walker: A Study in the Political, Social, and Cultural Life of the Old Southwest* (Tuscaloosa: University of Alabama Press, 1964), 76–77.

24. Thomas Perkins Abernethy, *From Frontier to Plantation in Tennessee—A Study in Frontier Democracy* (Chapel Hill: University of North Carolina Press, 1932), 271–72; James, *The Life of Andrew Jackson*, 277; Burke, *Emily Donelson*, 56.

25. John Coffee Papers, 1818–1831, SPR709, ADAH, Montgomery, Alabama.

26. Lewis, "John Coffee," *Encyclopedia of Alabama*.

27. Jon Meacham, *American Lion: Andrew Jackson in the White House* (New York: Random House, 2008), 6–7.

28. Greg O'Brien, "Treaty of Dancing Rabbit Creek (1830)," *Encyclopedia of Alabama* http://www.encyclopediaofalabama.org/article/h-3426 (accessed July 5, 2015), 161; "Levi Colbert to President Andrew Jackson, 22 Nov. 1832," Chickasaw Letters—1832, Chickasaw Historical Research Website (Kerry M. Armstrong) (accessed 12 December 2011).

29. Johnson, *American Military Leaders: A-L*. vol. 2 (Santa Barbara, CA: ABC-CLIO, 1999); James, *The Life of Andrew Jackson*, 408.

Chapter 4

1. Thornton, *Politics and Power in a Slave Society*; J. Mills Thornton III, "Broad River Group," *Encyclopedia of Alabama*, http://www.encyclopediaofalabama.org/article/h-1137.

2. Hugh C. Bailey, "The Petersburgh Youth of John Williams Walker," *Georgia Historical Quarterly* 43 (June 1959): 123–24.

3. Ibid.; Thornton, *Politics and Power*, 7–9.

4. Bailey, *John Williams Walker*; Daniel S. Dupre, *Transforming the Cotton Frontier* (Baton Rouge: Louisiana State University Press, 1997), 25.

5. Owen, *History of Alabama and Dictionary of Alabama Biography*, 1374–74; Hugh C. Bailey, "John W. Walker and the 'Georgia Machine' in Early Alabama Politics," *Alabama Review* 8 (July 1955): 179, 181; Bailey, *John Williams Walker*, 31, 68.

6. Thornton, *Politics and Power*, 7–9; Bailey, *John Williams Walker*, 68–69, 71–72; Dupre, *Transforming the Cotton Frontier*, 29.

7. Others believe that LeRoy Pope was merely an admirer of the English poet but of no relation.

8. Betts, *Early History of Huntsville*, 23; Dupre, *Transforming the Cotton Frontier*, 37; *Statutes of Mississippi Territory* (1816), 98, 14–15; Frank Alex Luttrell III, ed., *Historical Markers of Madison County* (Huntsville-Madison County Historical Society, 50th Anniversary, 1951–2001), 3.

9. Betts, *Early History of Huntsville*, 23; *Statutes of Mississippi Territory* (1816), 177–78, cited in Betts, *Early History of Huntsville*, 14, 19–21.

10. Bailey, *John Williams Walker*, 68–72; Dupre, *Transforming the Cotton Frontier*, 30, 37; Rohr, "Jackson's Victorious Return," 1, 17–20.

11. Anne Newport Royall, *Sketches of History, Life, and Manners in the United States* (New Haven, CT: np, 1826; reprint, New York: Johnson, 1970), 14; Royall, *Letters from Alabama 1817–1822*, ed. Lucille Griffith (Tuscaloosa:

University of Alabama Press, 1969), 246.

12. Betts, *Early History of Huntsville*, 32; Dupre, *Transforming the Cotton Frontier*, 80.

13. Dupre, *Transforming the Cotton Frontier*, 84, 89.

14. Owen, *Dictionary of Alabama Biography*, 1374–75; Betts, *Early History of Huntsville*, 34, 66–69.

15. Betts, *Early History of Huntsville*, 77–78; Rohr, "Jackson's Victorious Return," 3, citing Royall, *Letters*, 286.

16. His tombstone says he died in 1845. Thomas Owen gives a date of June 17, 1844, as Pope's date of death. Owen, *Dictionary of Alabama Biography*, 1374–75; Jonathan D. White, "LeRoy Pope Walker," *Encyclopedia of Alabama*, http://www.encyclopediaofalabama.org/article/h-1854 (accessed July 18, 2015).

Chapter 5

1. George R. Gilmer, *Sketches of the First Settlers of Upper Georgia, of the Cherokees, and the Author* (1855; reprint, Baltimore: Genealogical Publishing Co., 1965), 84–85; Daniel S. Dupre, "William Wyatt Bibb (1819–20)," *Encyclopedia of Alabama*, http://www.encyclopediaofalabama.org/article/h-1416 (accessed July 19, 2015).

2. Gilmer, *Sketches of the First Settlers of Upper Georgia*, 84–85; Bailey, *John Williams Walker*, 39.

3. Lewis, *Clearing the Thickets*, 113; Gilmer, *Sketches of the First Settlers of Upper Georgia*, 84–85.

4. Charles Edgeworth Jones, "Governor William Wyatt Bibb," *Transactions of the Alabama Historical Society* 3 (1898–99): 128–30; Dupre, "William Wyatt Bibb," *Encyclopedia of Alabama*; *Guide to Congress,* 7th ed. (Washington, DC: Congressional Quarterly Press, 2013), 920.

5. McMillan, *Constitutional Development in Alabama*, 24; Thornton, *Politics and Power*, 10–11; Thomas Perkins Abernethy, *The Formative Period in Alabama, 1815–1828* (Tuscaloosa: University of Alabama Press, 1995), 38, reprinted from Alabama State Department of Archives and History (Montgomery: Historical and Patriotic Series, no. 6), 1922; Bailey, *John Williams Walker*, 87.

6. Brantley, *Three Capitals*, 24–25, 229.

7. *Journal of the Legislative Council of the Alabama Territory at the First Session of the General Assembly in the Forty-third Year of American Independence* (St. Stephens, AL: Thomas Eaton, 1818), 1–12.

8. *Acts Passed at the First Session of the First General Assembly of the Alabama Territory in the Forty-second Year of American Independence* (St. Stephens, AL: Thomas Eaton, 1818), 3–116.

9. Bailey, *John Williams Walker*, 83–86.

10. *Journal of the House of Representatives of the Alabama Territory at the Second Session of the First General Assembly in the Forty-third Year of American Independence* (St. Stephens, AL: Thomas Eaton, 1818), 38.

11. Dupre, "William Wyatt Bibb"; Gilmer, "Sketches of the Settlers of Upper Georgia," 86.

12. Brantley, *Three Capitals*, 27, 31–39.

13. Ibid., 27, 31; William Wyatt Bibb (Coosada) to Senator Charles Tait, September 19, 1818, Tait Family Papers, ADAH, Montgomery, Alabama. In this same letter, Bibb complains, "As usual my private interests have been completely sacrificed. My overseer has been drunk most of his time." Bibb further asserts that the overseers' neglect in tending to his crops caused him to lose between $10,000 and $20,000.

14. Bailey, *John Williams Walker*, 88–91, 8–9; Brantley, *Three Capitals*, 27, 31–39. The apportionment bill was based upon white population and almost assured north Alabama of control of the General Assembly. Samuel Earle Hobbs, "The History of Early Cahaba, Alabama's First State Capital," *Alabama Historical Quarterly* 31 (Fall-Winter 1969): 155–63.

15. *Ala. Acts* (2 Sess. 1818), 46–49. As Secretary of the US Treasury, William H. Crawford presided over the General Land Office, which was responsible for the surveying, platting, and sale of public lands. He had established a land office at Milledgeville, Georgia, in 1816, some 150 miles away from the choice Creek cession lands, to make it difficult for the squatters who had already arrived in the area to purchase the land they had already begun to cultivate. Many of these squatters were too poor to travel such a distance to compete against wealthy planters at a public auction. Steven P. Brown, *John McKinley and the Antebellum Court: Circuit Riding in the Old Southwest* (Tuscaloosa: University of Alabama Press, 2012), 40.

16. Dupre, "William Wyatt Bibb," *Encyclopedia of Alabama*; Brantley, *Three Capitals*, 47, 230–31; Lewis, *Clearing the Thickets*, 144.

17. McMillan, *Constitutional Development in Alabama*, 38, 44–45; *Ala. Const.* Art. IV, Secs. 14, 23; Art. V, Secs., 2, 24; Lewis, *Clearing the Thickets*, 137–38.

18. Journal of the House of Representatives of the General Assembly (Cahawba, AL: Press Office, 1820), 8–16, hereinafter *Ala. House Journal* (1812); Bibb to Charles Tait, July 14, 1819, Tait Family Papers.

19. Bibb to Tait, April 15, 1820, Tait Family Papers.

20. Ibid.; Lewis, *Clearing the Thickets*, 162–63.

21. Brantley, *Three Capitals*, 71–72 (quoting, in part, *Eulogium in Commemoration of His Excellency, William W. Bibb, late Governor of the State of Alabama*, 9–10); *Journal of the Senate at the Second Session of the General Assembly of the State of Alabama* (Cahawba, AL: Allen and Drichell, 1819), cited hereafter as *Ala. Senate Journal* (1820); *Ala. Acts (1820)*, 63.

22. Dupre, "Thomas Bibb," http://huntsvillehistorycollection.org/hh/index.php?title=Person:Thomas_Bibb.

23. Dupre, *Transforming the Cotton Frontier*, 36–37.

24. Lewis, *Clearing the Thickets*, 123–24.

25. *Statues of Mississippi Territory* (1816), 177–78, cited in Betts, *Early*

History of Huntsville, 14, 19–21; *Ala. Const. 1819*, Art. IV, Sec. 18.

26.*Ala. Senate Journal* (1820), 10–11; Brantley, *Three Capitals*, 82.

27. Dupre, "Thomas Bibb"; *Huntsville History Collection*; Robert Sobel and John Raimo, eds., *Biographical Directory of the Governors of the United States, 1789–1978*, vol. 1 (Westport, CT: Meckler Books, 1978).

28. Brantley, *Three Capitals*, 83–85.

29. *Journal of the Senate at the Called Session of the General Assembly of the State of Alabama, 1821* (Cahawba: Allen and Brickell, 1821).

30. Brantley, *Three Capitals*, 84–87; *Ala. House Journal (Called Sess., 1821)* 59–61.

31. *Ala. House Journal* (1821), 11–15.

32. Ibid., 18–19.

33. Dupre, "Thomas Bibb"; *Huntsville History Collection*; Donna R. Causey, "Beautiful Bibb Mansions, Truth Versus Fiction," http://alabamapioneers.com/beautiful-bibb-mansions-truth-versus-fiction/#sthash.8o3F1pab.dpu (accessed August 14, 2015); Kelly Kazek, "Unincorporated town of Belle Mina, Population 68, Settled by State's 2nd Governor (Odd Travels)," http://www.al.com/living/index.ssf/2013/05/unincorporated_town_of_belle_m.html (accessed August 14, 2015); "300 Williams Avenue SE Thomas Bibb House, ca. 1836," Huntsville History Tour, http://www.huntsvillehistorytours.org/index.php?page=12&submit=Next&tour=hh2&last=12&ptgl=on&ftgl=on&atgl=on&dir=no (accessed August 14, 2015); Bibb's wife supposedly preferred living in Huntsville, but Bibb went back and forth between Huntsville and Belle Mina. "Thomas Bibb," Huntsville History Collection.

34. "300 Williams Avenue SE Thomas Bibb House, ca. 1836," Huntsville History Tour; "Thomas Bibb," *Huntsville History Collection*. Spinners of ghost tales insist that on a night with a full moon, a carriage carrying six white horses can be seen driving up to the Bibb grave and that an apparition of the former governor can then be seen getting into the carriage and riding through the cemetery in a desperate search for his beloved Bell Mina.

Chapter 6

1. Bailey, *John Williams Walker*, 39; Bailey, "John Williams Walker," *Encyclopedia of Alabama*, http://www.encyclopediaofalabama.org/article/h-1181 (accessed August 17, 2015); Walker to Tait, September 21, 1817, Tait Family Papers.

2. Bailey, *John Williams Walker*, 26–28.

3. Ibid., 28, 31; Bailey, "The Petersburg Youth,"123–28; John Newton Waddell*, Memorials of Academic Life: Being an Historical Sketch of the Waddell Family, Identified through Three Generations with the History of the Higher Education in the South and Southwest* (Richmond, VA: Presbyterian Committee of Publication, 1891), 168. A total list of prominent pupils includes two vice presidents, three secretaries of state, three secretaries of war, one assistant secretary of war, one US attorney general, several ministers to France, Spain, and

Russia, one US Supreme Court justice, eleven governors, seven US senators, thirty-two members of the US House of Representatives, twenty-two judges, eight college presidents, seventeen editors of newspapers or authors, five members of the Confederate Congress, two bishops, and three brigadier-generals. "Moses Waddell: Teacher Who Shaped South Carolina, America," *Educating South Carolina*, http://educatingsouthcarolina.blogspot.com/2012/01/moses-waddel-teacher-who-shaped-south.html (accessed October 6, 2015).

4. Bailey, *John Williams Walker*, 31; Bailey, "Petersburg Youth," 132–34; John Walker to James S. Walker, October 14, 1806, John W. Walker Papers, ADAH, Montgomery, Alabama.

5. Bailey, "Petersburg Youth," 134; John Walker to James S. Walker, October 14, 1806; Walker to Larkin Newby, November 29, 1806, John W. Walker Papers.

6. Bailey, "Petersburg Youth," 135–36; John Walker to James S. Walker, April 21, 1809, John W. Walker Papers, ADAH, Montgomery, Alabama.

7. Bailey, *John Williams Walker*, 68–70; Bailey, "Petersburg Youth," 136; Betts, *Early History of Huntsville*, 13; Thomas J. Taylor, "Early History of Madison County, and Incidentally of North Alabama," *Alabama Historical Quarterly* 1 (Summer 1930): 162; Lewis, *Lost Capitals of Alabama*, 42.

8. Bailey, *John Williams Walker*, 70–72.

9. Ibid., 73–74; Walker to Newby, December 25, 1811, John W. Walker Papers, ADAH, Montgomery, Alabama.

10. Bailey, *John Williams Walker*, 74–76.

11. Ibid., 76–77; Andrew Jackson to President Monroe, June 11, 1817, in Clarence E. Carter, ed., *The Territorial Papers of the United States*, vol. 18 (Washington, DC: Government Printing Office, 1937), 111–12.

12. Bailey, *John Williams Walker*, 78.

13. Ibid., 79–80; John Walker to Charles Tait, January 18, 1817, Tait Family Papers, ADAH, Montgomery, Alabama.

14. Bailey, *John Williams Walker*, 80–81 (LeRoy Pope Walker, the Walkers' third son, was born on February 7, 1817); Walker to Tait, February 1, 1818, Tait Family Papers.

15. Bailey, *John Williams Walker*, 83–84; Walker to Tait, February 1, 1818, Tait Family Papers; *Journal of the House of Representatives of the Alabama Territory*, 1 As.,1 Sess., pp. 1ff.

16. Bailey, *John Williams Walker*, 85; Ruth Ketring Neurmberger, "The 'Royal Party' in Early Alabama Politics," *Alabama Review* 6 (April and July 1953): 84–95.

17. *House Journal, Alabama Territory*, 1 As., 1 Sess., pp.100, 108; *House Journal, Alabama Territory*, 1 As., 1 Sess., pp. 83, 94, 108, 120, 140; *Ala. Acts*, 1 Sess., pp. 89–90, 113, 24; *Ala. Acts, 1 Sess.*, p. 92.

18. Bailey, *John Williams Walker*, 86–87; Walker to Tait, November 9, 1818, Walker to Tait, September 22, 1818, Tait Family Papers.

19. Walker to Tait, November 9, 1818, Tait Family Papers. Walker sided

with those who believed that three-fifths of each slave should be counted in determining the population for the Territory's admission. Bailey, "John Williams Walker," 88.

20. Walker to Tait, November 9, 1818, Tait Family Papers.

21. Walker to Tait, November 11, 1818, Tait Family Papers.

22. Walker to Tait, November 15, 1818, Tait Family Papers; William W. Bibb to Tait, September 19, 1818, Tait Family Papers; Brantley, *Three Capitals*, 27.

23. Bailey, *John Williams Walker*, 89–90; Brantley, *Three Capitals*, 31–39; Hobbs, "History of Early Cahabav," 155–63; Walker to Tait, November 15 and 20, 1818, Tait Family Papers.

24. Bailey, *John Williams Walker*, 91–92; Walker to Tait, November 15, 1818, Tait Family Papers.

25. Bailey, *John Williams Walker*, 92–93; Walker to Tait, January 19, 1819, and February 8, 1819, Tait Family Papers; *Alabama Republican*, April 17, 1819.

26. Walker to Tait, May 19 and June 17, 1819, Tait Family Papers.

27. *Alabama Republican*, June 5, 1819; Walker to Tait, June 17, 1819, Tait Family Papers.

28. Bailey, *John Williams Walker*, 96; Walker to Tait, June 17, 1819, Tait Family Papers.

29. The federal ratio originated as a compromise in the US Constitution that counted each slave as three-fifths of a person for enumeration for taxation and apportionment purposes.

30. Bailey, *John Williams Walker*, 97–98.

31. *Ala. Constitutional Journal*, 22–23, 29; Bailey, *John Williams Walker*, 100.

32. *Convention Journal*, 39–40; Walker to Tait, August 7, 1819, Tait Family Papers.

33. A. J. Pickett Papers, "Bibb Notes," ADAH, Montgomery; John Campbell to David Campbell, August 11, 1819, Campbell Collection, Duke University Library, Durham, NC.

34. Bailey, *John Williams Walker*, 101–2, 108–9. The fact that Walker named a son for Tait and spent his first few days in Washington lobbying for Tait's appointment as a federal judge is evidence of the closeness of their friendship.

35. Bailey, *John Williams Walker*, 102–3.

36. Ibid., 103–7; Henry Hitchcock to Walker, December 6, 1820, and January 5, 1821, Hitchcock to Walker, January 2, 1821, John W. Walker Papers, Montgomery, Alabama.

37. Walker to Tait, April 17, 1820, Tait Family Papers; Bailey, *John Williams Walker*, 124–25.

38. Bailey, *John Williams Walker*, 124–25, 133–36, 144–46; Tait to Walker, November 16, 1821, John W. Walker Papers.

39. Bailey, "John Williams Walker"; Bailey, *John Williams Walker*,

165–67.

40. A large portion of Walker's assets consisted of slaves, many of whom were inherited from his father. Bailey, *John Williams Walker*, 113; Bailey, "John Williams Walker," *Encyclopedia of Alabama*.

41. Bailey, "John Williams Walker," *Encyclopedia of Alabama*.

42. Walker to Israel Pickens, *Journal of the Alabama House of Representatives*, 2 Leg., 2 Sess., pp. 47–48.

43. Bailey, *John Williams Walker*, 208–9.

44. *Montgomery Republican*, April 28, 1823; *National Intelligencer*, as cited in the *Alabama Republican*, May 16, 1823.

Chapter 7

1. Charles H. Moffat, "Charles Tait: Planter, Politician, and Scientist of the Old South," *Journal of Southern History* 14 (May 1948): 206–7. The wooden leg has been preserved and is in the Alabama Department of Archives and History in Montgomery. A photograph of the wooden leg appears in Edwin C. Bridge's *Alabama: The Making of an American State* (Tuscaloosa: University of Alabama Press, 2016), 65.

2. Charles Tait Moffat, 207–8; Alma C. Tompkins, "Charles Tait" (Auburn: Alabama Polytechnic Institute Historical Studies, 1910); Herbert J. (Jim) Lewis, "Charles Tait," *Encyclopedia of Alabama*, http://www.encyclopediaofalabama.org/article/h-2338 (accessed November 4, 2015).

3. Also in 1798, the elder Tait died, leaving Charles several slaves and half of his lands. Tait Family Papers (LPR), ADAH, Montgomery, Alabama, Box 1, Folder 1.

4. Thompkins, *Charles Tait*, 2–3; James A. Tait's Memorandum Book, 1844; Moffat, "Charles Tait," 208–9.

5. Paul P. Pruitt Jr., David I. Durham, and Sally E. Hadden, *Traveling the Beaten Trail: Charles Tait's Charges to Federal Grand Juries (1822–1825)* (Occasional Publications of the Bound Law Library, No. 8: University of Alabama School of Law, 2013), 5.

6. The Yazoo Act enacted by the Georgia Legislature allowed over 35 million acres of public domain to be sold to several companies of speculators in complicity with the state legislature for less than one and a half cents per acre. Public outrage resulted in the Yazoo affair being eventually concluded by Georgia ceding its western claims to the United States in 1802. Pruitt et al., *Traveling the Beaten Trail*, 7.

7. Thompkins, *Charles Tait*, 3–4; George R. Lamplugh, "James Jackson (1757–1806)," New Georgia Encyclopedia, http://www.georgiaencyclopedia.org/articles/government-politics/james-jackson-1757-1806, September 15, 2014, accessed November 5, 2015; Lewis, "Charles Tait," *Encyclopedia of Alabama*.

8. Moffat, "Charles Tait," 209–10; J. E. D. Shipp, *Giant Days or the Life and Times of William H. Crawford* (Americus, GA: Southern Printers, 1909), 48–49; E. Merton Coulter, *A Short History of Georgia* (Chapel Hill: University

of North Carolina Press, 1933), 226–27; Lucian Lamar Knight, *A Standard History of Georgia and Georgians*, vol. 1 (Lewis Publishing Company: New York, 1917), 507.

9. Moffat, "Charles Tait," 210–12.

10. Ibid., 212.

11. Ibid., 213; Pruitt et al., *Traveling the Beaten Trail*, 11.

12. Moffat, "Charles Tait," 210–13; *Savannah Columbian Museum and Advertiser*, December 7, 1809; Lewis, "Charles Tait," *Encyclopedia of Alabama*.

13. The War Hawks were made up of about a dozen members of the Twelfth Congress who were staunch supporters of the War of 1812. They were led by Henry Clay and John C. Calhoun.

14. The term "the Orders in Council" is used collectively to refer to the group of orders issued by the Privy Council in Great Britain in the late eighteenth and early nineteenth centuries, which restricted neutral trade and enforced a naval blockade of Napoleonic France and its allies.

15. Moffat, "Charles Tait," 214–15.

16. Crawford to Tait, October 12, 1814, Tait Family Papers; Clay to Tait, October 25, 1814, Tait Family Papers.

17. Moffat, "Charles Tait," 217–18; *Annals of Congress*, 12 Cong. 2 Sess. (38 January 4, 1813) and 14 Cong., 2 Sess., 71 (January 17, 1817), 91 (January 31, 1817), and 139 (February 21, 1817).

18. Lewis, "Charles Tait"; *Encyclopedia of Alabama*; Walker to Tait, November 9, 1818 (Tait Family Papers).

19. Annals of Congress, 12 Cong., 2 Sess. 38 (January 4, 1813), and 14 Cong., 2 Sess., 71 (January 17, 1817), 91 (January 31, 1817), and 139 (February 21, 1817).

20. Moffat, "Charles Tait," 218; Walker to Tait, September 22, 1818 (Tait Family Papers).

21. Moffat, "Charles Tait," 219; Bailey, *John Williams Walker*, 91–92; "An Act to Enable the People of the Alabama Territory to Form a Constitution and a State Government," 1819, 3 Stat. 489–92; McMillan, *Constitutional Development in Alabama*, 45; *Official Journal of the Alabama Constitutional Convention, 1819*, 39–40.

22. *Annals of Congress*, 15 Cong., 2 Sess., 251 (February 22, 1819), 272–73 (February 27, 1819); Tait to Thomas Cobb, February 29, 1820 (John W. Walker Papers).

23. Moffat, "Charles Tait," 220; Tait to James A. Tait, January 20, 1817 (Tait Family Papers). The elder Tait named the family plantation as "Medina," which was located near the present town of Burnt Corn. Thompkins, *Charles Tait*, 18.

24. Moffat, "Charles Tait," 221–22; Tait to Walker, October 9, 1819 (John W. Walker Papers).

25. Moffat, "Charles Tait," 222; *Annals of Congress*, 17 Cong., 2 Sess., 463–67 (December 29, 1822), 715–18 (January 28, 1823); Pruitt et al., *Traveling the Beaten Trail*, 27.

26. Pruitt et al., *Traveling the Beaten Trail*, 24–25; Lewis, "Charles Tait," *Encyclopedia of Alabama*.

27. Lewis, "Charles Tait," *Encyclopedia of Alabama*. For a detailed discussion of this complex case, see Pruitt et al., *Traveling the Beaten Trail*, 32.

28. Pruitt et al., *Traveling the Beaten Trail*, 30.

29. Thompkins, *Charles Tait*, 28; Moffat, "Charles Tait," 226–27. Tait's interest in science and the liberal arts is reflected by the list of the type of books in his personal library. He divided his collection into nine subject areas: divinity, law, history, politics, biography, arts & science, literature, Greek, and Latin. Pruitt et al., *Traveling the Beaten Trail*, 21.

30. He was lucky enough to have immediate access to an area that a scientist described as offering "more charms for the fancy of a geologist than any spot probably in America." Moffat, "Charles Tait," 227.

31. Ibid., 228–32.

32. Pruitt et al., *Traveling the Beaten Trail*, 37.

33. Tompkins, "Charles Tait," 29.

34. Pruitt et al., *Traveling the Beaten Trail*, 1.

Chapter 8

1. J. Mills Thornton III, "Clement Comer Clay," *Encyclopedia of Alabama*, http://www.encyclopediaofalabama.org/article/h-1496 (accessed Nov. 19, 2015).

2. Ibid.; Ruth Ketrlug Nuermberger, *The Clays of Alabama: A Planter-Lawyer-Politician Family* (Lexington: University Press of Kentucky, 1958), 5.

3. Nuermberger, *The Clays of Alabama*, 1; Anne Royall to Mathew Dunbar, Huntsville, January 1, 1818, in Royall, *Letters from Alabama on Various Subjects*, 10, 118–19.

4. Thornton, "Clement Comer Clay"; *Encyclopedia of Alabama*; Carol Bleser, ed., *In Joy and Sorrow: Women, Family, and Marriage in the Victorian South* (Oxford: Oxford University Press, 1991), 137.

5. Nuermberger, *The Clays of Alabama*, 19; James Campbell to David Campbell, March 8, 1819, David Campbell MSS; Alabama Territorial Legislature, House Journal, 1st Sess., pp. 3–47, January 19–February 14, 1818.

6. John Campbell and James Campbell to David Campbell, July 10, 13, August 11, 1819, David Campbell MSS; Nuermberger, *The Clays of Alabama*, 20–21; Clay Sr. to Susanna Clay, November 11, 1818, Clay MSS; John Campbell to David Campbell, April 27, 1821, David Campbell MSS; Alabama Territorial Legislature, House Journal, 2nd Sess., 3–117, November 2–21, 1818; *Huntsville Alabama Republican*, February 20, 1819.

7. Owen, *History of Alabama*, 342–43; Nuermberger, *The Clays of Alabama*, 21–23.

8. Clement Comer Clay, *The Huntsville History Collection*, www.huntsvillehistorycollection.org (accessed November 24, 2015); James Edmonds Saunders, *Early Settlers of Alabama, Part 1* (New Orleans: L. Graham & Son,

Ltd., 1899), 283; Nuermberger, *The Clays of Alabama*, 22; *Huntsville Democrat*, November 25, 1823. LeRoy Pope, president of the Huntsville bank and a member of the Broad River Group, made the clash edgier when he said, "That the country people were a parcel of ignorant animals and not able to determine whether this Bank acted correctly or incorrectly."

9. Dupre, *Transforming the Cotton Frontier*, 186; Nuermberger, *The Clays of Alabama*, 25.

10. Thornton, "Clement Comer Clay," *Encyclopedia of Alabama*.

11. Ibid.

12. Ibid.; Nuermberger, *The Clays of Alabama*, 33, 45–46.

13. Ibid., 46.

14. William Warren Rogers et al., *Alabama: The History of a Deep South State* (Tuscaloosa: University of Alabama Press, 1994), 138; Jessup to Clay, Administrative files, RSG00707, Folder 12, ADAH, Montgomery. Thornton, "Clement Comer Clay," *Encyclopedia of Alabama*; Lewis, *Clearing the Thickets*, 210–11.

15. Rogers et al., *Alabama*, 138–39; Brantley, *Banking in Alabama: 1816–1860*, 2 vols. (Birmingham: Birmingham Printing, 1961), 2: 6.

16. The independent subtreasury scheme was a system for the retaining of government funds in the US Treasury and its subtreasury, independently of the national banking and financial systems.

17. On the other hand, Owen's *Biography* indicates that the digest, "after examination by the judiciary committee, was accepted and approved . . . and in 1843 was published and has been used as authority in the courts since that time."

18. Thornton, "Clement Comer Clay," *Encyclopedia of Alabama*; Owen, *History of Alabama*, 342–43.

19. Thornton, "Clement Comer Clay," *Encyclopedia of Alabama*. Many years earlier, Clay had received a letter from Dr. Thomas Fearn, a prominent Huntsville physician who was at the time visiting in London, in which he revealed that he was working on a plan to emancipate the slaves in Alabama. Dr. Fearn characterized slavery as a "damning curse entailed on us by our forefathers, that glaring inconsistency between republican principles and despotic practice—Slavery." He continued, "To plead equal rights of man & at the same time make the heavenly principle bend & yield to convenience or even necessity is too great an absurdity." It is apparent that Clay did not adopt Dr. Fearn's feelings on the matter. Fearn to Clay, July 29, 1818, in the Clement Comer Clay Letter #692-z, Southern Historical Collection, Wilson Library, University of North Carolina at Chapel Hill.

20. Owen, *History of Alabama*, 341–42.

21. Ibid.; *A Belle of the Fifties: Memoirs of Mrs. Clay, of Alabama, Covering Social and Political Life in Washington and the South, 1853–66* (New York: Doubleday, 1905), 32; Joseph Howard Parks, *General Edmund Kirby Smith, C.S.A., 1954* (reprint; Baton Rouge: Louisiana State University Press, 199?), 122.

22. Thornton, "Clement Comer Clay," *Encyclopedia of Alabama*.

Chapter 9

1. Herbert J. "Jim" Lewis, "Henry Hitchcock," *Encyclopedia of Alabama,* http://www.encyclopediaofalabama.org/article/h-1095 (accessed December 7, 2015).

2. George P. Houghton, "History of Burlington, Chittenden County, Vermont," *Vermont Historical Magazine* 11 (October 1867): 590–92 (Internet version, www.rockvillemamma.com/chittenden/hitchcockhenrysamuel.txt (accessed December 7, 2015).

3. William H. Brantley Jr., "Henry Hitchcock of Mobile, 1816–1839," *Alabama Review* 5 (January 1952): 5; Houghton, "History of Burlington," 590–92; Darrel E. Bigham, "From the Green Mountains to the Tombigbee: Henry Hitchcock in Territorial Alabama, 1817–1819," *Alabama Review* 26 (July 1973): 210–11.

4. Bigham, "From the Green Mountains," 212.

5. Ibid., 213–16, quoting Hitchcock to Pomeroy, April 12, 1817 (collection formerly in possession of Darell E. Bigham, now in the special collections unit of the University of Vermont Libraries). Hitchcock would come to change his original position that there was nothing that could persuade him to purchase a slave. He justified this change of position on the basis that he, as a lawyer, would only use slaves for domestic work and would not increase their number nor abuse them. He also recognized that slaves were "the most profitable species of property that we had." He also observed that slaves would destroy themselves if freed.

6. Brantley, "Henry Hitchcock," 6; Bigham, "From the Green Mountains," 217 (quoting Hitchcock to Pomeroy, August 14, 1817).

7. This William Crawford is not the William H. Crawford of Georgia, who was secretary of the treasury under Presidents Madison and Monroe and who later ran for president himself.

8. Brantley, "Henry Hitchcock," 6; Bigham, "From the Green Mountains," 218; Houghton, "History of Burlington," 590–92; Hitchcock to Pomeroy, March 24, 1818.

9. Bigham, "From the Green Mountains," 220–21.

10. Ibid., 219–24; Hitchcock to Pomeroy, March 24, 1818; Brantley, "Henry Hitchcock," 6; Hitchcock to Pomeroy, May 11, 1819.

11. Brantley, "Henry Hitchcock," 7; Bigham, "From the Green Mountains," 226–27.

12. Brantley, "Henry Hitchcock," 8; *Ala. Senate Journal* (1820), 167.

13. Houghton, "History of Burlington," 590–92.

14. *A Eulogium in Commemoration of His Excellency William W. Bibb, Late Governor of the State Alabama, Delivered at the Request of the Citizens of the Town of Cahawba*, August 16, 1819. . . (Cahawba, 1820).

15. Brantley, "Henry Hitchcock," 10; Philip D. Beidler, *First Books: The Printed Word and Cultural Formation in Early Alabama* (Tuscaloosa: University of Alabama Press, 1999), 25.

16. Brantley, "Henry Hitchcock," 11; Henry Hitchcock to US Senator

John W. Walker, August 11, 1821, September 9, 1821, and December 6, 1821, John W. Walker Family Papers, ADAH, Montgomery, Alabama.

17. Hitchcock would travel to Vermont two or three more times prior to his death in August 1839. Houghton, "History of Burlington," 590–92.

18. Brantley, "Henry Hitchcock," 12.

19. Ibid., 14.

20. Brantley, "Henry Hitchcock," 15–16; Houghton, "History of Burlington," 590–92; Lewis, "Henry Hitchcock"; *Encyclopedia of Alabama*; James Sanders Day, *Diamonds in the Rough: A History of Alabama's Cahaba Coal Field* (Tuscaloosa: University of Alabama Press, 2013), 8.

21. Brantley, "Henry Hitchcock," 16–17.

22. Ibid., 18; Houghton, "History of Burlington," 590–92; Lewis, "Henry Hitchcock," *Encyclopedia of Alabama*.

23. Henry Hitchcock, *Marching with Sherman: Passages from the Letters and Campaign Diaries of Henry Hitchcock*, ed. M. A. DeWolfe Howe (1927; reprint, Lincoln: University of Nebraska Press, 1995), 2–4.

Chapter 10

1. Owen, *Dictionary of Alabama Biography*, 1360; Roy Parker Jr., "Israel Pickens," *NCPedia*, http://ncpedia.org/biography/pickens-israel (accessed December 21, 2015); Daniel S. Dupre, "Israel Pickens," *Encyclopedia of Alabama*, http://www.encyclopediaofalabama.org/search/node/israel%20pickens (accessed December 21. 2015).

2. Dupre, "Israel Pickens," *Encyclopedia of Alabama*; Hugh C. Bailey, "Israel Pickens, People's Politician," *Alabama Review* 17 (April 1924): 84.

3. Bailey, "Israel Pickens," 84.

4. Ibid., 85; Dupre, "Israel Pickens," *Encyclopedia of Alabama*. http://www.encyclopediaofalabama.org/article/h-1912 (accessed September 3, 2017).

5. Lewis, *Clearing the Thickets*, 169–70.

6. *Ala. House Journal* (1821), 58–64.

7. Ibid., 40–43; Brantley, *Three Capitals*, 98.

8. *Ala. Acts (1823)*, 3–11; Brantley, *Three Capitals*.

9. Dupre, "Israel Pickens," *Encyclopedia of Alabama*; Rogers et al., *Alabama,* 79–80; Lewis, *Clearing the Thickets*, 178–79.

10. *Ala. Senate Journal* (1823) 12; Brantley, *Three Capitals*, 136–37.

11. Tennant S. McWilliams, "The Marquis and the Myth: Lafayette's Visit to Alabama, 1825," *Alabama Review* 22 (April 1969): 136; Edwin C. Bridges, "The Nation's Guest: The Marquis de Lafayette's Tour of Alabama," *Alabama Heritage* (Fall 2011): 8–17; Lewis, "Lafayette's Visit to Alabama," *Encyclopedia of Alabama*.

12. Abernethy, *Formative Period*, 130; Moore, *History of Alabama*, 119.

13. Dupre, "Israel Pickens," *Encyclopedia of Alabama*; Bailey, "Israel Pickens," 100–101.

14. Bailey, "Israel Pickens," 100–101.

Chapter 11

1. Rossiter Johnson and John Howard Brown, eds., *The Twentieth Century Biographical Dictionary of Notable Americans* (Boston: The Biographical Society, 1904), s.v. "Saffold, Rueben."

2. Owen, *History of Alabama and Dictionary of Alabama Biography*, s.v. "Saffold, Reuben" 1488.

3. Lengel, "The Road to Fort Mims," 16–36; Halbert and Hall, *The Creek War*, 141, 279; Pickett, *History of Alabama*, 24–25. At the time of the massacre at Fort Mims, August 30, 1813, Mrs. Saffold and her sons were in a neighboring fort out of harm's way. Mildred Reynolds Saffold, "Belvoir, Home of Chief Justice Reuben Saffold," *Alabama Historical Quarterly* (1930): 235; Owen, *History of Alabama*, 1488.

4. *Saffold History and Genealogy Book*; McMillan, "Alabama Constitution of 1819," 79; *Montgomery Daily Confederation*, July 8, 1859, 2.

5. Anna M. Gayle Fry, *Memories of Old Cahaba* (Nashville: Publishing House of the Methodist Episcopal Church, South, 1908), 33, 66; Harvey H. Jackson III, introduction to Phillip Henry Gosse, *Letters from Alabama, Chiefly Relating to Natural History* (reprint, Tuscaloosa: University of Alabama Press, 1993), xx.

6. Lewis, *Clearing the Thickets*, 158, 162; *Saffold History and Genealogy Book*.

7. McMillan, *Constitutional Development in Alabama*, 47–51.

8. Ibid.; Henderson Middleton Somerville, "Trial of the Alabama Supreme Court Judges in 1829," *Alabama State Bar Association Proceedings*, June 1899; Ala. Const. 1819 Art. V, Sec. 13.

9. *Saffold History and Genealogical Book*; "Reuben Saffold II," *Saffold Roots*, http://saffold.com/history/?p=6 (accessed January 7, 2016); Brantley, *Banking in Alabama*, II: 204.

10. Pickett, *History of Alabama*, 657–58; *Mobile Register and Journal*, April 22, 1844, April 27, 1844, 2.

11. Willis Brewer, *Alabama: Her History, Resources, War Record, and Public Men from 1540 to 1872* (reprint, Baltimore: Genealogical Publishing Company, 2000), 215.

12. *Mobile Register and Journal*, February 22, 1847, 2.

Chapter 12

1. Charles D. Rodenbough, "Gabriel Moore," *NCPedia*, http://ncpedia. org/biography/moore-gabriel (accessed January 10, 2016); Harriet E. Amos Doss, "Gabriel Moore, 1829–March 1831," in *Alabama Governors: A Political History of the State*, ed. Samuel Webb and Margaret E. Armbrester (Tuscaloosa: University of Alabama Press, 2001), 24.

2. Rodenbough, "Gabriel Moore," *NCPedia*; John M. Martin, "The Early Career of Gabriel Moore," *Alabama Historical Quarterly* 29 (Fall-Winter 1967), 89.

3. Doss, "Gabriel Moore," in *Alabama Governors*, 24–25; Lewis, *Clearing the Thickets*, 109.

4. Harriet Amos Doss, "Rise and Fall of an Alabama Founding Father," *Alabama Review* 52 (July 2000): 163–71; *Acts Passed at the Second Session of the First General Assembly of the Alabama Territory in the Forty-third Year of American Independence* (St. Stephens, AL: Thomas Easton, 1818), 10.

5. Martin, "Early Career of Gabriel Moore," 90.

6. Ibid., 90–91.

7. Doss, "Gabriel Moore," in *Alabama Governors*, 25; Rodenbough, "Gabriel Moore," *NCPedia*.

8. Martin, "Early Career of Gabriel Moore," 90–93; *Annals of Congress*, Seventeenth Congress, First Session, 1269, and Second Session, 676–78.

9. *Annals of Congress*, Eighteenth Congress, First Session, 1580–85; Martin, "Early Career of Gabriel Moore," 94.

10. Martin, "Early Career of Gabriel Moore," 94–95; John McKinley to Henry Clay, September 29, 1823, Clay Papers, Library of Congress; *Huntsville Democrat*, February 15, 1825.

11. W. F. Withers to Clay, May 10, 1825; A. W. H. Clifton to Clay, May 7, 1825, Clay Papers, Duke University Library, Durham, NC; *Huntsville Democrat*, June 21, August 12, 1825; Martin, "Early Career of Gabriel Moore," 96; Doss, "Gabriel Moore," in *Alabama Governors*, 25.

12. Martin, "Early Career of Gabriel Moore," 96.

13. Ibid., 98–99.

14. Doss, "Gabriel Moore," in *Alabama Governors*, 26; Martin "Early Career of Gabriel Moore," 100–101; *Huntsville Democrat*, December 4, 1829.

15. Doss, "Gabriel Moore," in *Alabama Governors*, 26.

16. Ibid., 26–27.

17. Dupre, *Transforming the Cotton Frontier*, 176; Doss, "Gabriel Moore," in *Alabama Governor*, 27; Rodenbough, "Gabriel Moore," *NCPedia*.

18. Doss, "Gabriel Moore," in *Alabama Governors*, 27; Doss, "Rise and Fall of an Alabama Founding Father," 163–71.

19. Doss, "Gabriel Moore," in *Alabama Governors*, 27–28.

Chapter 13

1. Willis Brewer, *Alabama: Her History, Resources, War Records, and Public Men from 1540 to 1872* (reprint, Baltimore: Genealogical Publishing Company, 2000), 211; John Milton Martin, "William Rufus King: Southern Moderate" (PhD diss., University of North Carolina, 1955).

2. John M. Martin, "William Rufus Devane King," *NCPedia*, *http://ncpedia.org/biography/king-william-rufus-devane* (accessed February 1, 2016); Daniel Fate Brooks, "The Faces of William Rufus King," *Alabama Heritage* (Summer 2003): 14.

3. It should be noted that in those days both branches of the Congress occasionally overlooked the minimum age requirement, which only was applied to the date of taking office, not the date of election. Mark O. Hatfield, with

the Senate Historical Office, *Vice Presidents of the United States, 1789–1993* (Washington, DC: Government Printing Office, 1997), 181–87n.8.

4. Ibid., 181–87; Brooks, "The Faces of William Rufus King," 16.

5. Brooks, "The Faces of William Rufus King," 16–17; Hatfield, *Vice Presidents*, 181–87.

6. Walter M. Jackson, *Alabama's First United States Vice-President: William Rufus King* (Decatur, AL: Decatur Printing Co., 1952), 6–7.

7. Brooks, "The Faces of William Rufus King," 17; John Updike, *Memories of the Ford Administration* (New York: Random House, 1992), 250; Hatfield, *Vice President*, 181–87.

8. Martin, "William Rufus Devane King," *NCPedia*; Brantley, *Three Capitals*, 113–14.

9. John M. Martin, "William R. King: Jacksonian Senator," *Alabama Review* 18 (October 1965): 243–45; Hatfield, *Vice President*, 181–87.

10. Brewer, *Alabama*, 212.

11. Leada Gore, "Senator, slave owner and quite possibly gay, Alabama's William Rufus King was country's 13th VP," AL.com, July 4, 2014 (http://www.al.com/news/index.ssf/2014/07/senator_slave_owner_and_quite.html (accessed February 6, 2015); Brooks, "The Faces of William Rufus King," 18.

12. Martin, "William R. King: Jacksonian Senator," 247–51, 253, 256, 262; Martin, "William Rufus King: Southern Moderate," 77.

13. Martin, "William Rufus Devane King," *NCPedia*. The Distribution Act of 1836 provided for a system of distributing federal surpluses to state banks and restricting legal tender to gold and silver. Those who opposed it were supporters of hard money (or specie, i.e., gold and silver) who feared speculative banking and the contraction of the money supply. Some who were also concerned sent the government's surplus tax revenue back to the states on an equalized basis. Polk objected to the bill because it gave the money only as a loan, for which the states might be liable for repaying later.

14. Hatfield, *Vice Presidents*, 181–87; Phillip Shriver Klein, *President James Buchanan* (University Park: Pennsylvania State University Press, 1962), 111.

15. Hatfield, *Vice Presidents*, 181–87, quoting an account of this encounter in Robert V. Remini, *Henry Clay: Statesman* (New York: W.W. Norton & Company, 1993), 574. See also *Congressional Globe* (26th Cong., 2d sess., 245, 247–249, 256–257).

16. Hatfield, *Vice President*, 181–87; John M. Martin, "William R. King and the Vice-Presidency," *Alabama Review* 16 (January 1963): 43–44.

17. Hatfield, *Vice Presidents*, 181–87; Brooks, "The Faces of William Rufus King," 20–21; Jackson, *Alabama's First United States Vice-President*, 30.

18. Martin, "William Rufus Devane King," *NCPedia*; Jackson, *Alabama's First United States Vice-President*, 31.

19. Jackson, *Alabama's First United States Vice-President*, 34; Martin, "William Rufus King: Southern Moderate," 274–281, 290–291, 300–303. After two days of voting without gaining a majority, King withdrew his name

from the race in the 1847 contest for Dixon Hall Lewis's Senate seat. The resulting defeat was King's only loss in a state election. Brooks, "The Faces of William Rufus King," 21.

20. For a good discussion of William Lowndes Yancey and the Alabama secessionists, see Christopher Lyle McIlwain Sr., *Civil War Alabama* (Tuscaloosa: University of Alabama Press, 2016), 11–26.

21. Hatfield, *Vice Presidents*, 181–87; Remini, *Henry Clay: Statesman for the Union*, 746–47; Brooks, "The Faces of William Rufus King," 21.

22. Hatfield, *Vice Presidents*, 181–87.

23. Ibid.; Jackson, *Alabama's First United States Vice-President*, 41–42; Brooks, "The Faces of William Rufus King," 23.

24. *Mountain Sentinel* (Ebensburg, Pennsylvania), March 31, 1853.

25. Brooks, "The Faces of William Rufus King," 23; Joel Campbell Du Bose, *Alabama History* (Richmond, VA: B. F. Johnson Publishing Company, 1915), 93.

26. Jackson, *Alabama's First United States Vice-President*, 42–43, 46.

27. *Obituary Addresses on the Occasion of the Death of the Hon. William R. King* (Washington, DC: Robert Armstrong, 1854), 6–7, 12, 16.

28. Ibid., 24–33, 33–39, 39–46, 47–49, 49–54, 54–56, and 57–58.

Conclusion

1. References to founders in this conclusion pertain to the group of Alabama founders focused upon in this book, and not necessarily to the delegates to the Constitutional Convention of 1819, even though quite a few of the founders focused upon herein were also delegates to that convention.

SELECTED BIBLIOGRAPHY

Primary Sources

Archival Material

A Eulogium in Commemoration of His Excellency William W. Bibb, Late Governor of the State Alabama, Delivered at the Request of the Citizens of the Town of Cahawba, August 16, 1819 . . . (Cahawba, 1820).

Bibb, William Wyatt, to Charles Tait, September 19, 1818; July 14, 1819; and April 15, 1820, Tait Family Papers, ADAH, Montgomery, Alabama.

Campbell, John, to David Campbell, August 11, 1819, Campbell Collection. Duke University Library, Durham, North Carolina.

Campbell, James, to David Campbell, March 8, 1819, Campbell Collection, Duke University Library, Durham, North Carolina.

Campbell, John, and James Campbell to David Campbell, July 10, 13, August 11, 1819. Campbell Collection, Duke University Library, Durham, North Carolina.

Campbell, John, to David Campbell, April 27, 1821, David Campbell Collection, Duke University Library, Durham, North Carolina.

Clay, Henry, to Tait, October 25, 1814, Tait Family Papers, ADAH, Montgomery, Alabama.

Clay Sr., Clement to Susanna Clay, November 11, 1818, Clay MSS.

Coffee, John, to Mary Coffee, from Camp Batey near Huntsville [undated], "Letters of John Coffee," transcribed by Jan Grant, *Tennessee Historical Magazine* 2, no. 4, December 1916.

Coffee, John, to Mary Coffee, from Headquarters 24 miles south from Ditto's Landing, October 24, 1813, "Letters of John Coffee."

Coffee, John, to Mary Coffee from Ten Islands, Coosey [*sic*] River, November 4, 1813, Grant, "Letters of John Coffee."

Coffee to Commissioners, February 14, 1816, John Coffee Papers, LPR27, 1818–1831, Box 1, ADAH, Montgomery, Alabama.

Crawford, Charles, to Tait, October 12, 1814, Tait Family Papers, ADAH, Montgomery, Alabama.

Dale, Samuel, to Governor William Wyatt Bibb, September 23, 1818, *Creek War Military Records Collection*, SPR359, ADAH, Montgomery, Alabama.

Fearn, Thomas, to Clement Comer Clay, July 29, 1818, in the Clement Comer Clay Letter #692-7, Southern Historical Collection, Wilson Library, the University of North Carolina at Chapel Hill, North Carolina.

Hitchcock, Henry, to Walker, December 6, 1820, John W. Walker Papers,

ADAH Montgomery, Alabama.

Hitchcock to Walker, January 5, 1821, John W. Walker Papers, ADAH, Montgomery, Alabama.

Hitchcock to Walker, January 2, 1821, John W. Walker Papers, ADAH, Montgomery, Alabama.

Hitchcock, to Senator John W. Walker, August 11, 1821, September 9, 1821, and December 6, 1821, John W. Walker Papers, ADAH, Montgomery, Alabama.

James A. Tait's Memorandum Book, 1844.

Jackson, Andrew, to President Monroe, June 11, 1817. In Clarence E. Carter, ed., *The Territorial Papers of the United States*, vol. 8. Washington, DC: Government Printing Office, 1937.

Jefferson, Thomas, from Rodominick H. Gilmer, 8 November 1804, Founders Online, National Archives (http://founders.archives.gov/documents/Jefferson/99–01–02- 0611).

Jessup, Maj. Gen. to Governor Clay, Administrative files, RSG00707, Folder 12, ADAH, Montgomery, Alabama.

McKinley, John, to Henry Clay, September 29, 1823, Clay Papers, Library of Congress.

Madison, President James, from Caleb Wallace, April 20, 1804 (Abstract), Founders Online, National Archives http://founders.archives.gov/documents/Madison/02-07-02-0087.

Madison, President James, from Harry Toulmin, November 5, 1804, Founders Online, National Archives (http://founders.archives.gov/documents/Madison/02-08-02-0262).

McKinley, John, to Henry Clay, September 29, 1823, Clay Papers, Library of Congress.

The Papers of James Madison, Secretary of State Series, vol. 7, April 2–August 31, 1804, ed. David B. Mattern, J. C. A. Stagg, Ellen J. Barber, Anne Mandeville Colony, Angela Kreider, and Jeanne Kerr Cross. Charlottesville: University of Virginia Press, 2005.

Pickett, A. J., Papers, "Bibb Notes." Alabama Department of Archives and History (ADAH), Montgomery, Alabama.

Tait, Charles, to James A. Tait, January 20, 1817, Tait Family Papers, ADAH, Montgomery, Alabama.

Tait to John W. Walker, October 9, 1819, John W. Walker Papers, ADAH, Montgomery, Alabama.

Tait to Thomas Cobb, February 29, 1820, John W. Walker Papers, ADAH, Montgomery, Alabama.

Tait to Walker, November 16, 1821, John W. Walker Papers, ADAH, Montgomery Alabama.

R. Thomas's account of the "Traders in the Creek Nation," taken from American Indians, A Select Catalog of National Archives Microfilm Publications M1334. 13 rolls.

Walker to Charles Tait, September 21, 1817, Tait Family Papers (LPR), ADAH, Montgomery, Alabama, Box 1, Folder 1.

Walker, John W., to James S. Walker, April 21, 1809, John W. Walker Papers, ADAH, Montgomery, Alabama.

Walker to Walker, October 14, 1806, John W. Walker Papers, ADAH, Montgomery, Alabama.

Walker to Larkin Newby, November 29, 1806, John W. Walker Papers, ADAH, Montgomery, Alabama.

Walker to Newby, December 25, 1811, John W. Walker Papers, ADAH, Montgomery, Alabama.

Walker to Charles Tait, January 18, 1817; February 1, 1818; September 22, 1818; November 9 1818; November 11, 1818; November 15, 1818; November 20, 1818; January 19, 1819; February 8, 1819; May 19, 1819; June 17, 1819; August 7, 1819; and April 17, 1820; Tait Family Papers, ADAH, Montgomery, Alabama.

Withers, W. F., to Clement Clay, May 10, 1825, Clay Papers, Duke University Library, Durham, NC.

Toulmin to Secretary of State, July 6, 1805, General Correspondence, 1795–1815, Mississippi Territorial Transcripts, 58-A.

Toulmin to Brigadier General Ferdinand Claiborne, July 23, 1813, *Harry Toulmin Letters*, SPR234, Folder 2, ADAH, Montgomery, Alabama.

Newspapers

Alabama Republican, April 17, 1819.

Alabama Republican, June 5, 1819.

Alabama Republican, May 16, 1823.

American Beacon (Norfolk, VA), vol. 2, issue 58, April 15, 1816.

Bibb Blade, February 24, 1881.

Cahawba Press and Alabama Intelligencer, November 1, 1823.

Cincinnati Commercial Tribune, June 29, 1894.

Columbus Daily Enquirer, January 22, 1887.

Columbus Daily Enquirer, December 1, 1887.

Huntsville Democrat, November 25, 1823.

Huntsville Democrat, February 15, 1825.

Huntsville Democrat, December 4, 1829.

Macon Telegraph, December 2, 1887.

Memphis Appeal, July 30, 1859.

Mobile Register and Journal, April 22, 1844.

Mobile Register and Journal, April 27, 1844.

Mobile Register and Journal February 22, 1847.

Montgomery Advertiser, June 7, 1893.

Montgomery Advertiser, February 27, 1881.

Montgomery Daily Confederation, July 8, 1859.

Montgomery Flag and Advertiser, October 5, 1847.

Montgomery Republican, April 28, 1823.

Mountain Sentinel (Ebensburg, PA), March 31, 1853.

New York Times, September 4, 1883.

New York Times, April 28, 1886.

Niles' Weekly Register, April 5, 1817.

Republican Farmer (Bridgeport, CT), volume 6, issue 317, May 15, 1816.

Shelby Sentinel, April 4, 1878.

Shelby Sentinel, February 24, 1881.

Shelby Sentinel, January 4, 1883.

Savannah Columbian Museum and Advertiser, December 7, 1809.

Legal References, Government Resources, and Public Documents

"An Act to Enable the People of the Alabama Territory to Form a Constitution and a State Government," 1819, 3 Stat. 489–92.

Acts Passed at the First Session of the First General Assembly of the Alabama Territory in the Forty-second Year of American Independence. St. Stephens: Thomas Eaton, 1818.

Acts Passed at the Second Session of the First General Assembly of the Alabama Territory in the Forty-third Year of American Independence (St. Stephens, AL: Thomas Easton, 1818), 1818.

Ala. Acts (1820), 63.

Ala. Acts (1820), 104.

Ala. Acts (1821), 53, 60–61, 115–16.

Ala. Acts (1822), 138.

Ala. Acts (1823), 3–11; 115.

Ala. Acts (2 Sess. 1818), 46–49.

Ala. Acts, 1 Sess. (1819) pp. 89–90, 113, 24, 92.

Ala. Acts (1845), 207.

Ala. Const. 1819, Art. IV, Sec. 18.

Ala. Const. Art. IV, Secs. 14, 23; Art. V, Secs. 2, 24.

Ala. House Journal (1819), 8–16.

Ala. Senate Journal (1820), 18–19.

Ala. Senate Journal (Cahawba 1820), 167.

Ala. Senate Journal (1823), 12.

Ala. House Journal (1821), 11–15; 58–64.

Ala. Territorial Legislature, House Journal, 1st Sess., pp. 3–47, January 19–February 14, 1818.

Ala. Territorial Legislature, House Journal, 2nd Sess., 3–117, November 2–21, 1818.

Annals of Congress, 12th Cong. 2 Sess., 38, January 4, 1813.

Annals of Congress, 14th Cong., 2 Sess., 71 (January 17, 1817), 91 (January 31, 1817), and 139 (February 21, 1817).

Annals of Congress, 15th Cong., 2 Sess., 251 (February 22, 1819, and February 27,

1819).

Annals of Congress, 17th Cong, 1 Sess. 1269 and 2d Session, 676–78.

Annals of Congress, 17th Cong., 2 Sess. (December 29, 1822, and January 28, 1823).

Annals of Congress, 18th Cong. 1 Sess., 1580–85.

Appendix, Mississippi Territorial Register of Appointments, Civil and Military. 1805–1817.

Barren County, Kentucky, Tax List (1806–1819).

Dale vs. the Governor, 3 Stewart 387.

House Journal, Alabama Territory, 1 Sess., pp.100, 108.

Journal of the House of Representatives of the Alabama Territory, 1 Sess., pp. 1ff.

Journal of the House of Representatives of the Alabama Territory at the Second Session of the First General Assembly in the Forty-third Year of American Independence (St. Stephens, AL: Thomas Eaton), 1818.

Journal of the Legislative Council of the Alabama Territory at the First Session of the General Assembly in the Forty-third Year of American Independence (St. Stephens, AL: Thomas Eaton), 1818.

Journal of the Senate at the Second Session of the General Assembly of the State of Alabama (Cahawba, AL: Allen and Drichell), 1820.

Journal of the Senate at the Called Session of the General Assembly of the State of Alabama, 1821 (Cahawba: Allen and Brickell, 1821).

Journal of the Alabama House of Representatives, 2 Leg., 2 Sess., pp. 47–48.

McAdams, Eileen B., Compiled Index to the Compiled Military Service Records for the Volunteer Soldiers Who Served During the War of 1812. M602, National Archives and Records Administration, Washington, DC.

Official Journal of the Alabama Constitutional Convention of 1819, 22–23, 29, 39–40.

Records of the Creek Factory of the Office of Indian Trade of the Bureau of Indian Affairs, 1795–1821.

Statutes of Mississippi Territory (1816), cited in Betts, *Early History of Huntsville*, 14, 19–21.

US Statutes at Large, III, 371–73.

Secondary Sources

Books

A Belle of the Fifties: Memoirs of Mrs. Clay, of Alabama, Covering Social and Political Life in Washington and the South, 1853–66. New York: Doubleday Page & Company, 1905.

Abernethy, Thomas Perkins. *From Frontier to Plantation in Tennessee—A Study in Frontier Democracy*. Chapel Hill: University of North Carolina Press, 1932.

———. *The Formative Period in Alabama, 1815–1828*. Tuscaloosa: University of Alabama Press, 1995.

Bailey, Hugh C. *John Williams Walker: A Study in the Political, Social, and Cultural Life of the Old Southwest.* Tuscaloosa: University of Alabama Press, 1964.

Beidler, Phillip D. *First Books: The Printed Word and Cultural Formation in Early Alabama.* Tuscaloosa: University of Alabama Press, 1999.

Bernstein, R. B. *The Founding Fathers Reconsidered.* New York: Oxford University Press, 2009.

Betts, Edward Chambers. *Early History of Huntsville Alabama, 1804–1870,* rev. ed. Montgomery, AL: Brown Printing Co., 1916.

Bleser. Carol ed., *In Joy and Sorrow: Women, Family, and Marriage in the Victorian South.* Oxford: Oxford University Press, 1991.

Borneman, Walter R. *1812: The War That Forged a Nation.* New York: HarperCollins, 2004.

Brantley, William H. *Three Capitals, A Book about the First Three Capitals: St. Stephens, & Cahawba, 1818–26.* 1947. Reprint, Tuscaloosa: University of Alabama Press, 1976.

———. *Banking in Alabama: 1816–1860.* 2 vols. Birmingham, AL: Birmingham Printing, 1961.

Brewer, Willis. *Alabama: Her History, Resources, War Record, and Public Men from 1540 to 1872.* Reprint, Baltimore: Genealogical Publishing Company, 2000.

Bridges, Edwin C. *Alabama: The Making of an American State.* Tuscaloosa: University of Alabama Press, 2016.

Brown, Steven P. *John McKinley and the Antebellum Court: Circuit Riding in the Old Southwest.* Tuscaloosa: University of Alabama Press, 2012.

Buchanan, John. *Jackson's Way: Andrew Jackson and the People of the Western Waters.* Edison, NJ: Castle Books, 2005.

Burke, Paulin Wilcox. *Emily Donelson of Tennessee.* Knoxville: University of Tennessee Press, 2001.

Cheatham, Mark R. *Andrew Jackson, Southerner.* Baton Rouge: Louisiana State University Press, 2013.

Claiborne, J. F. H. *Life and Times of Gen. Sam. Dale, the Mississippi Partisan.* New York: Harper & Brothers, 1860.

Clarke, Hewitt. *Thunder at Meridian.* Spring, TX: Lone Star Press, 1995.

"Crawley Deposition." In *Correspondence of Andrew Jackson*, ed. John Spencer Bassett. Washington, DC: Carnegie Institution, 1926–1935.

Coulter, E. Merton. *A Short History of Georgia.* Chapel Hill: University of North Carolina Press, 1933.

Cox, Isaac J. *The West Florida Controversy, 1798–1813: A Study in American Diplomacy.* Baltimore: John Hopkins University Press, 1918.

Day, James Sanders. *Diamonds in the Rough: A History of Alabama's Cahaba Coal Field.* Tuscaloosa: University of Alabama Press, 2013.

Dick, Everett. *The Dixie Frontier: A Social History of the Southern Frontier from the First Transmontane Beginnings to the Civil War.* Lincoln: University of Nebraska Press, 1964.

Du Bose, Joel Campbell. *Sketches of Alabama History.* Philadelphia: Eldridge and Brothers, 1901.

———. *Alabama History.* Richmond, VA: B. F. Johnson Publishing Company, 1915.

Dupre, Daniel S. *Transforming the Cotton Frontier: Madison County, Alabama (1800–1840).* Baton Rouge: Louisiana State University Press, 1997.

Foster, Thomas. ed. *The Collected Works of Benjamin Hawkins, 1794–1810.* Tuscaloosa: University of Alabama Press, 2003.

Fry, Anna M. Gayle. *Memories of Old Cahaba.* Nashville: Publishing House of the Methodist Episcopal Church, South, 1908.

Goldenberg, David, M. *The Curse of Ham: Race and Slavery in Early Judaism, Christianity, and Islam.* Princeton, NJ: Princeton University Press, 2003.

Gosse, Phillip Henry. *Letters from Alabama, Chiefly Relating to Natural History.* Introduction by Harvey H. Jackson III. Reprint, Tuscaloosa: University of Alabama Press, 1993.

Griffith, Benjamin W. Jr. *McIntosh and Weatherford: Creek Indian Leaders.* Tuscaloosa: University of Alabama Press, 1988.

Griffith, Lucille. *Alabama: A Documentary History to 1900.* Rev. ed. Tuscaloosa: University of Alabama Press, 1972.

Halbert, Henry T., and T. J. Ball. *The Creek War of 1813 and 1814.* 1895. Reprint, Tuscaloosa: University of Alabama Press, 1995.

Hamilton, William Baskerville. *Anglo-American on the Frontier: Thomas Rodney and His Territorial Cases.* Durham, NC: Duke University Press, 1953.

Hatfield, Mark O. *Vice Presidents of the United States, 1789–1993.* Washington, DC: Government Printing Office, 1997.

Hitchcock, Henry. *Marching with Sherman: Passages from the Letters and Campaign Diaries of Henry Hitchcock.* Ed. M. A. DeWolfe Howe. 1927. Reprint, Lincoln: University of Nebraska Press, 1995.

Haynes, Robert V. *The Mississippi Territory and the Southwest Frontier, 1795–1817.* Lexington: University Press of Kentucky, 2010.

Jackson, Walter M. *Alabama's First United States Vice-President: William Rufus King.* Decatur, AL: Decatur Printing Co., 1952.

James, Marquis. *The Life of Andrew Jackson.* New York: Bobbs-Merrill Company, 1938.

Johnson, Fredirksen. *American Military Leaders:* A-L. Vol. 1. Santa Barbara, CA: ABC- CLIO, 1999.

Johnson, Rossiter, and John Howard Brown, eds. *The Twentieth Century Biographical Dictionary of Notable Americans,* s.v. "Saffold, Rueben." Boston: Biographical Society, 1904.

Kennedy, Roger G. *Burr, Hamilton, and Jefferson: A Study in Character.* New York: Oxford University Press, 2000.

Knight, Lucian Lamar. *A Standard History of Georgia and Georgians,* vol. 1. New York: Lewis Publishing Company, 1917.

Klein, Phillip Shriver. *President James Buchanan.* University Park: Pennsylvania State University Press, 1962.

Lewis, Herbert James. *Clearing the Thickets: A History of Antebellum Alabama.* New Orleans: Quid Pro Books, 2013.

———. *Lost Capitals of Alabama.* Charleston, SC: History Press, 2014.

Luttrell, Frank Alex III, ed. *Historical Markers of Madison County.* Huntsville-Madison County Historical Society, 50th Anniversary, 1951–2001.

McMillan, Malcolm Cook. *Constitutional Development in Alabama, 1798–1901: A Study in Politics, the Negro, and Sectionalism.* Chapel Hill: University of North Carolina Press, 1955.

McIlwain, Christopher Lyle Sr. *Civil War Alabama.* Tuscaloosa: University of Alabama Press, 2016.

Matte, Jacqueline Anderson. *The History of Washington County First County in Alabama.* Chatom, AL: Washington County Historical Society, 1982.

Moore, Albert B. *History of Alabama.* 1934. Reprint, Tuscaloosa: Alabama Bookstore, 1951.

Nuermberger, Ruth Ketring. *The Clays of Alabama: A Planter-Lawyer-Politician Family.* Lexington: University Press of Kentucky, 1958.

Obituary Addresses on the Occasion of the Death of the Hon. William R. King. Washington, DC: Robert Armstrong, 1854.

Owen, Thomas McAdory. *History of Alabama and Dictionary of Alabama Biography.* Chicago: S. J. Publishing Company, 1921.

Owsley, Frank Lawrence Jr. *Struggle for the Gulf Borderlands: The Creek War and Battle of New Orleans.* Gainesville: University Press of Florida, 1981.

Parks, Joseph Howard. *General Edmund Kirby Smith, C.S.A.* 1954. Reprint, Baton Rouge: Louisiana State University Press, 1992.

Pickett, Albert James. *History of Alabama and Incidentally of Georgia and Mississippi from the Earliest Period, 1851.* Reprint, Birmingham, AL: Birmingham Book and Magazine Co., 1962.

Pruitt, Paul M. Jr. *Taming Alabama: Lawyers and Reformers, 1804–1929.* Tuscaloosa: University of Alabama Press, 2010.

Pruitt, Paul M. Jr., David I. Durham, and Sally E. Hadden. *Traveling the Beaten Trail: Charles Tait's Charges to Federal Grand Juries (1822–1825).* Occasional Publications of the Bound Law Library, No. 8: University of Alabama School of Law, 2013.

Putnam, Richelle. *Lauderdale County, Mississippi: A Brief History.* Charleston, SC: History Press, 2011.

Remini, Robert V. *Henry Clay: Statesman.* New York: W. W. Norton & Company, 1993.

Rogers, William Warren et al. *Alabama: The History of a Deep South State.* Tuscaloosa: University of Alabama Press, 1994.

Roland, Dunbar, ed. *Courts, Judges, and Lawyers of Mississippi, 1798–1935.* Jackson: State Department of Archives and History and the Mississippi Historical Society, 1935.

Rowland, Eron. *Mississippi Territory in the War of 1812.* 1921. Reprint, Baltimore: Genealogical Publishing Company, 1968.

Royall, Anne. *Letters from Alabama on Various Subjects* Washington, DC, 1830.

————. *Sketches of History, Life, and Manners in the United States.* New Haven, CT, 1826. Reprint, New York: Johnson, 1970.

————. *Letters from Alabama 1817–1822.* Ed. Lucille Griffith. Tuscaloosa: University of Alabama Press, 1969.

Saunders, James Edmonds. *Early Settlers of Alabama*, Part 1. New Orleans: L. Graham & Son, Ltd., 1899.

Schafer, Elizabeth D. *Lake Martin: Alabama's Crown Jewel.* Charleston, SC: Arcadia Publishing, 2003.

Sellers, James Benson. *Slavery in Alabama.* Tuscaloosa: University of Alabama Press, 1950.

Shipp, J. E. D. *Giant Days or the Life and Times of William H. Crawford.* Americus, GA: Southern Printers, 1909.

Sobel, Robert, and John Raimo, eds. *Biographical Directory of the Governors of the United States 1789–1978*, vol. 1. Westport, CT: Meckler Books, 1978.

Thornton, J. Mills III. *Politics and Power in a Slave Society.* Baton Rouge: Louisiana State University Press, 1978.

Tompkins, Alma C. *Charles Tait.* Auburn: Alabama Polytechnic Institute Historical Studies, 1910.

Tinling, Marion, and Godfrey Davies, eds. *The Western Country in 1793: Reports on Kentucky and Virginia by Harry Toulmin.* San Marino, CA: Huntington Library, 1948.

Updike, John. *Memories of the Ford Administration.* New York: Random House, 1992.

Waddell, John Newton. *Memorials of Academic Life: Being a Historical Sketch of the Waddell Family, Identified through Three Generations with the History of the Higher Education in the South and Southwest.* Richmond, VA: Presbyterian Committee of Publication, 1891.

Waselkov, Gregory A. *A Conquering Spirit: Fort Mims and the Red Stick War of 1813–1814.* Tuscaloosa: University of Alabama Press, 2006.

Webb, Samuel, and Margaret E. Armbrester, eds. Harriet E. Amos Doss, "Gabriel Moore, 1829–March 1831." *Alabama Governors: A Political History of the State.* Tuscaloosa: University of Alabama Press, 2001.

Periodicals

Abernethy, Thomas Perkins. "Aaron Burr in Mississippi." *Journal of Southern History* 15 (February 1949).

Alabama Historical Quarterly 6, no. 1 (Spring 1944).

Bailey, Hugh C. "The Petersburgh Youth of John Williams Walker." *Georgia Historical Quarterly* 43 (June 1959).

————. "John W. Walker and the 'Georgia Machine' in Early Alabama Politics." *Alabama Review* 8 (July 1955).

————. "Israel Pickens, People's Politician." *Alabama Review* 17 (April 1924).

Bigham, Darrel E. "From the Green Mountains to the Tombigbee: Henry Hitchcock in Territorial Alabama, 1817–1819." *Alabama Review* 26 (July

1973).

Brantley, William H. Jr. "Henry Hitchcock of Mobile, 1816–1839." *Alabama Review* 5 (January 1952).

Briceland, Alan V. "Ephraim Kirby, Mr. Jefferson's Emissary on the Tombigbee-Mobile Frontier in 1804." *Alabama Review* 24 (April 1971).

Bridges, Edwin C. "The Nation's Guest: The Marquis de Lafayette's Tour of Alabama." *Alabama Heritage* (Fall 2011).

Brooks, Daniel Fate. "The Faces of William Rufus King." *Alabama Heritage* (Summer 2003).

Burton, Gary. "Pintlala's Cold Murder Case: The Death of Thomas Meredith in 1812." *Alabama Review* 63 (July 2010).

Charles Tait to David B. Mitchell, February 20, 1812. *Georgia Historical Quarterly* 21, no. 4 (December 1937): 385.

"Comments on America and Kentucky, 1793–1802." *Register of the Kentucky Historical Society* 47 [1949].

Cruzat, Héloise H., trans. "Records of the Superior Council of Louisiana." *Louisiana Historical Quarterly* 5 (January–October 1922).

Doss, Harriet E. Amos. "Rise and Fall of an Alabama Founding Father." *Alabama Review* 52 (July 2000).

Doster, James F. "Early Settlers on the Tombigbee and Tensaw Rivers." *Alabama Review* 12 (April 1959).

Guice, John D. W. "The Cement of Society: Law in the Mississippi Territory." *Gulf Coast Historical Review* 1 (Spring 1986).

Haynes, Robert. "Early Washington County Alabama." *Alabama Review* 20 (July 1965).

———. "Law Enforcement in Frontier History." *Journal of Mississippi History* 22 (January 1960).

Hobbs, Samuel Earle. "The History of Early Cahaba, Alabama's First State Capital." *Alabama Historical Quarterly* 31 (Fall-Winter 1969).

Houghton, George P. "History of Burlington, Chittenden County, Vermont." *Vermont Historical Magazine* 11 (October 1867).

Jones, Charles Edgeworth. "Governor William Wyatt Bibb." *Transactions of the Alabama Historical Society* 3 (1898–99).

Lengel, Leland L. "The Road to Fort Mims: Judge Harry Toulmin's Observations on the Creek War, 1811–1813." *Alabama Review* 29 (January 1976).

Lowery, Charles D. "The Great Migration to the Mississippi Territory, 1798–1819." *Journal of Mississippi History* (August 1968).

McLemore, Richard A. "Division of the Mississippi Territory." *Journal of Mississippi History* 5 (1943).

Martin, John M. "The Early Career of Gabriel Moore." *Alabama Historical Quarterly* 29 (Fall-Winter 1967).

———. "William R. King: Jacksonian Senator." *Alabama Review* 18 (October 1965).

———. "William R. King and the Vice-Presidency." *Alabama Review* 16 (January 1963).

Moffat, Charles H. "Charles Tait: Planter, Politician, and Scientist of the Old South." *Journal of Southern History* 14 (May 1948).

Pearson, Theodore Bowling. "Early Settlement Around McIntosh Bluff: Alabama's First County Seat." *Alabama Review* 20 (October 1978).

"Portrait of Judge Toulmin Presented." *Alabama Lawyer* (April 1950).

Neurmberger, Ruth Ketring. "The 'Royal Party' in Early Alabama Politics." *Alabama Review* 6 (April and July 1953).

"Register of Gubernatorial Appointments: Civil and Military." *Alabama Historical Quarterly* 6 (Summer 1944).

Stumpf, Stuart O., ed. "The Arrest of Aaron Burr: A Documentary Record." *Alabama Historical Quarterly* 42 (Fall-Winter, 1980).

Saffold, Mildred Reynolds. "Belvoir, Home of Chief Justice Reuben Saffold." *Alabama Historical Quarterly* (1930).

Somerville, Henderson Middleton. "Trial of the Alabama Supreme Court Judges in 1829." *Alabama State Bar Association Proceedings.* June 1899.

Taylor, Thomas J. "Early History of Madison County, and Incidentally of North Alabama." *Alabama Historical Quarterly* 1 (Summer 1930).

Wyman, William Stokes. "Early Times in the Vicinity of the Present City of Montgomery." *Transactions from the Alabama Historical Society* 2 (1897–98).

Dissertation

Martin, John. "William Rufus King: Southern Moderate." PhD dissertation, University of North Carolina, 1955.

Internet

Bailey, Hugh C. "John Williams Walker." *Encyclopedia of Alabama.* http://www.encyclopediaofalabama.org/article/h-1181.

"Clement Comer Clay." *The Huntsville History Collection.* http://www.huntsvillehistorycollection.org.

Coffee, Jerry. "Coffees of Gravesend, Kent." *Roots Web,* http://archiver.rootsweb.ancestry.com/th/read/COFFEE/2009-07/1247520022.

Colbert, Levi, to President Andrew Jackson. November 22, 1832, Chickasaw Letters–1832, *Chickasaw Historical Research Website* (Kerry M. Armstrong).

Dupre, Thomas Bibb. *Huntsville History Collection,* http://huntsvillehistorycollection.org/hh/index.php?title=Person:Thomas_Bibb.

———. "Israel Pickens." *Encyclopedia of Alabama.* http://www.encyclopediaofalabama.org/search/node/israel%20pickens.

Grant, Jan, transcriber. "Letters of John Coffee." *Tennessee Historical Magazine* 2 (December 1916). *http://genealogytrails.com/ala/history_jcoffee1.html.*

Lamplugh, George R. "James Jackson (1757–1806)," *New Georgia Encyclopedia.* 15 September 2014. Web. November 5, 2015. http://www

georgiaencyclopedia.org/articles/government-politics/james-jackson-1757-1806.

Lewis, Herbert J. "Jim." "Charles Tait." *Encyclopedia of Alabama.* http://www.encyclopediaofalabama.org/article/h-2350.

———. "Henry Hitchcock." *Encyclopedia of Alabama,* http://www.encyclopediaofalabama.org/article/h-1095.

———. "John Coffee." *Encyclopedia of Alabama.* http://www.encyclopediaofalabama.org/article/h-3041.

———. "Lafayette's Visit to Alabama." *Encyclopedia of Alabama,* http://www.encyclopediaofalabama.org/article/h-2152.

———. "Samuel Dale." *Encyclopedia of Alabama,* http://www.encyclopediaofalabama.org/article/h-2460.

Luckett, Robert E. "Macon County." *New Georgia Encyclopedia.* http://www.georgiaencyclopedia.org/articles/counties-cities-neighborhoods/macon-county.

Martin, John M. "William Rufus Devane King." *NCPedia,* http://ncpedia.org/biography/king-william-rufus-devane.

"Moses Waddell: Teacher Who Shaped South Carolina, America." *Educating South Carolina.* http://educatingsouthcarolina.blogspot.com/2012/01/moses-waddel- teacher-who-shaped-south.html.

O'Brien, Greg. "Treaty of Dancing Rabbit Creek (1830)." *Encyclopedia of Alabama.* http://www.encyclopediaofalabama.org/article/h-3426.

Parker, Roy Jr. "Israel Pickens." *NCPedia.* http://ncpedia.org/biography/pickens-israel.

Rodenbough, Charles D. "Gabriel Moore." *NCPedia.* http://ncpedia.org/biography/moore-gabriel.

Saffold History and Genealogy Book. https://sites.google.com/a/saffoldfamily.org/www/home/chapters/chapters-and-family-group-sheets/william-saffold-i/reuben-saffold-i.

Smith, Gerald J. "War of 1812 and Georgia." *New Georgia Encyclopedia.* September 25, 2014. http://www.georgiaencyclopedia.org/articles/history-archaeology/war-1812-and-georgia.

Thornton, J. Mills III. "Broad River Group." *Encyclopedia of Alabama.* http://www.encyclopediaofalabama.org/article/h-1137.

———. "Clement Comer Clay." *Encyclopedia of Alabama.* http://www.encyclopediaofalabama.org/article/h-1496.

White, Jonathan D. "LeRoy Pope Walker." *Encyclopedia of Alabama,* http://www.encyclopediaofalabama.org/article/h-1854.

INDEX